HIGH PRAISE FOR *YOUR LIFE'S RIPPLE EFFECT*

"Jeff Janssen's *Your Life's Ripple Effect* is the book I have not only been waiting for; it's one I wish I had written! Jeff shows the reader how to learn from the most important feature of near-death experiences, the Life Review, and does a masterful job drawing out its implications for one's daily life. It is a cliché to say 'this book could change your life', but in this case, it really will once you begin to absorb its lessons. I simply cannot recommend this book strongly enough! Now pick it up and learn how near-death experiences can teach us how to live."

DR. KEN RING
Author of *Lessons from the Light*

"If everyone read *Your Life's Ripple Effect* I believe it could change the world. If you really want to understand the impact our thoughts and actions have on the people around us and the world as a whole, then this is a must read! What we think of as small, insignificant actions really do matter just as much as the 'big events' in our lives. Through studying thousands of Near-Death Experiences, Jeff Janssen has compiled their wisdom into a thought-provoking, easy to read book. His expertise in the subject matter enhances the stories and adds great insight into the vast amount of knowledge offered to us from the Other Side. I'm grateful that Near-Death Experiencers have shared this priceless knowledge with us so we can live our best lives right now!"

MELISSA HERRIN, RN

"Jeff has done it again! *Your Life's Ripple Effect* not only offers a deep-dive into the value of a Life Review and what we can learn from those who have had a near-death experience, but it also translates those insights into a simple framework you can put into practice to transform your life. After the loss of a loved one, we feel lost. I recommend this book to all grievers as they seek to rebuild their life and redefine their purpose."

EMILY GRAHAM
Child Loss Survivor and Grief Coach at After Child Loss

OTHER BOOKS BY JEFF JANSSEN

10 Life-Changing Lessons from Heaven: Discover Who You Really Are, Why You're Here, and How to Find and Fulfill Your Life's Sacred Purpose

What You'll Learn in Heaven: A Comforting Story for Those Who've Lost a Loved One

LifeLessonsFromHeaven.com

YOUR LIFE'S RIPPLE EFFECT

Discover How and Why Your Life Really Matters

JEFF JANSSEN

Published by Life Lessons from Heaven
Website: LifeLessonsFromHeaven.com

ISBN 978-1-7330850-7-6

First printing in the United States of America

DEDICATION

To the people who have had a profound Ripple Effect on my life:

Jodi, Lari, Bob, Ken, Mike, Anson, Randy, Ken, Tammy, Cathy, Kristi, Ryan, Jill, Tom, Mary, Jaclyn

You've each taught me a great deal about life and love. Some of you positively changed the trajectory of my life while for others I am deeply sorry for the negative impact I had on your life and hope you will find it in your heart to forgive me.

This book is dedicated to you and the influence you've had on my life. May your Ripple Effect be shared through this book to positively impact others.

TABLE OF CONTENTS

INTRODUCTION

Do you realize the tremendous impact your life has on others? Imagine if you could see, feel, and understand exactly how every word you said, choice you made, and action you took (or didn't take) throughout your whole lifetime actually impacted others?

Would you be curious to find out the millions of ways your life positively or negatively affected others?

For example, imagine if you could experience how a simple encouraging word and a big heartfelt hug you gave someone kept them from giving up on a dream of starting a non-profit organization that ended up helping thousands of people.

Or if you could see how a local grade school boy you once coached was so inspired and influenced by your belief in him that he went on to become a Hall of Fame basketball coach, win national championships, and positively impact thousands of people's lives.

What if you could really see, feel, and understand the positive difference your life had on countless others?

Conversely, what if you could also see, feel, and fully grasp how a few harsh words, said in a heated moment of frustration and anger, unfortunately destroyed a close friendship that was never the same again?

Or what if you could experience how making fun of a grade school classmate contributed to him becoming depressed throughout his lifetime, abuse alcohol, struggle to keep a job, and pass that same hopelessness along to his kids?

If you could somehow see, fully feel, and completely comprehend exactly how your entire lifetime of choices impacted others, would it change the way you speak and act TODAY?

Well guess what . . .

At the end of your life *you will experience exactly how your life impacted others . . .*

You will certainly see, fully feel, and unforgettably realize how your life affected others in what many call a Life Review. The question is: Will you be happy about or haunted by what you see?

"Your life matters. You can't live through a day without making an impact on the world. And what's most important is to think about the impact of your actions on the world around you."

Jane Goodall, Primatologist

Your Life "Flashes" Before Your Eyes—and So Much More!

You've probably heard people talk about their life "flashing before their eyes" when facing a life-threatening situation. Here is an example from a man named Deroan as he stared death in the face.

> "As I lost control of the car, I remember seeing a guardrail coming at me. The guardrail was dead on center of the car. I was going normal speed, maybe 35 to 40 mph or so. I remember seeing the guardrail coming at the car, I remember the headlights shining on the guardrail, and that was the moment I KNEW I was going to die. In that instant, something happened to me, some kind of 'rush' and in that one instant, prior to contact, my entire life 'flashed before my eyes', just like they describe it on TV shows or in movies or what not, my life flashed from start to end and in the one moment I knew every moment of my life." Deroan

It's really true. Your entire life does indeed flash before your eyes! You see all the things you ever did and all the people you interacted with and impacted in a way that will absolutely blow your mind, expand your heart, and stir your soul.

Here's another example from a woman named Angie, who briefly died at age 27, and saw her whole life appear before her eyes before coming back to life:

> "I was being drawn into a three-dimensional slideshow of my life that played out before my eyes chronologically, while I experienced every part of it from all points of view and all points of understanding. I knew exactly how each person felt who had ever interacted with me. In particular, however, I was being shown in vivid detail exactly what my childhood was really like. The pictures flew past me, but I easily absorbed every moment, each one triggering an entire memory or a chunk of my life. So this was what people meant when they said, 'My life flashed before my eyes.' The closer I came to the end of my life, the faster the pictures flew past me. It was incredible! In an instant I had experienced the entirety of the twenty-seven years from my birth until the moment that I found myself dying on the couch and passing into the warm tunnel." Angie Fenimore

Like Deroan, Angie's life of 27 years may have "flashed" before her eyes, but as we'll soon discover from millions of others who've had this same death-defying experience, this so-called "flash" contains infinitely more information and knowledge than an entire library and tons of valuable insight into the meaning of life, death, and the Afterlife.

> "I didn't just understand the events; I relived them. I was that person again, doing those things to my mother, or saying those words to my father or brothers or sisters, and I knew why, for the first time, I had done them or said them. Entirety does not describe the fullness of this review. It included knowledge about myself that all the books in the world couldn't contain. I understood every reason for everything I did in my life." RaNelle Wallace

> "What was given to me at the time, would not fit in a whole library. It was as if in a moment, all my questions had been answered. There was nothing I didn't know." Miguel A.

How do I know about the amazing Life Review and why should you take my word for it?

Studied 3,500+ People Who Died and Lived to Tell About It

Over the last decade, after nearly dying myself from a 99% blockage in my widowmaker artery, I've spoken with, studied, and analyzed over 3,500 people who have temporarily died and lived to tell about it in what are known as Near-Death Experiences. In fact, Gallup polls show that roughly 5% of people report having Near-Death Experiences (NDEs), or over 16 million people across the United States alone with millions more in other countries.

While each person's experience is slightly different, respected researchers like Dr. Bruce Greyson at the University of Virginia and Dr. Ken Ring at the University of Connecticut who have intensely studied the phenomenon for roughly 50 years, have discovered many common features of Near-Death Experiences across age, culture, gender, religion, etc.

At the moment of death, millions of people report experiencing:

- rising up and painlessly leaving their physical body
- floating above the scene of the hospital, accident, etc.
- feeling a strong sense of peace and unconditional love
- entering and moving along a tunnel
- seeing a bright, warm, irresistible, loving Light

- entering into a different realm or dimension outside of the physical earth
- seeing and communicating with deceased friends and family members and/or religious figures
- having a Life Review where they see all of their life experiences
- coming to a kind of barrier or border they are not able to cross
- returning, often reluctantly, back to their physical body a profoundly changed person

Each of these experiences is amazing enough in its own right. However, one of them powerfully, persuasively, and permanently alters people so much so that it significantly changes how they approach their life and their interactions with others for the rest of their life.

> "It is the Life Review that has the greatest effect on people who have had a near-death experience. Although passing up a tunnel, seeing dead relatives, and being bathed in the mystical light all have a great effect, the panoramic Life Review instills in people a sense of who they are and how they fit in. The Life Review will let us see everything we have done and become everyone we have ever met. It also gives us true understanding of justice and equality. During the experience you become the judge and jury over events in your life. Through that experience, you will know just how it is that you have affected the world . . . The panoramic Life Review remains the pinnacle point of my time spent in Heaven." Dannion Brinkley

The Powerful and Persuasive Impact of the Life Review

Near-Death Experiencers (NDErs) tell us one of the most powerful and life-changing parts of their death-defying near-death experience is when they see their entire lifetime of situations, relationships, conversations, and choices appear before them in what is known as a Life Review. The Life Review shows people exactly how their whole life impacted others in both positive and negative ways.

Here are two compelling examples from NDErs Dianne Morrissey and Marion Rome describing aspects of their Life Reviews and what they learned when their life "flashed" before their eyes:

> "As the Life Review continued, I was shown two very special deeds I had performed. I saw myself at seventeen, when I'd worked at a convalescent hospital after school. I had grown fond of a toothless old woman who was no longer able to speak clearly, and who never had visitors. She liked to

suck on graham crackers before going to bed, but no one wanted to serve her because when she had finished, she would drool as she kissed the entire length of the arm of the person feeding her. While others avoided her, I willingly fed her the cookies she adored, seeing how happy this made her. When that scene was replayed for me, I felt as if every loving spirit in God's kingdom was thanking me in unison. I was amazed that such an act could have meant so much to God—and to me. I felt humbled and very honored. As these scenes were displayed before me, every emotion I had originally felt returned in full force. I also felt as if God and the angelic being were honoring me for having performed those deeds. I will never forget the love that surrounded me at that moment, or the joy that ran through me. Can you imagine being hugged by God and your angel? It's an experience that defies description!" Dr. Dianne Morrissey

"I had been shown my entire life from birth to my 'death.' During this Life Review, I saw the consequences of my actions for other people . . . Throughout my life, I have done many things I regretted. Like anyone, there have been times when I have made poor choices and bad decisions . . . There was a time when a classmate of ours got a Superman outfit on his birthday. Every little boy at the party wanted to try it on and so did Oliver. Alas, he was too heavy for the costume and, when his turn came to put it on, he couldn't close the zipper. Everyone was laughing and I said: 'He's not Superman, he's Superfat,' and I kept repeating this over and over again, along with the other kids, amid the general laughter. Now my soul could feel every single bit of his pain. Emotion by emotion—and in a much more powerful way than we can experience it on earth—I could feel everything he felt that day because of me: sadness, shame, distress, anger . . . I could see him after the party crying alone in his room, wondering why other kids always made fun of him. It broke my heart in a way I can't begin to explain . . ." Marion Rome

As you can see, the Life Review is so much more than a quick flash of images of your life. These comprehensive, intensive, mind-blowing, emotionally-charged, and spiritually-enlightening Life Reviews deeply impact the NDErs and transform them into much more conscious, kind, compassionate, loving, and empathetic people the rest of their lives. Reviewing and re-experiencing all of their life choices and seeing their previously unknown powerful and long-lasting Ripple Effect on others for seemingly simple acts changes them for the better.

"Life Reviews teach us how to live. It is as simple as that. There are certain values—universal values—we are meant to live by, and Life Review episodes contain vivid and powerful reminders of these values. No one who undergoes one of these encounters can avoid becoming aware of these teachings, because they are shown to be self-evident and it is impossible

> not to be affected by them. You see, you remember, and you change your life accordingly. Nothing compels like a Life Review . . ." Dr. Ken Ring

> "If I had any preconceptions about death, it would have been to assume that a Life Review would be the stereotypical image of one's life flashing before their eyes. That is not what my experience was. I was shown events in my life, not in isolation but in the context of their unseen Ripple Effects. It is easy for us all to see the impact our words or actions may have on our immediate surroundings, but to see the impact of events or words dozens of times removed was profoundly powerful. Through this experience, I was able to clearly see that every action, every decision, and every human interaction impacts the bigger world in far more significant ways than we could ever be capable of appreciating. As one might imagine, this was a profound part of my experience." Dr. Mary Neal

The Life-Changing Impact of Life Reviews on Everyone

Interestingly, it's not just the NDErs who are changed from their Life Reviews: we are too when we hear about them, learn their lessons, and implement their long-lasting effects. Researchers have discovered we don't need to experience a death-defying NDE and comprehensive Life Review to experience these same life-changing benefits. Noted NDE researcher Dr. Ken Ring found that educating people about the Life Review and exposing them to these life-changing stories and ideas is enough to impact all people, shift their paradigms, and change their behavior, even if they didn't have a Life Review themselves.

> "No feature of the NDE is more important as a guide to daily life for those who have not had an NDE than the Life Review . . . Persons who are exposed to the stories and views of NDErs—as long as they are open to such matters—become influenced by them and begin to express beliefs and attitudes about death that are very similar to NDErs themselves . . . They have not had the experience, but 'they get the message,' and it, in turn, becomes theirs . . .. The near-death experience isn't given just to those who have the experience, it's given to all of us to learn from because all of us can profit from the lessons that near-death experiencers learn in the course of a Life Review or other aspects of their experience. We can grow from these lessons. We can apply these lessons in our daily lives." Dr. Ken Ring

In fact, that is exactly why I invested over a decade researching thousands of NDEs and wrote this book for you—and myself quite honestly. I've seen and felt the influential and indelible impact of the life-changing lessons from the Life Review on my own life. Learning about the Life Review was a critical catalyst in my continuing effort to transform myself from a selfish, scared, materialistic, elitist, impatient, and judgmental person to someone who now tries to be a more helpful, accepting, loving, kind, patient, positive person. It literally changed my life for the better—and I know it will for you too.

I've also seen the Life Review's incredible impact across hundreds of people, many of whom have endured life's toughest challenges like losing a child or being in prison, and want to share this powerful understanding with you and others.

So the question becomes for you: *What if you had the opportunity to reexamine every choice you made, interaction you had with others, and action you took throughout your lifetime?*

Would you smile and feel satisfied with the life you lived?

Or would you have some regrets about the choices you made, the unkind and downright mean ways you treated some people, and experience regret because your life's purpose was unfulfilled?

If you're like most people, it is probably a combination of both.

Throughout this book, we will share and explore the wisdom of roughly 200 Life Reviews and learn all about the profound and highly valuable life lessons learned.

6 LESSONS FROM THE LIFE REVIEW

To help us better understand the priceless value of the Life Review and how it masterfully teaches and transforms us by experiencing it either as an NDEr or learning about it as a reader, we will use the 6 Lessons from the Life Review to guide our discussions and provide a valuable framework for our chapters.

1. Examine Your Life (Chapter 1)

We'll learn how the comprehensive Life Review allows us to examine all of our choices, words, and deeds with all the people and situations we encountered throughout our entire life from birth until death.

2. Experience Your Life (Chapter 2)

We'll then look at how we actually re-experience our life not just from our own eyes but from the eyes and unique perspective of every single person with whom we ever interacted throughout our entire life in astounding detail in our Life Review.

3. Empathize with Others (Chapter 3)

By seeing ourselves through other's eyes in our Life Review, we'll also

6 LESSONS FROM THE LIFE REVIEW

1. **Examine your whole life from birth to death.**
2. **Experience your life from everyone's perspective.**
3. **Empathize with others you both helped and hurt.**
4. **Evaluate how well you lived and loved.**
5. **Enlighten yourself about what really matters.**
6. **Exemplify love in your thoughts, words, and deeds.**

learn how we get to fully feel and experience exactly how all of our choices, words, and actions made others feel and realize how our behavior either helped or hurt everyone we ever met.

4. Evaluate Your Life (Chapter 4)
Once we explore our lifetime of choices and how they impacted others through the Life Review, we'll then look at how our life is evaluated to determine how well we lived, loved, and fulfilled our life's sacred purpose.

5. Enlighten Yourself (Chapter 5)
After learning how our life is evaluated, we'll then learn how much our life really matters and that everything we do matters to someone or something. The Life Review helps us fully realize our powerful impact on the people in our lives and our concentric and cascading Ripple Effect on the world around us.

6. Exemplify Love (Chapter 6)
Finally, based on fully understanding our effect on others through our Life Review, we will consciously and compassionately choose to think, speak, and act differently with much more love, kindness, compassion, patience, and forgiveness with everyone.

The Long-Lasting Lessons from the Life Review
Learning about Life Reviews powerfully, profoundly, and permanently changes people. Understanding how much our life positively or negatively impacts others can't help but encourage us to be much more conscious of, careful about, and compassionate with our actions.

After learning the 6 Lessons from the Life Review, we will:

- recognize the powerful Ripple Effect we have on our family, friends, and the world
- realize we really do matter and everything we do matters to someone or something
- treat people with much more compassion, kindness, patience, and forgiveness
- understand life, death, and the Afterlife much differently than we did previously

- have a much clearer understanding about God, Heaven, and our heavenly guides
- seek to find and fulfill our special mission and purpose here on earth
- gain comfort in knowing our deceased loved ones are alive and well in Heaven
- live our life fully and fearlessly with more purpose, peace, passion, and perspective

Special Final Chapter on How to Do Your Own Life Review

To help implement the lessons into your own life, you'll find an entire chapter at the end of the book on how you can conduct your own comprehensive and intensive Life Review to learn valuable lessons you can use the rest of your life. You'll also find a special Practical Reflections and Exercises section at the end of each chapter. These reflections and exercises help you better apply the lessons from each chapter to your own life. Invest the time to do them to take your learning and application to a whole new level.

So if you too desire to become a better person by getting a rare, behind the veil glimpse of what thousands of NDErs learned about life, death, and the Afterlife and what it means for your life, let's get started!

HOW YOU CAN GET THE MOST OUT OF THIS BOOK/PROGRAM

Through sharing this book and piloting this Spiritual Development Program with many people, we've learned various ways you can get the most out of it. Explore these options to see what might work best for you to meet your goals and needs.

Read the Book

If you simply want to better understand how your life influences others, you can read the book to learn how your words and deeds impact the world. However, all good books should not only inform you but inspire you to act. If you're interested and willing, this book invites and encourages you to take a deep dive into yourself and act on your insights. Thus, you may also desire to use it as your own personal Spiritual Development Program.

Create Your Own Personal Spiritual Development Program

This book can also be used as a weekly Spiritual Development Program. You can read a chapter a week and complete the Practical Reflections and Exercises at the end of each chapter to apply the lessons. These exercises provide you with the opportunity to not just learn the lessons but to implement them into your daily life. Further, you can conduct your own comprehensive Life Review using the detailed process at the end of the book. The intensive Life Review reveals so much about your life thus far and shows you specifically where and how you can develop and improve. It is challenging to do your own Life Review but you'll gain priceless and practical insights in doing so.

Book Club Discussion with Your Friends, Family, Church Groups

We've found significant spiritual growth occurs when you read and discuss the book with a group of people (friends, family, church members, etc.) on a weekly basis using each of the chapters as your theme for the week. You can gather a small group, anywhere from 3-15 people typically works best, and read and discuss the book together over the course of 8 weeks. After reading a chapter each week, you can get together for 30-60 minutes in person or online to discuss your thoughts on the lessons, talk about how you can implement them into your daily lives, and challenge and support each other in doing so. You can even divide up the chapters and put one or two people in charge of leading the discussion for one particular chapter. Having been a member of several of these groups in piloting the book and program, I can tell you it is a very powerful way of learning, implementing, and infusing the spiritual concepts into your life as well as connecting with your fellow participants on a much deeper level.

Soul Peeps Discussion Groups

We also offer Soul Peeps Discussion Groups for individuals and groups who would like to take a deep dive into the material with author Jeff Janssen and his team. Affectionately called the Soul Peeps, you'll find that discussing the material with a group of like-minded spiritual seekers allows you to go in-depth into the lessons from each chapter. Visit our website at LifeLessonsFromHeaven.com to see our schedule of upcoming Soul Peep Discussion Groups for this book and the *10 Life-Changing Lessons from Heaven*.

AUTHOR'S NOTE ABOUT NDE ACCOUNTS AND TERMS USED

Special thanks to all the NDErs who share their life-changing near-death experiences and profound Life Review lessons. I've included insights from roughly 200 NDErs throughout the book (set apart in a different font) to provide context, depth, and validation to the concepts. Many readers love to hear directly from the NDErs and request more quotes while other readers prefer less. Each NDE quote adds a unique layer of understanding to the mysteries of the Afterlife but if you prefer less quotes simply read one or two in each section to understand the concept and move on to the next paragraph.

The inspiring and enlightening NDE accounts come from a variety of sources including direct interviews with them as well as their presentations, videos, books, blog posts, and accounts shared on nderf.com, near-death.com, ndestories.com, and elsewhere. Some NDErs have their full names listed while others' experiences come from nderf.com, a fantastic site of 5,000 NDE accounts which only lists their first name and last initial for privacy reasons. All NDE sources are listed in the references section at the end of the book.

I will use the term "Heaven" to refer to the realm beyond physical death but will also use the terms Afterlife and the Other Side interchangeably. Additionally, I will use the word "God" to refer to the Divine but please feel free to substitute any other terms like Source, Spirit, Universe, Creator, Allah, Being of Light, etc., that may better align with your religious or spiritual views and comfort level.

> "I was shown how people waste precious time fighting over what name to call God, when instead they should be acknowledging His existence and realizing that He wants nothing but the very best for us." Casper

> "I did not have an experience of seeing God as an old man in a big white robe, sitting on a throne . . . God was all around and in everything. God no longer felt male to me. I didn't sense a gender, if there was one. The idea of that just seemed silly from the Other Side. God was just all that is beautiful and peaceful and One, and all that is Good. Even using the name 'God' for what I experienced seems

unfitting. God is so much more than what can be imagined through naming." Amy Call

Because most NDErs say God transcends the concept of gender, I will alternately use the pronoun "He" for God in even-numbered chapters and "She" in odd-numbered chapters.

Finally, my intent with this book is neither to promote nor denigrate any particular religion or spiritual path, just to share the voluminous and valuable wisdom learned by studying thousands of NDErs on their death-defying and life-changing visits to the Afterlife and what they learned in their profound and paradigm-shattering Life Reviews. I sincerely hope you enjoy and find value in the book.

Jeff Janssen

WHAT IS HEAVEN LIKE?

"My idea of heaven is a great big baked potato and someone to share it with."

Oprah Winfrey

Steve B's Description of Heaven

"My journey was the ultimate excursion of a lifetime as I eventually came to realize. To have actually crossed over the thin fine line that separates us from this reality and then return was an enlightening experience. Limitations in our human language have made it difficult for me to articulate certain aspects of my NDE. It was like returning from a foreign land, a place that no one in my circle of life has ever visited and then trying to explain to them what it's like.

It seems that words can only scratch the surface when it comes to describing the awesome wonder. And, perhaps if I were to give it a try, the only possible way that I can think of to help anyone understand even the most basic wonder is to try to create a picture.

So, imagine for just a moment if you will a place void of any and all negativity. A place void of fear, famine, dread, hunger, greed, hate, anger, pain, racial and religious bigotry, jealousy, disease, pestilence, violence and all other possible forms of human suffering. A place of total bliss, overflowing with harmony where only complete unconditional love and understanding exists. One filled with such magnificent splendor, color, beauty, and wonder that it escapes all human comprehension.

A place that at first seems so foreign and almost frightening, yet as you continue begins to feel so familiar and wonderful. One where nothing is obscure or hidden. Infinite wisdom and knowledge abounds. Barriers or limitations of this physical world simply do not exist. One where there is no measure of time, no days passing, no seconds, minutes, or hours ticking away on the clock. Everything is perfect and, everything makes perfect sense. A place that I have come to call 'home'. Can you imagine such a place? Wow, I still get a rush just thinking about it.

Even though it wasn't my intention to end up in this wonderful place, once I was there and aware of what was happening I didn't want to leave. I didn't want to come back to this world with all of its turmoil, but, that wasn't my choice to make. Against my strong desire to stay in this glorious place, the message was conveyed to me that I couldn't.

There was a problem with what we in this physical world consider the 'ego' and its unwillingness to let go, and, there was unfinished business here on earth. I had more to experience—more to accomplish—more to teach my son—more to learn from life itself, and, I had to set the record straight. So, in an instant I found myself on another unimaginable excursion. I was shrouded in a layer of warmth like I had never known before—a blanket of intense love—and thrown into a vortex of beautiful colors swirling around me as I spiraled downward with incredible velocity when suddenly, bam! I was slammed with intense force back into my physical body."

Almost all of us at some point in our life wonder if there is life beyond death, especially when our own life is threatened, a friend or family member is diagnosed with a terminal illness, or we lose a loved one. We wonder what happens after physical death, if our spirit will still be alive in some way, where we will go, what it's like, and if our deceased family and friends will be there with us.

Fortunately, NDErs not only assure us there is life after physical death based on their visits to Heaven, they tell us it is a magnificent realm that is far more amazing and different from this earthly world than we ever could imagine.

Key Understandings about How Heaven is Different than Earth

Before we jump directly into the Life Review, we must first cover some critical ground regarding how Heaven is different than earth. NDErs tell us to fully comprehend and accept all that transpires in an NDE and especially a Life Review, we'll need to exponentially expand our minds and make a significant mental shift out of what isn't physically possible in this earthly world to what is possible in Heaven, the Afterlife, the Other Side, Paradise, etc., whatever you prefer to call it.

This foundational chapter covers several critical concepts about how Heaven is different than earth to help us better understand how certain things happen in the Life Review, especially if you are newer to NDEs and what they entail. Understanding this essential information about the wonders of Heaven, as shared with us from the NDErs who've been there, prepares us to better grasp the logistics and lessons of the Life Review.

We're Not in Kansas Anymore

As Steve B. shares in his NDE to begin this chapter, we must realize that Heaven is a significantly different dimension or realm that is not subject to the same physical laws of time and space that we have grown accustomed to on earth. In this earthly realm, we obviously navigate our way through the physical world via three spatial dimensions (length, width, and height) and one dimension of time. We function primarily as physical beings using our human brains and bodies in a 3D, material, time-bound, gravity-governed, physical world here on earth because it is all we have ever known since birth.

However, on the Other Side, NDErs tell us Heaven is not only multidimensional but infinite, existing outside of both time and space. Rather than just the basic three-dimensional world we experience as humans here on earth, physicists believe there may actually be as many as 10, 11, or even 26 dimensions as proposed by String Theory, all of which we likely sense once we leave our physical body and experience these expanded dimensions as spiritual beings in Heaven.

> "Everything seemed to be happening at once; or time stopped or lost all meaning in each experience. Space and time are relative to our dimension but have no meaning at the Universal level." Julio M.

> "The barn, the horses, the people, and the fences all began to fade away into an intensely bright fog . . . I felt the separation from the ranch increase as another world developed . . . As my world in Tucson gradually grew dimmer, another realm slowly emerged . . . As this new world came more into view, selfless love covered me and filled me with the purest and most intense sensation of indescribable joy . . . The transition from the earth plane to this place—whatever it was—happened so seamlessly that I wondered if this realm had always surrounded my life in Tucson but on another level of energy that existed beyond the human scope of perception and comprehension . . . I knew I was in Heaven." Lesley Lupo

> "In this state there is no concept of time, and most people remark upon the timelessness of this out-of-body state. It is as if the out-of-body experience takes you out of the dimension of time and space that we know and into another dimension—an infinite and boundless dimension—that is beyond our physical reality." Rene Jorgensen

Our Five Physical Senses Only Detect a Sliver of Reality

Ironically, our marvelous human brain and miraculous body can only sense a small sliver of the multidimensional and infinite world NDErs say is all around us. Dr. Eben Alexander, a Duke trained neurosurgeon who taught at Harvard and also had a profound NDE detailed in his riveting book *Proof of Heaven*, says our human body and brain can only detect a small portion of the physical world. "The brain does not produce consciousness," Dr. Alexander says. "The brain is, in fact, a reducing valve—a filter—that constricts primordial consciousness down to the limited trickle of our perceived reality through our physical brain and body. It actually works as a reducing valve or filter. It's a veil, hiding a reality that's far more real and powerful." Essentially, our human brain filters our consciousness down to only see the limited physical world in front of us.

Dr. Alexander and other scientists say our brain actually limits the total amount of stimuli we can perceive and doesn't allow us to sense everything occurring in the environment around us. We know this is true because our human eyes can only perceive a very narrow amount of the total light waves available in the electromagnetic spectrum. While we see some light waves, we don't detect radio waves, microwaves, infrared waves, x-rays, gamma waves and a whole host of other vibrations occurring all around us that can be sensed by electronic equipment. The visible light our earthly eyes can see makes up less than 1% of the total electromagnetic spectrum; meaning we miss 99% of all the sights happening around us.

Similarly, our human ears can only hear a small sliver of the total sound vibrations available and miss high-pitched sounds that other animals like bats, dolphins, and dogs can hear. Bloodhounds and beagles have such a powerful sense of smell they can detect scents 55 times better than our human noses. Even though our five senses and brains are miraculous, they only detect and inform us about a super small segment of the world happening around us. NDErs tell us there is so much more out there and we get to sense and experience it all when we leave our clunky bodies and discard the limiting filter of our brains when we enter the fullness of Heaven.

> "I recall thinking how we human beings have limited our perception of reality by accepting only as truth anything that can be observed, tested, or reproduced by scientific methodology. What I experienced was yet another dimension greater in truth and perception than our physical reality. There is another part of our existence that is viable at the same time we are experiencing this observable reality. The other dimension, the intangible non-observable through our physical senses, is the actual, genuine and pure reality." Nancy Clark

"It's not what you look at that matters,
it's what you see."
Henry David Thoreau, Author

Illuminating Our Darkened Warehouse

NDEr Anita Moorjani, author of *Dying to Be Me,* uses a great example of a darkened warehouse to help us understand how our physical senses limit us. She says we should imagine ourselves standing inside an unknown, pitch-dark room. However, the room is actually a huge, vast warehouse, one like Amazon has that contains millions of items (toys, books, TVs, shoes, etc.) on every shelf stacked stories high and encompasses an entire city block. But, the warehouse is completely dark and we can't see the vast majority of items in it because all we have is a single, tiny flashlight projecting a faint, thin beam of light. We can only see just a few things at a time where we shine our little light, but we miss millions of things in the massive warehouse because we are unaware they even exist. This is what physical life is like Anita says.

Then imagine if suddenly all the powerful warehouse floodlights turn on. In the illuminating brilliance of all the lights, our vision and awareness expand significantly and we now notice millions of items stacked stories high on the shelves which seem to run for miles. We now see numerous items in shapes, sizes, and colors we've never seen before. We also notice hundreds of workers busily working as they send out thousands of items and bring in new ones. We stand in utter awe and amazement by everything happening around us and realize we had no idea about the multitude, complexity, vastness, and fantastic things all happening right in our midst.

And then, as soon as they came on, all the floodlights turn off and all we have is our measly little flashlight to see with. It is much like having an NDE. NDErs briefly get to see and experience all the wonder and grandiosity of the entire warehouse/universe and all its glory, activity, and multiple dimensions, but then the lights are turned out and they are thrust back into their limited 3D bodies and brains. NDErs know all the same millions of fantastic things are still there on the shelves all around them, and know the previously invisible workers are still scurrying about doing important behind-the-scenes work, they just can't physically see them anymore. Not only do they have to try to process

"Reality is merely an illusion,
albeit a persistent one."

ALBERT EINSTEIN

the mind-blowing sights they briefly experienced, they also have to try to explain what they saw in the indescribably brilliant Light to the rest of us who are stumbling around in the pitch-dark warehouse with our tiny little flashlights thinking we are trapped inside a small coat closet.

> "Suddenly, I was in a place FULL OF LIGHT, and I realized that all I had experienced on earth was to get there. Finally I was where I belonged, I was home. It was a feeling of complete happiness and well-being. I was realizing that all made sense. The most striking feature of the place was the light. It cannot be described if you have not had the experience. Everything was light, there were no shadows. Everything was happiness and love. Everything made sense and was understandable. Finally I had made it; all my life had been lived to get to that place. I felt no anxiety. There was no Time. There was only knowing, being, loving, and felicity. I realized that we were out of Time. That as such, Time had ended and it was a relief. It was a totally different dimension. In that place there were other people. Like everything else, they were light and all loved me. Specially and closest to me, there was one person who looked at me and smiled. In a sense I knew he/she was MY person and was there for me . . . I wonder on how should I describe the light? I cannot say that it was white, for it would make it sound dark. It is like asking what is the color of brilliance? Everything was made of light. I came back from REALITY, from the place where I belonged. I came back from my home to this dark, sad, and full-of-pain place." Juana DB

> "In the physical plane, however, our sensory organs limit us. Our eyes take in what they see in this instant; our ears hear in the same way. The mind can only exist in one moment, and then it strings those moments together to form a linear progression. But when we spill out of our bodies, we cross all time and space with awareness—not sight, hearing, touch, taste, or smell. We're pure consciousness. I experienced this while in the NDE state." Anita Moorjani

> "The immensity and infinite love of God is unbelievably overwhelming . . . And I knew that every single human being was loved in the same way. But the difference between the human beings and me was that they couldn't see. They were still in the world with a veil not knowing the immensity of love. They couldn't know it, not built into the structure. But still loved nonetheless." Peter Panagore

Based on thousands of NDErs' descriptions of what they experienced in the Afterlife, Heaven is such a different dimension than what we currently "see" (or don't see) on earth and it is important to discover these distinctions to prepare us for delving deeply into the Life Review.

12 WONDROUS WAYS HEAVEN IS DIFFERENT THAN EARTH

Hopefully the previous quotes from NDErs help us start to grasp the possibilities and perfection of Heaven. A whole volume of books could be written just to try to explain how the heavenly realm is different than earth and we still would only be scratching the surface. But, for the purposes of this book and to help us understand how Life Reviews can somehow record, download, and reveal essentially trillions of terabytes of information in such a lightning-fast period of time, here are 12 key ways NDErs tell us the heavenly realm is different than what we've grown accustomed to on earth.

HEAVEN IS . . .

1. Heaven is Ineffable

First, NDErs say there really are no words to describe the wonder, beauty, bliss, awe, expansiveness, comfort, eternity, majesty, peace, and unconditional love of Heaven. Try as they might to encapsulate, express, and explain what they saw and experienced during their NDE, they eventually say it is ineffable, or utterly impossible to describe with mere words. As much as I will try to capture and relay their experiences in this book, Heaven far transcends words, analogies, categorization, and human comprehension.

> "Please understand that for anyone who has had a near-death experience, to try and explain it, is taking on a monumental task. The whole experience is truly ineffable. The world beyond this one is so very different that there are no words for the many things I saw and experienced. All of our words are created to describe a three-dimensional physical world which exists in time and space . . . I found myself in a realm of reality in which there was not time, nor space, nor all the limitations which we live with in this reality."
> Reinee Pasarow

> "When I talk about my experience I try to give a chronological order but everything that happened to me happened at the same time. But it was separate. And I know that's really hard to wrap our minds around and it's even hard for me to this day. When I talk about my experience, it's really hard for me still to articulate it because I'm not doing it justice. I'm not able to articulate to you really that love and that warmth and that peace and that contentment. And it was just beautiful. We don't have the vocabulary. We don't have the colors. We don't have the smells. We don't have the sights and tastes. It's magnified beyond what we could imagine here."
> Heidi Craig

"The peace, the love, the joy, the Godly feelings that I had were just amazing and overpowering. It was such a wonderful feeling. I'm not doing an explanation of my feelings any justice at all because all I know are earthly words. And earthly words don't get it. Earthly words are very insignificant when you're describing Heaven. There is so much more that we're missing living here . . . I've authored 25 books but I'm telling you I don't know how to describe what I experienced in Heaven. There are no words for it in English." David Rose

2. Heaven is All about Unconditional Love

NDErs are absolutely blown away by the amount of pure, powerful, and unconditional love they experience in Heaven. The unconditional love is one of the most comforting aspects of the NDE and is fully shared with everyone. In Heaven, we understand we are loved completely and fully no matter what we did or didn't do during our time on earth.

"I saw how this Light absolutely loved everything on earth, a billion times more than love, as we know it. Even the fine hair underneath plant's leaves were not only loved, but also somehow accounted for. I laughed at the notion that we did not know how much we are loved. It was stupendous in emotion. I did not want to ever leave that love . . . No woman, child, animal, or belief has ever been able to even approach this Love." Loran G.

"The most amazing part was a pure feeling of the most intense love I can barely describe. It was just wave after wave of pure love. It was within me, it was around me, it was EVERYTHING. It felt like heartbeats of love, one wave of love after another. Yet there was love in the interim as well, then the wave would come with even more and more. It was endless, eternal and complete. I had no fear whatsoever, I had no feeling other than LOVE. I had no thought other than reaching the LIGHT. I felt pure happiness and joy. It was the most beautiful feeling that words could never even come close to describing. The closest thing I can think of to relate it to on this earth would be the moment I brought my child into this world. That moment of pure unconditional love that I'm sure most mothers and some fathers have felt. Still that is only but a very small fraction of what I am trying to explain. Words seem so small and insignificant in comparison to the experience." Nichole BD

"The Light then told me, 'You are here to learn how to love and to gain knowledge.' When I was told this, all the implications of the word love and knowledge were imparted to me. With the word 'love', it wasn't just about physical love but the love of nature, accepting all people as the same, everything that pertained to love. I was being told this is why you are here on earth to learn how to love and accept each other." Barbara S.

3. Heaven is Blissful and Beautiful

NDErs also struggle to capture the sheer bliss they feel and the indescribable beauty they see in Heaven. They say everything seems to be fully alive and joyously and effortlessly emanates a light from within. They describe amazing colors they have never seen before on earth and that everything seems to be oozing love at them.

> "I stayed in an area of beautiful gardens. These gardens were greener than green is on earth and the colors were vivid and rich. While I was in this place, I was weightless. I could access all knowledge I could think of. I also felt no pain because I didn't have a body. No weight, no pain. It was like it was impossible to be clumsy. It was also impossible to be anything other than truly myself. I felt as if I was more myself there than here on earth." Katherine I.

> "I went into the 'Light', I put emphasis on this because I haven't words to express how this Light made me feel. There seemed to be serenity, peace, happiness, everything right with the world. I've told others multiply your most happiest feelings, your most contented feelings, times a hundred million; and the feelings I had doesn't even come close." Mary Lu R.

> "It was and is Truth, Love, Compassion, Joy, and All. There is no way to describe the immaculate beauty of this experience, though every day for the last 35 years I wish I could find a way. Bliss is a mere descriptive word, yet does not give to you what I wish I could, but yes 'bliss' is close." Yazmine S.

4. Heaven is Hyperreal

NDErs say Heaven is hyperreal and the most authentic and real experience they have ever had. Many talk about living on earth as being a fuzzy, dull, drab, dream-like world in comparison. They say the clarity, authenticity, and aliveness they experience in Heaven is our true reality.

> "Ultra-real, frequently mentioned in descriptions of NDEs, is a key concept here . . . I was astonished to find that more than half of NDErs report that realm to be far more real than this one . . . That realm is far more real than this murky, dream-like material realm." Dr. Eben Alexander

> "This experience was more real than my life on earth. Even though I can distinguish between being asleep or awake, it was as if life on earth is also a type of dream state and that my near-death-like experience was the real life." Nancy Clark

> "What I experienced was ultra-real. It's reality. And what I came back to is not real." Daniel Giroux

5. Heaven is Our True Home

"Home" is one of the most frequent words used by NDErs in describing Heaven. They are often told and fully believe Heaven is our true home and we just visit earth for a short time. As we'll discuss in future chapters, NDErs say coming to earth is like going away to boarding school or summer camp but getting to return to Heaven is like coming home again where we belong, feel most comfortable, and are joyously welcomed with open arms.

> "The place where I went wasn't here, wasn't this universe . . . I've never found adequate words for what to call it, except for 'HOME.' I just knew it was HOME, my real HOME. When I did return back to here, I felt totally out of place. This wasn't where I belonged anymore—it was only where I'm meant to be, just for a time. They promised that when I'm done, or when I've done all I can do, then I could go HOME again. To express what HOME was like has been impossible for me to do. Everything HOME is connected. It is all One. It's Light. Light is love, or what beings here call 'love,' I think. Peace. It is all at peace . . . While I was HOME, I was more alive and at peace than I have ever been here." Carl D.

> "Everything was so well known, so familiar and so self-evident. Nearly as if I had been away on a long, long journey in a foreign country, and after a time I finally had come back again! I was home where everything was so familiar and safe. I felt the exuberant joy of returning home, of being able to come back." John S.

> "Upon arrival to this place, it had an unmistakable familiarity. It was home. In fact, it was all of our homes. In fact, it was the place from where we all had originated. Much like here on earth, when you come home from work at night, you cross the threshold of the doorway, you know you're home. You don't need to say it out loud. You just know. That is how I know. I had been to this place before. It was comfortable. It was glorious." Dr. Jean Hausheer

---

"My home is in Heaven. I'm just passing through this world."

Billy Graham, Preacher

---

6. Heaven is Timeless

An important concept to grasp, especially when considering Life Reviews, NDErs consistently tell us that time is different and even nonexistent in Heaven. The absence of time is a hard concept to believe because so much of our existence on earth revolves around time. We hear the tick of a clock measure the passage of time. We see planes and trains come and go based on a schedule. We turn the page on the calendar and see the seasons change. We see time pass as people age and we laugh at old pictures and videos of our younger selves. Life on earth is extremely time-focused and time-bound. However, time is basically non-existent in Heaven.

> "When I think of this review now, I imagine it must have taken up a very long time in earth-time had I done the same thing here. However, at this place, the concept of time didn't translate very well. Time was now and it only passed in a linear fashion because I organized the different events as happening in a certain order when I reflect on it. It's extremely hard to explain, but it was nothing like time on earth." Katherine I.

> "The very fact I saw so much in Heaven, during such a brief period of time, gave me the realization that time is man's measure for order on earth but totally unnecessary in Heaven. Heaven is forever, without limitations." Diane C.

> "I saw that time was only real in the physical realm to satisfy our one-dimensional linear thinking, but it was an illusion in the Ethereal. Instead, time was constantly in flux between past and present, creating the ultimate paradox." Rob Gentile

---

"We are living in a culture entirely hypnotized by the illusion of time."

Alan Watts, Author and Theologian

If you're having trouble understanding or believing Heaven exists outside of earth time, check out highly-respected physicist Brian Greene's *Fabric of the Cosmos: The Illusion of Time* video online to see that he actually validates the concept of time being an illusion from a physics point of view. Instead of the usual linear time we experience on earth, NDErs say Heaven is a realm outside of earth time. Many say time basically stops, becomes suspended, or doesn't exist there—or all time somehow happens simultaneously.

> "Everything seemed to be happening at once; or time stopped or lost all meaning. Absolutely. There didn't seem to be the concept of time in this forever-land. Although it seemed like things moved, which doesn't make sense to Newtonian physics or to Einstein's postulates, this place was a magnificent creation. It was ineffable and reminds me of how does one explain the beauty of Mozart's symphony?" Heather V.

"It is impossible for me to say how long the Life Review actually lasted. The entire review appeared to last for only a split-second, because all the events of my entire life were shown to me simultaneously. Yet I was free to examine each and every part of my life, piece by piece, to the finest detail. Time was subjective and distance was non-existent, because I was in every place at the same time. When my attention was drawn to a particular situation or set of circumstances, there I was already experiencing the moment. In other words, I literally saw every last detail of my entire life, compressed into a split second." Malcolm Miller

"Everything in this experience merged together, so it is difficult for me to put an exact sequence to events. Time as I had known it came to a halt; past, present and future were somehow fused together for me in the timeless unity of life." George Rodonaia

7. Heaven is a Realm with Instantaneous Thinking and Processing Speeds

Without the limits and filters of the human brain, NDErs tell us we can instantaneously think and process information at infinitely higher speeds, greater volumes, and enhanced clarity than we can on earth. It's as if we can instantly understand all the knowledge of our life and the universe all at once.

"I was suddenly able to think hundreds or thousands of times faster—and with greater clarity—than is humanly normal or possible . . .Time itself suddenly became infinite or irrelevant. In 'earth time' only about ten seconds had gone by until my heart re-started beating, but I was also in 'zero time' (for lack of a better word), or actually outside of time . . . There was an automatic review of my entire life—every event ever experienced complete with emotions (but viewed objectively)—rolling in front and around like a panoramic movie. From birth to death in linear fashion, observed without sadness or remorse. Yet in 'earth time', it only took a quarter second. Yet it seemed to be weeks spent replaying my life." Daniel A.

"I reviewed almost every moment of my life and analyzed it. Oh, and I also FELT every emotion that went along with these experiences, although because it all happened so fast, I felt them all at once, which was a bit overwhelming to me. It was like my brain was running on an energy-drink speed. It didn't slow down until the end. I was thinking the entire time—REMEMBERING would be a more correct term for it." Brandy M.

"According to my medical documents, I came back to life 32 minutes after I was pronounced dead. But during these 32 minutes, I saw so many things. It was like several months to me, if not several years." Mohammed Z.

8. Heaven is a Dimension with Simultaneous Multi-Perspective Awareness

NDErs can see and process things from multiple perspectives in Heaven all at once. Often called multilocation, it means our minds and consciousness can somehow split into multiple points of awareness and can adopt multiple perspectives and perceive multiple situations all at the same time. For example, NDEr Anita Moorjani could not only perceive herself in her hospital bed as she was dying, she could sense what her husband was thinking, hear conversations her doctors were having about her down the hall, fully perceive her brother hurriedly getting on a plane thousands of miles away in India to be by her bedside, and her mother and sister talking in their home in India—all at the same time. Understanding simultaneous multi-perspective awareness is a key part of comprehending the Life Review. Here are some examples:

> "I was aware of what my family members were going through, their anguish, their desperation. I couldn't understand it. I could hear the doctor telling them that these were my last hours; I had 36 hours at best, if even. Then I was aware that my husband was frantically trying to call my brother, who was in India, to tell him to come here. Then I was even aware that my brother was already on a plane. He had sensed something was going on, so he'd already left his home. He packed his bags, left his home, and got on a plane to come to Hong Kong. It was as though my awareness was just expanding. It still chokes me up every time I recall it or think about it. So it was like I was expanding, and then I was encompassing everything. So I became my husband, and I became my brother. I was aware that my brother was frantically wanting to get to me before I actually died." Anita Moorjani

> "I started to think to myself, 'Am I dead? Is this my body on the bed? My God, my mom would be so devastated. She is expecting me back home tomorrow.' As soon as I thought about my mom, I immediately found myself in front of her in our house in Isfahan. It is hard to explain, but strangely I was still in the hospital too. I was aware and seeing everything there as well, without any difficulty and confusion. My presence at home did not decrease my awareness and presence in the hospital at all. It was like I had split into two pieces with equal awareness. During this period as I thought about various friends and relatives, I instantly went to them while still present in previous places of the hospital, home, etc. For example when I thought about one of my teachers who I loved so much back in the days of high school, suddenly I was beside him, while still in the hospital and also in my house in Isfahan beside my mom." Mohammed Z.

> "I found myself 20 or 30 feet above my body looking down watching what was happening but it was not that straightforward. I was still alive. I was

still swimming to shore. It was actually like my consciousness was two places at the same time. And how I describe it was it was like a split screen TV. Everyone is used to that now where you can have a little tiny picture within a big picture. It was like my consciousness was two places at the same time. The little tiny picture was the little bit of consciousness that was still in my body swimming to shore desperately, desperately, desperately trying to swim this long distance to shore. But the main part of my consciousness had risen and was above my body, it felt like 20 or 30 feet above my body. And then I went even higher into this realm that was filled with light." Yvonne Kason

9. Heaven is a Realm Where We Can Experience Other's Thoughts and Feelings

Another amazing aspect during an NDE is that somehow we can merge with other people's thoughts and emotions and experience exactly what they are thinking and feeling. We can actually step into their shoes and skin and see what they see, think what they think, feel what they feel, and adopt their unique perspective on the world and essentially temporarily become them. Further, we also understand their complete life history, what motivates them, as well as their goals, fears, and frustrations. Feeling others' thoughts and feelings and knowing their life history inside and out is another critical aspect of comprehending the Life Review.

"My perceptions were expanded. I knew each person I saw perfectly. I knew their joys and their sorrows. I knew their love, their hate, their pain, and their secrets. I knew everything about them, every detail, every motivation, and every outcome. I knew every emotion they were feeling, and I knew intuitively why they were feeling it. In an instant, I knew them as well as I knew myself. I knew their hearts. I looked into the face of a woman in her early thirties and felt her elation at the anticipated marriage proposal from her boyfriend. I instantly knew that this was the second time around for her, but also that this was Mr. Right . . . Another woman walked toward me . . . I experienced her pain from the abuse she had received as a child. I saw how broken it made her feel. I felt how damaged and unworthy she had viewed herself for years and how she still felt that way. At the same time, I felt her capacity to love and her strength because of what she had been through . . . A young, heavy man in scrubs passed by near me . . . I felt his self-loathing because of his obesity. As he waddled past me and down the hallway, I saw the magnificence of his spirit. He was feeding his loneliness with food, yet he was brilliant. I encountered many more people. I felt spontaneous, intense love for each and every one of them . . . I felt their true essence and marveled at the connection I had to each of them, even though I had never met them before. I wondered about what I was experiencing . . . What if I could feel every person's hurt and joy and know every motivation for his or her every action or thought? They were, in a strange sense, me!" Jeff Olsen

"I could feel what he's feeling. I could feel what my husband was feeling. My husband wouldn't leave my side because he was just sitting riveted watching all the dials above my bed, and he didn't want to move because he didn't know when I would take my last breath. I would feel their feelings and I would feel their emotions . . . In fact, it's like I became them. It's like there's no separation. It's as though the body keeps us separate, but when we're not in our body it's like we're all one. It's like I was able to feel every emotion they were feeling. It was really like I became whatever I focused on. It also felt like it was all happening simultaneously, so it was like in that state the awareness is like 360-degree peripheral vision. Distance is not an issue. It doesn't matter how far, but even the time is not an issue. It's as though everything is happening simultaneously." Anita Moorjani

"I became aware of myself hovering over my hospital bed while looking down at my body. Now I began to observe the nurses on my floor moving in and out of patients' rooms. It was like watching multiple televisions screens at once, with each of their lives playing out before me like a movie trailer . . . The film was going backward, from present day to childhood . . . I was peering into their lives, observing their mistakes and watershed events, both good and bad, that brought them to this place. Anytime something destructive happened, like abuse, bad personal choices, or circumstances beyond their control, it has contributed to this moment, revealing a portrait of who this person had become. Now, overwhelming feelings of their collective pain and sufferings become part of me." Rob Gentile

10. Heaven is a Realm with Telepathic Communication

NDErs say communication occurs instantly and telepathically in Heaven. Instead of having to use our mouths to speak words, God and the angels simply transfer their thoughts to us telepathically and instantaneously, and we can do the same. The communication comes instantly in complete chunks of detailed information so there is no misunderstanding about what is meant.

"We communicated through telepathy, I suppose. It was like 'voices', which came and went immediately between us. A complete clear and direct communication, that didn't allow any sort of lies, only clean and clear communication. We talked about the meaning and the purpose of my life, about the world of God, and everything around order and meaning, and much more." John S.

"The Light and I talked for quite a long time. Oh, yes! On the Other Side, communication is done via telepathy (thought transfer). I must tell you that

God has a fantastic sense of humor; I never laughed so much in all my life! We laughed about the way I had so seriously reacted to an event. Life on earth is a big drama! It should not be taken too much in earnest!" Leonard

"Everything was communicated telepathically—whether with the Light or other beings, friends, or loved ones. It did not matter. It was always honest, open, and real and it was always done with love. There is no such thing as 'putting on airs' and no need to hide on the Other Side. No one is there to hurt you in any way—not in the least—because there is no sense of lack . . . or the need to 'steal' someone else's power or energy. You are operating as a soul, not centered in ego or personality." Juliet Nightingale

11. Heaven is a Realm with Universal Downloads of Knowledge

Many NDErs also experience what they call a universal download of knowledge. They instantly know everything there is to know about the universe. They can think of a topic and all the knowledge on the topic instantly downloads into them and they completely understand it from all angles.

"You realize you are suddenly in communications with absolute, total knowledge . . . You can think of a question and immediately know the answer to it. As simple as that. And it can be any question whatsoever. It can be on any subject. It can be on a subject that you don't know anything about, that you are not in the proper position even to understand and the Light will give you the instantaneous correct answer and make you understand it." Tom Sawyer

"Floodgates of knowledge opened and truth poured into me without end or constraint. Its source was the light and truth all around me . . . The truths were comprehensive and complete and rushed upon me in such an enormous volume that I thought my head would explode." RaNelle Wallace

"One thing I should mention is this biographical movie I saw. I had the feeling that it was very extraordinary and dense. I saw a lot of images and these images where combined with situations. I could see all the feelings and see all the things that played a role in each respective scene. But here I am also of the opinion that the wealth of images that I received from birth until the moment that I had reached in my life were so intense and shown at such a high pace that no human brain could ever work or think like that." Sabine Mehne

"Knowledge of how the universe works was understood in a flash. I sensed complex mathematical equations, along with their solutions, floating in the air, surrounding me. The nature of the universe and the laws that govern it are elegant. To learn the answer to any question, all I had to do was observe." Rob Gentile

12. Heaven is Where We'll Reunite with Loved Ones

Finally, Heaven is also the realm where NDErs tell us we will reunite with our loved ones who have physically died, which is super comforting to know. Many NDErs report having joyous reunions with their family, friends, relatives, and pets who have passed on. Further, no matter what illnesses, diseases, accidents, amputations, etc., their loved ones may have had on earth, they are all whole and healthy in Heaven.

> "When you die you are greeted by loved ones first so that you may understand what has happened. There is a big celebration, like a birthday party, heralding your arrival. Family and friends who have gone on before you are there to celebrate your arrival." Betty Bethards

> "There were enormous shade trees scattered around and beyond the field was a small river about 30 feet across. On the opposite bank of this river was my father, who had died when I was seven, and my brother, who had been killed in a car accident when I was 23, and various aunts and uncles who had passed away. And even there were four people that I had never met in this life, but I certainly knew who my four grandparents were even though they died before I was born. It was this huge welcoming, homecoming, and family reunion feeling. They were as thrilled to see me as I was to see them." Karen Thomas

> "At first, I thought these men were angels, but, then, I realized who they were. These two men were my younger brothers who had died as babies. I was only age 1 when my first brother died shortly after birth and I was age 2 when my mother lost the other one due to a miscarriage although she was far enough along to know she was having a boy. I knew of these men but was too young to have remembered anything about them. My parents never spoke of them. We were so happy to see each other; it was like a family reunion. They had beautiful smiles and they both looked so much like my dad. I knew he would be so proud of them both." Sharon Milliman

> "I saw a beautiful light and heard this amazing music that just brought me such peace. Eventually I found myself in a big yard where I'd grown up. I saw Sadie, my best childhood friend, a cute little Schnauzer. She was running toward me, wagging her tail. I'd missed her so much when she died. Yet, there she was, coming to greet me. She was licking me like crazy and I was laughing with joy." Alma

What is Heaven Like Summary

As you can see, things on the Other Side are WAY different than they are on earth. From our earthly mind's perspective, these things seem absolutely amazing yet totally unbelievable at the same time. As we learn more about the Life Review, realize and accept that things are definitely different in the Afterlife dimension. By exploring and understanding these 12 Wondrous Ways of Heaven, we can better try to wrap our human heads around how the Life Review can download and display a whole lifetime of experiences and insights in what seems like just a flash of time. We'll begin by exploring what we are actually shown in our Life Review, who shows it to us, and how we are shown our life in the next Examine Your Life chapter.

WHAT IS HEAVEN LIKE?
PRACTICAL REFLECTIONS AND EXERCISES

WHAT IS HEAVEN LIKE EXERCISE #1

Consider your views on Heaven, the Afterlife, or the Other Side and who taught you them.

Have you believed in Heaven, the Other Side, the Afterlife and if so, how have you pictured it?

What have you been taught about Heaven and how does what NDErs say about Heaven fit or not fit with what you were taught?

Which aspect of Heaven according to the NDErs most intrigues and excites you and why?

Which aspect of Heaven according to the NDErs most confuses or causes you to question it and why?

WHAT IS HEAVEN LIKE EXERCISE #2
Bring Heaven to Earth Day

Pick a day this week to bring Heaven down to earth. You goal is to bring the unconditional love of Heaven to earth by unconditionally loving every person you interact with throughout the day. Whether the person is your spouse, child, neighbor, friend, stranger, or nemesis, treat them with unconditional love and total acceptance. See how approaching them with unconditional love changes your mindset toward them and your interactions with them. Assuming this exercise goes well and is transformative for you and others, apply it for as many days as possible this week.

WHAT IS HEAVEN LIKE EXERCISE #3
Most Impactful NDEr Quote

Which of the NDEr quotes from this chapter most impacted you and why? When you reflect on the quote in relation to your own life, how does it lead you to think and feel?

1.
EXAMINE YOUR LIFE

"The unexamined life is not worth living."

Socrates

David Bennett's Life Review

"It was as if we entered a sphere. Once this sphere was completely around us, I started to experience my life. I got to experience it in a way that is very difficult to explain. It was as if I was looking at it from inside out, from other people's perspectives. This view was wondrous and wonderful. The depth of the Life Review was incredible and ineffable. I'll try to put words to it so that you may envision it. I like to say it was all-encompassing but that falls short as an explanation.

The review moved along fairly sequentially. But, I could see multiple effects and ripples, from my original actions and reactions, all at the same time moving beyond the area of the sphere. Not only were they images, but I also experienced feelings. I could sense the feelings of others and how my actions in this life had touched them. I could feel the joy, happiness, heartaches, disappointments, and love. I felt all of their emotions in regard to my actions.

I have difficulty explaining the intensity, speed, and the flow because everything was flowing continuously in my Life Review. It was distracting because I could also feel that my Soul Family was excited to be here and to get to experience this along with me.

There were parts of my Life Review that I wished that they didn't have to see. I didn't want to have to admit things that I had done. They didn't judge it, not even the parts that were sorrowful, suffering, or things I was not too proud of. They were merely observing it.

Beyond the group's support, I was also aware of the consciousness of the Light. When I think of God, I think of this consciousness of the Light . . . I can tell you this. It was observing, supporting, and an incredibly loving constant during my experience.

Along with not having a physical body, I was there without my life's drama wrapped around me. All the fiction I had created in my life of who I thought I should be was stripped away because the consciousness of the Light knew me better than I knew myself. I experienced my true self.

I felt as though I was reviewing my life so that I might grow and evolve from this life's experience. I was surprised that some of the things I had done had taken on so much importance because when they actually happened it didn't feel that critical. But they took on a bigger significance in the Life Review once I saw the after effects, especially how my actions affected others.

In life we are always thinking about leaving a mark and trying to make our life matter. The accomplishments we think are important, like building something that will live beyond us or getting a promotion aren't necessarily the things that are going to be the most important in our Life Review.

I learned that what is more important than focusing on these grand plans of leaving a mark is to try to live your life, day by day, the best you can. Cherish your experiences, good and bad, big and small. Try to be as helpful, compassionate, and loving as you physically can."

The Life Review: The Ultimate "This is Your Life" Experience

The Life Review provides us with the unbelievable opportunity to examine our entire lifetime from birth to death. Every situation we experienced, word we said, action we took, person we met, and even every thought we had from our first day of human life until our very last breath is all there for us to see and re-experience.

From our first messy and smelly diaper as a baby, to our first steps as a toddler, to learning how to ride a bike as an elementary school kid, to our first kiss as a teenager, to our first professional job as a young adult, to getting married, to having kids, to growing old, to our final breath (and EVERYTHING in between) is all miraculously shown to us in our Life Review. Yes, every naughty and nice thing we ever did is all there for us to see. ABSOLUTELY EVERYTHING!

> "I saw me as I was as a baby, a child, a teen, and adult, all at once. At the same time, I saw everything I ever did, everything I ever thought, everything. I saw events and people in my life that I previously considered important. Also, I saw many things that seemed not so important. I was aware of everything in my life all at once and I was aware of every response that others had to what occurred in my life. It was all there for me to understand . . . everything 'good', 'bad', or 'indifferent.'" Grace Bulbulka

> "In the life passing before my eyes, there was nothing left out. It was going fast. I knew that was my life. It was like somebody put on a reel in a motion

> picture, and they speeded up the film. Your life! Your whole life! There was nothing spliced or cut out. It was your whole life, from the day you were born, to the time you went to kindergarten, to when you stole a piece of bubble gum out of the dime store. It was continuous! Driving cars, stealing hubcaps, having sex. Nothing was left out! It was the whole life!" Larry

Amazing isn't it!?! Somehow our ENTIRE lifetime has been cosmically captured by the Universe and compressed into a kind of virtual video file that instantly downloads into our mind when we die and uploads onto a kind of massive heavenly screen so we have the opportunity to examine our life all over again in what seems like a mere matter of milliseconds or minutes at most. Even a 100-year-old person, who lived a full 10 decades on earth, has their lifetime fully encapsulated and experienced within a couple of seconds in a Life Review in Heaven.

> "I would now go through my Life's Review. During this review, which lasted about one second or less, I saw all that I had previously seen while living on earth. I relived every conversation I had had. I saw each pet I had owned. I saw again each piece of clothing I had worn. I relived every class I had attended in school. I saw everything again." John F.

> "I could see every part of my life, every event and incident all at once. Although it seemed instantaneous, I knew that every moment was there. These days, I might say that I downloaded my whole hard drive. At the time, I think I tried to compare it to a replay of a cassette tape in fast forward." Brian T.

> "The review of my life consisted of a series of events, both big and small, something like watching a documentary unfolding before my eyes. Naturally, I became intensely absorbed in my past and reflected upon it carefully. Everything that I had done, as well as everything that I hadn't done, was there for me to see. All the good stuff as well as the bad. Every word, every look, every smile, every tear, all the pain and all the pleasure. Everything that I had ever experienced on earth was there. So too was every person with whom I had had an encounter, even if it was merely a fleeting conversation on a bus or in an elevator. And so, I saw everything . . . Nothing was omitted or misrepresented." Malcolm Miller

Obviously, from our human perspective, it seems totally impossible to review an entire lifetime of experiences and information and process it all at lightspeed within a second of time, so let's break it all down in this chapter into some bite-sized chunks so we can have a much better and more thorough understanding of this amazing "Movie of Our Whole Life" known as the Life Review.

Let's start by setting the scene. To help us know what to expect when it is eventually our turn to watch the epic feature film of our life we surreptitiously made and unwittingly starred in, we'll begin by exploring the medium, mechanics, logistics, and details of the Life Review based on what thousands of NDErs tell us.

We'll examine the what, how, and why aspects of Life Reviews as reported by NDErs including:

- the setting of Life Reviews
- the format Life Reviews are presented to us
- the order of our life's events during the Life Review
- who watches our Life Review with us
- what role our hosts play in the Life Review process

NDEs are Customized to Each Individual

Let's begin by understanding that while many NDEs include the same common elements we mentioned earlier of leaving our physical body, traveling along a tunnel, seeing the bright loving Light, entering into an otherworldly realm, and having a Life Review, the specifics of each NDE are unique to the individual. Many NDErs actually feel like the experience is customized to them so they get the most learning from it. Here are the primary ways NDErs experience their Life Review.

LIFE REVIEW SETTING: In the Room Where It Happens

Life Reviews can be presented to us in a variety of ways on the Other Side. We'll share several of the modes NDErs experienced. However, while we will examine the different venues and formats in which they can occur to provide us with some general context, we need to understand the setting of the Life Review is subordinate to the actual wisdom we gain from it—as we will focus on for the majority of the book.

Large Spherical Arena or Planetarium

Many NDErs say their Life Review occurred in what seemed like a large sphere similar to a big basketball arena or a huge planetarium. As they watch and re-experience their life from the center of the sphere, millions of scenes from every stage of their life appear before them as if they are on 360-degree screens surrounding them.

"As I got closer to the light, all of a sudden I popped into a giant sphere. It was about the size of a basketball coliseum. And I was suspended in the middle of this sphere. All around me, in all parts of the sphere—up, down, sideways, left, right, all over—were miniature motion pictures of my lives and what was going on. And I could see, I could touch, I could feel, I could sense every emotion that was taking place in all of those lifetimes. When I would concentrate on one, I would immediately be there; I would be reliving what I had lived and I would remember the reliving. Then I would think about another area. I would pop into another movie. And I would do this for some period of time." Andy Petro

"The next thing I knew I was standing in what seemed to be a circular room with MASSIVE movie screens at a complete 360-degree view. All time seemed to stop. However, my Life Review seemed to take mere seconds. Everything I had ever done, good or bad. Everyone I had ever known no matter how important or trivial. All my life experiences played out in a matter of fleeting seconds." Traci P.

"I was in a large soap bubble, which was like a planetarium. I was sitting in very comfortable reclining chair and viewing snippets of past experiences in my recent past. There were many snippets, like videos being shown on a screen, of random acts of kindness which I had performed." Bryan C.

"A shimmering, luminescent sphere enveloped me, making me feel as if I had stepped into a crystal globe . . . My Life Review was about to begin . . . The visual reality of the crystalline sphere was different from any concept of reality that I had ever experienced. I was enveloped in a realm of consciousness devoid of time or space . . . My Life Review began as the surface of the sphere came alive with a vivid and lifelike scene that took me back to my infancy." Ned Dougherty

Movie Screen

Others say their Life Review seemed to occur in a heavenly theatre type setting with a large movie screen before them. The cosmic curtains draw back and the movie of their life begins.

"One of the first things I remember experiencing was the Life Review—which included everything that I had experienced in my physical incarnation up to that point. It was like being at the cinema—watching a movie of my life and everything happening simultaneously." Juliet Nightingale

"I watched with fascination as I saw the highlights of each stage of my life. It was like seeing a circular movie screen and many different scenes flashing by at tremendous speeds. Somehow, I was able to see and grasp not only what was happening, but the feelings I was experiencing at the time as well as the emotions I caused in others." Mary

3D Super-Fast Slideshow

Some NDErs said their Life Review was like a high-speed, three-dimensional slide show that quickly passed before them, yet they instantaneously absorbed every moment of their life as it quickly slid by.

> "The room was dark and I was in a chair. A being behind me began clicking images from my life through my brain really fast like a slide projector. The slide show stopped at four times in my life where I was being encouraging to people. At each moment I was launched back in time and into the event." Mike

Other NDErs said the Life Review was much like quickly swiping through photos on an iPhone, with each photo being roughly a second of their life. In a similar vein, some NDErs said experiencing their Life Review was like quickly flipping through a deck of cards with each card being a moment in their life.

> "Scenes from my life became visible in front of us, as though projected onto a large three-dimensional multisensory screen . . . The scenes moved quickly past, from right to left in sequential order. It was like swiping through the chain at the bottom of 'all photos' on an iPhone. This forward motion intermittently slowed when Jesus reached his hand forward to pluck a scene from the strand of my life. Rather than just seeing the scene in front of me, I would immediately re-experience it with absolute understanding, and from every vantage point." Dr. Mary Neal

> "All of a sudden, my life started passing in front of my eyes. It went from a little pink dot and it was like a deck of cards being flipped so fast, that's how fast this was going. You can't stop it. That's how fast my life was passing before my eyes. It was a continuous motion picture, passing nonstop. I could see myself. I was probably 8 years old, holding a little BB gun. Then suddenly I see this oil well I used to play on in the backyard. Here's me in the Marine Corps, holding a rifle. Armed forces. Zip! That was it! It went that fast!" Larry

Holographic Images of Our Life

Some NDErs saw 3D holographic images of their entire life playing out before them. Every life situation appeared in a holographic form and they could even re-enter and re-immerse themselves in the scenes.

> "I was told that I would be shown my Life Review. When it started, it was like a holographic image that came up in front of me from out of the surroundings, and then I became completely immersed in the experience, connecting my soul as one with it." David N.

"My life appeared before me in the form of what we might consider well-defined holograms, but at tremendous speed. I was astonished that I could understand so much information at such a speed." Betty Eadie

"We continued to a back room where some Spiritual Beings were sitting in chairs that circled around a screen in the floor that was like a glass bottomed boat. They communicated that I was to watch my life and then scenes like a 3D hologram appeared. I was able to re-experience myself in all these events in my life, but just as importantly, I was able to experience the impact of my actions and words on those other people with whom I had interacted." Karen Thomas

The Characters of Our Life on a Stage

A small number of NDErs reviewed their lives in a unique way: the major characters of their life appeared before them on a suspended stage. Each main character came out on the stage as if during an encore of a play and they discussed the impact the person had on their life.

"On a stage that seemed to be suspended in front of me, I witnessed, with my grandmother, what seemed to be an encore performance of my life. Ninety degrees to my right was what I perceived to be a doorway, just within the range of my peripheral vision. It was from this doorway that every character who had played in my life's drama emerged. In turn they walked to center stage, where they faced me . . . I was greeted by acquaintances, friends, my grandparents, my father's best friend, as well as a school chum from seventh grade . . . For the first time I saw the depth of the impression we make on one another's lives." Lynnclaire Dennis

"I was in a large theater, with a stage and velvet curtains on both sides. No one else was there. I was sitting in the middle of the row. I didn't know how I got there or why. I waited, and then one of my earliest childhood friends came out onto the stage. She looked at me, and she let me know that she loved the games that we played and all the laughs that we had. Then it was my turn to tell her how I always had so much fun, but that I was sad when they moved away. We stayed there until we had exchanged love and admiration for each other. A young boy from my block came out. I thanked him for teaching me how to tie my laces, and he let me know that he loved the running races we had. I was enjoying every aspect of this. I never knew who was coming out next. But each time it ended in giving, and getting, love." Anonymous NDEr

---

"All the world's a stage, And all the men and women merely players;
They have their exits and their entrances."

William Shakespeare

As these various examples and formats show us, there is no one set way we review our life. Each person seems to have their life presented in a way that is most helpful to them. Rather than focusing on the venue or mode, the primary point of the Life Review is to encapsulate, examine, and extract the situations, choices, relationships, and lessons from our entire lifetime in what seems like a mere matter of seconds from an earthly perspective.

The Chronological Order of Life Reviews

Now that we have explored the various settings of the Life Review, let's briefly examine the order of events of our lives. Many Life Reviews progress in chronological order showing the events of our lives starting from birth to death.

> "A 'movie' for want of a better word, began to play. It was black and white and huge. As if I were staring at a giant screen that filled the whole of every which way I turned. The 'movie' was my life from birth to death, every minute of it, every event I had ever experienced." Rachel F.

> "There was an automatic review of my entire life—every event ever experienced complete with emotions (but viewed objectively)—rolling in front and around like a panoramic movie. From birth to death, in a linear fashion." Daniel A.

Interestingly, several NDErs say that every event of their life appeared before them simultaneously rather than in an individual sequence. Of course this is hard to picture but imagine yourself in a large spherical planetarium with millions of stars projected above you. Also picture the sphere extending below you through the floor with an equal number of millions of stars both above and below you as well as on the sides of you. Now picture each one of those millions of stars as an instance from your life from your birth until your death and you see them all happening simultaneously. But you also have the ability to focus in on a single star and know it completely.

> "Everything happened instantaneously. The whole thing happened all at once but we are bound by the restraints of language . . . It is like an explosion, it is all there. When my life went before my eyes . . . there was an enormous screen in front of me . . . Way over on the left was my memory at thirteen months, and way over on the right was July, 1972, age thirty-eight. Everything in between was right there and I could see the whole thing, all at the same instant." Nel

"At some point, I underwent what has been called the 'Life Review process,' for I saw my life from beginning to end all at once. I participated in the real-life dramas of my life, almost like a holographic image of my life going on before me—no sense of past, present or future, just now and the reality of my life. It wasn't as though it started with birth and ran along to my life at the University of Moscow. It all appeared at once. There I was. This was my life." George Rodonaia

"It was like watching an immense, very clear TV. I was watching images of every event that had taken place in my life. My entire life all in pictures. The most interesting part of it was that with each picture, with all the pictures (there were more than I could count), I re-experienced the original feelings that had accompanied each one. And this was happening all at the same time! I could actually see my life in picture form and feel the emotion or the lesson in each one! All together and in complete unison. It was the most phenomenal experience! Not at all like we experience life. Here, you see a picture, for example, a photograph, and you have a memory. Then you pick up another picture and have another memory. But in this experience, I received complete knowledge of all my life events in picture form, reliving each picture's memory at the same moment! I have never forgotten what it was like to have the ability to relate to my life that way. Everything was so clear, so vivid! Mine was like 'plugging' into my whole memory bank all at once. It was a total engulfing experience of my life events, no matter how mundane or uneventful. A normal experience of life to me would be going through events one after the other, but here I had a quiet understanding that it all belonged as one experience, and it displayed itself through pictures of my life, spanning everything, people, animals, and everything else." Samantha H.

While most NDErs see their lives chronologically or simultaneously, a smaller number say they saw their lives going backwards in time from their "death" to their birth.

"My life was going backwards. I remember thinking 'How bad can this be? I'm only eight years old.' The first image I saw was something bad that I did (I used a key to scratch a car). I could feel the pain that I caused because of my actions . . . This movie was showing, second by second, my entire life; everything I saw I could feel the results of it . . . As my life was going backwards I saw me as a baby inside my mother, then just a molecule of life, really, really small but alive." Glauco S.

"I saw the events of my life passing in front of my eyes. I couldn't stop this, either. The events were passing in front of me like on a projector. They were going backwards until I was a baby and crawler, which was surprising me very much." Birgit S.

> "I saw, as in a cinema, the film of my life. Images from the present went gradually backwards to my birth, as if it was a tomography scan, with cross-sections. Then it moved back from the birth to the present time, showing the answers I have searched for all my life, all the whys of my paths." Nilda P.

Again, the order of how our lives are shown to us might be interesting but matters much less than the actual lessons learned by viewing and examining our lives, whether we watch them moving forwards, occurring simultaneously, or proceeding backwards.

Entire Life or Key Snippets

Let's also explore the content of the Life Review in terms of the events and situations NDErs were shown. Some said they didn't see their entire life play out before them but were shown a montage of key moments and snippets, usually related to highly emotional times in their life.

> "It wasn't a review of my entire life and every detail, but only those moments of intense love that I felt in a shared experience with other people . . . I didn't relive receiving my first bicycle or events like that. It wasn't any of that. But rather moments of such shared love." Manuala Fazzi

> "My life unfolded in the form of movie highlights. Important events were replayed in short black and white snippets from a reel-to-reel movie projector." Greg L.

> "I watched with fascination as I saw the highlights of each stage of my life. It was like seeing a circular movie screen and many different scenes flashing by at tremendous speeds." Mary

However, the vast majority of NDErs say their Life Review included absolutely EVERYTHING they ever thought, said, and did during their entire lifetime. Nothing was spared; they saw every millisecond of their life.

> "I watched a movie of my life, every tiny detail. So quickly it passed, but it took forever. I saw everything I had done right, every wrong, how each of those actions affected others and I saw when I should have done things and didn't; those were the worst, I understood." Sandy D.

> "I was taken to a big room and shown myself on a screen for a life reading. I saw everything in my life that I had done, frame by frame, and in slow motion. I re-experienced every moment and its cause and effect." Vernon C.

> "Just before I hit the van I saw everything in my life, from major to something as small as putting my shoes on. I saw every little detail, big or small, within a millisecond." Grady R.

> "I saw my whole life; every microsecond, every thought, and every feeling. The Beings escorted me through my complete life. It was like a Life Review. I could ask everything and got answers that were healing to my soul. There was no sense of time and space." Koppi H.

DIVINELY GUIDED REVIEW OF OUR LIFE

Fortunately, we almost always get some help and guidance as we witness our lightning quick yet completely comprehensive Life Review. Rarely are we alone but often we have our own spiritual support team in the form of a group of spiritual guides or guardian angels who lovingly initiate and shepherd us through our Life Review as they watch it with us. Some NDErs refer to them as spiritual guides, guardian angels, a Council of Elders, or simply beings of light as we will see in the following examples.

Spiritual Guides/Guardian Angels

Many NDErs talk about seeing and interacting with spiritual guides or guardian angels in Heaven who encourage, support, and love on us as we examine all of our life's choices, triumphs, and tragedies during our Life Review. Oftentimes these guides seem to orchestrate the Life Review process but do so collaboratively with us so we can gain the most value and learning from it.

> "I noticed two of the most intelligent beings I had ever seen. They were very large, approximately eight or nine feet, androgynous, with long shoulder-length hair and composed more of light than solid form. I call them angels only because I have no other term for them . . . The angels were trustworthy and there to help and comfort me, so I did not question their authority. They sent waves of light which transferred messages to me in the form of completed thoughts and feelings, not individual words." Tricia Barker

> "I became conscious of two 'Beings,' illuminated by the most stunning backdrop of fluid light . . . They greeted me with a love and joy so pure; it was as if I could feel myself melt right into them . . . The stories of Divine Beings who lovingly watch over us were true! These were my guides, my spiritual watchdogs. They really did exist! They were there to assist me in my transition from incarnation on the physical to life on the spiritual plane. I was ready to examine the story of my life. With the interest of an actress critiquing her own performance, it was as if I was watching a film with my best friends. My spiritual cheerleaders enveloped me in their love, proceeding to guide me, step by step, through twenty-one years on Earth as Mary Helen Hensley: the marvelous, the mediocre, and the dreadfully disappointing bits of my intriguing young life." Dr. Mary Helen Hensley

"I see a guardian angel with everyone, regardless of their religion or nationality. I have never seen anyone anywhere in the world without a guardian angel. Your guardian angel is with you from before you are conceived until after your death and never leaves you even for one moment. It loves you unconditionally and will do everything possible to guide you through life and keep you filled with hope."

LORNA BYRNE

"My guardian angel, she was holding my hand, rubbing my arm while I was dying, telling me, 'It's going to be OK, baby. It's going to be OK.' That was the most beautiful human being or entity I have ever seen or witnessed in my entire life. That woman was absolutely flawless. Gorgeous. The most beautiful color skin and hair and eyes. And her touch was so soft and gentle, just soothing. And you just knew who she was; that she's always been there. She's still here. And you've got one too! She's standing right beside you, holding your hand. And it's going to be OK." Cecil Willy

NDErs say the heavenly guides are extremely excited, supportive, and understanding throughout the entire Life Review. It's as if the review of our life is some kind of billion-dollar blockbuster movie they can't wait to see, are eager to show us, and relish sharing the experience with us, no matter what kind of "good" or "evil" life we feel we might have lived.

"Excited is such a limited word to describe the reaction from my group of beings as we viewed this experience. They didn't have any judgment pro or con. They seemed to relish the experience." David Bennett

Further, these spiritual guides or guardian angels encourage us and seem to applaud us when we observe and re-experience our loving and unselfish acts.

"To my amazement, I was re-living my entire twenty-eight years simultaneously! The best experiences brought me feelings of great joy, as if God were talking to me through the angelic being, sharing the highest moments of my life. I felt as if every spirit in Heaven was watching with me, applauding me and letting me know that God approved of my caring, unselfish deeds." Dr. Dianne Morrissey

In addition to our acts of love and compassion, of course there will be many embarrassing moments we would absolutely cringe to have others, especially angelic beings, see in our Life Review. However, our spiritual guides help us see them from a higher perspective so we can learn and grow from them.

"I judged and condemned myself for many things, but the whole time the angels kept on loving me (I can't imagine going through it without them). They let me feel guilt and remorse, but also helped me forgive myself and see each experience from a different perspective, the perspective of love and spiritual growth." Cree Dean

Council of Elders

Other NDErs report watching their Life Review with a Council of Elders, or group of wise spiritual beings, who watch over us throughout our lifetime and guide us during the Life Review.

> "I saw how much grief my bad temper had caused, and I suffered this grief. I saw my selfishness, and my heart cried for relief. How had I been so uncaring? Then in the midst of my pain, I felt the love of the council come over me. They watched my life with understanding and mercy." Betty Eadie

> "There were these twelve golden lights in white robes with golden cords. You couldn't see a lot of them at all, but you knew they were there. They introduced themselves as the Council of 12." Virginia Drake

Interestingly, as NDEr Amy Call describes, our Council of Elders sometimes finds humor in our human life when we put too much emphasis on trivial matters and stress out about them; much like a parent might find it humorous when a young child cries over spilled milk.

> "I could feel how the 'Elders' as I will call them (these are those who are Helpers on the Other Side . . . who have mastered themselves in many or all ways, and help work with us) see us and find so much humor in the way we do things. It might seem brutally annoying to consider when we are in the midst of a great argument or drama that is playing out in our lives, that the Elders view these things very much like when a mother sees her two-year-old scream and cry and bop another child on the head with a stuffed animal. The mother doesn't want her child to 'fall apart' and become hysterical and cry. She feels for her child, but at the same time, she sees a little bit of comedy in how seriously the child takes what is usually a trivial drama. She continues to love her child and thinks the world of it, hoping it will go on enjoying the day, living and learning. This was a big light bulb moment for me, because I had entertained the dark idea, during my life, that every little less than perfect action of mine, was being watched 'by God,' and judged with anger or great sadness. I felt constant guilt for my mistakes and belabored over the dread of 'being watched' with severe or at least very stern eyes. I wanted to please, and I believed that I was so often falling short. This had been a maddening way to live. So getting the chance to view others from a much Higher Frequency, was wonderful, to say the least. And knowing how much Love I felt as I watched or sensed others in their personal situations, made me want to live more in joy rather than guilt and worry. No one was mad at me. I am forever grateful for my Life Review and what I took from it. It is one of my favorite memories." Amy Call

NDErs tell us the heavenly beings on the Other Side don't laugh at us as they observe our life; they simply find some things we stress over as humans during our time on Earth as comical because they know we will see them in their proper perspective once we observe our life with them in Heaven through our Life Review.

Whether we want to call them spiritual guides, guardian angels, light beings, or a Council of Elders, we should be comforted to know we are guided, supported, and unconditionally loved when viewing our intensive and instructive Life Review.

Ability to Control, Pause, and Zoom In Our Life

If having a Life Review isn't amazing enough in its own right, we and our guides can control the movie of our life as if we have our own heavenly remote control. Many NDErs say at any point during our Life Review we can pause, stop, and even zoom in on the various situations of our lives we want to more closely explore and learn more about.

> "I reviewed my life like a movie except that I could pause it and zoom into different important times during my life. I could examine these times from multiple perspectives, such as the people they affected." Katherine I.

> "Although moving with incredible speed, as though someone had put my Life Review on superfast forward, I quickly discovered I could linger on any scene that caught my interest, re-experiencing it moment by moment if I desired. My Life Review was extremely enlightening . . ." Dr. Joyce Brown

> "I was given a Life Review while inside the void. During this review, I told the being to pause. I wanted to better examine the parts of my life. I was then able to view these events from overhead." Niels W.

According to NDErs, sometimes our guides, Jesus, and God pause and zoom in on certain key, highly emotional situations of our lives for us so we can re-examine them, see them in a new light, and extract the valuable learning from them. This process seems similar to how a sports coach shows their athletes video of a past competition so they can see the game from a different, paused, and slow-motion perspective. The video review allows the athletes to see how the situation developed, objectively observe how they reacted in the moment, and learn how to respond more effectively for the next competition. Similarly, with the help of our spiritual coaches, the Life Review allows us to observe and analyze our life from a variety of perspectives and pause and zoom in on key moments of our life so we can learn and grow from them.

"We just watched my life from beginning to the end. Some things they slowed down on, and zoomed in on, and other things they went right through. My life was shown in a way I had never thought of before." Howard Storm

"A giant screen appeared next to us. It was so gigantic that I can naturally compare it to the large screens that used to be in the old drive-in theaters of the 40s, 50s, 60s, and early 70s. On this screen, in random order, different scenes of incidents that had happened in my life while here on Earth were being played out. Jesus would select one scene and it would expand to the point that it encompassed almost the whole screen. I could still see other scenes playing in the background around the edges of the main scene that we were reviewing. The scene we were reviewing was a most accurate depiction of an incident that I was involved in at that point in my life, and He questioned me as to why I did the things that I had done." Odell H.

"My Life Review was quick and zeroed in only on what I should learn and what I could do better in life. I judged myself and my actions mainly because I could see into the hearts and minds of others and observed my limited thinking. God seemed to be guiding this Life Review and let me feel what I needed to feel from these scenes. I understood that people I had written off had love and concern for my well-being, and I wished that I had been more open and kinder to them both in my thoughts and in my actions. I saw that God sees our hearts much more than anything else." Tricia Barker

OMG!!! God Watches Our Life Review Too!?!

As Tricia Barker and many other NDErs experienced, God watched their Life Review right along with them. Of course this sounds infinitely intimidating! How can it not be? The Supreme Being who created us along with seven billion other humans, all the planet's animals and plants, our Milky Way solar system, and the entire Universe will sit beside us to watch our Life Review!?! OMG! How embarrassing! No thanks times infinity!

"I was mortified as I watched the movie of my life unfold. I'd hurt so many people and acted out in so many cruel and ugly ways. From the kids I teased in the schoolyard to the enemies whose lives I targeted for my country, I had lived a life that was harsh and violent . . . Viewing my actions in the way others had viewed them now evoked tremendous shame and guilt within me. Very quickly, I wished I had spent my life being a kinder, more loving person." Dannion Brinkley

Yes, it's true. God is often right there with us observing our entire Life Review. But instead of acting like an impossible to please movie critic, stern judge, or merciless executioner, listen closely to what the NDErs say about how God responds when watching our Life Review.

> "I think most NDErs will agree that the Life Review is one of the most difficult aspects of the NDE. Viewing your entire life before you—with every thought, word, action, etc.—can be most unsettling, indeed. Yet, what happened was the fact that no one passed judgment on me! I only felt the constant enveloping of divine love from the Being of Light that was always with me. What I came to realize, then, is that we judge ourselves! There was no 'He-God' sitting on some throne, passing judgment on me, (not that I even expected to see such a being in the first place). I never subscribed to such religious myths anyway. I seemed to be the only one who was uncomfortable and most critical of myself." Juliet Nightingale

> "At the end of the Life Review, a Being came forward in very deep humbleness and told me three times, 'It's okay the way it happens.' Today, I call this Being God." Koppi H.

> "During this Life Review I experienced what I can only describe as 'in the eyes of Jesus Christ.' Meaning, I watched and observed this entire event as if I were in the eyes of Jesus Christ; which means unconditionally. It's not judgmental or negative. I can't describe it other than with the unconditional love of Christ, the Christ who has absolute unconditional love." Tom Sawyer

NDErs assure us the same unrelenting and unconditional love they received from God as they entered the Afterlife continues to be showered upon us during our Life Review. God lets us know it's all okay. No matter who watches with us, God and/or the spiritual beings love us unconditionally and support us through our Life Review whether we are humanity's and history's worst human being or best human being—or likely somewhere in between.

Examine Your Life Summary

The Examine Your Life chapter helps us initially understand what to expect when we someday have our own intensive and instructive Life Review. Although it will be customized to each individual, we should expect to see images of our life replayed before us from birth until death with our guardian angels often eagerly running the projector and God with a universal remote control watching by our side. Although the mechanics of the Life Review are important to set the scene, the things we will learn in our next chapter about how we get to see our life from multiple perspectives in our Life Review will likely blow your mind!

Author's Note: It is important to acknowledge that not all NDErs report having a Life Review as part of their NDE. As mentioned, each NDE is customized to the individual and may not include a Life Review. Statistics vary but Dr. Ken Ring found that 24% of NDErs reported having a Life Review as part of their NDE, but don't let that seemingly small number mislead you.

In discussing the research numbers with Dr. Ring, one of the world's most respected NDE researchers who has studied thousands of NDEs over the past 50 years, we both agree that a person may not have a Life Review if their NDE is rather short and shallow. Many NDErs may briefly leave their body upon death and feel a sense of peace and love, but then quickly return to their body without having a Life Review. While this experience would often be accurately categorized as an NDE, it is such a short and shallow experience that they likely did not have a deep enough NDE to go through a Life Review, which typically happens later in a near-death experience. Most of the deeper and longer NDE accounts, what Dr. Ring calls core NDEs, include a Life Review. Thus, Dr. Ring and I believe the Life Review is a crucial and highly valuable part of the transitioning process from earth to Heaven and will likely be experienced by most if not all of us when we physically die.

> "I was shown during my multiple NDEs that we each go through a Life Review in which we get to FEEL all the pain we caused and all the joy we brought others." Mariel Martin

> "When you have a panoramic Life Review, and everybody has one, you're going to see the little things, the little acts of kindness, the smile, the pat on the back." Dannion Brinkley

EXAMINE YOUR LIFE
PRACTICAL REFLECTIONS AND EXERCISES

EXAMINE YOUR LIFE EXERCISE #1
Your Life's Characters Appearing on Stage

Imagine if the major characters in your life appeared before you on a stage at the end of your life:

Who are the main characters in your life?

Who are the supporting actors in your life?

What would the characters say about the role they played in your life?

What would the characters say about the role you played in their life?

EXAMINE YOUR LIFE EXERCISE #2
Guardian Angels and Guides in Your Life

Have you believed in having guardian angels or spiritual guides for your life? Why or why not?

If so, what role have they played during various times of your life?

If you don't believe in guardian angels, check out the Cokeville Elementary School bombing where over 154 students and teachers miraculously survived a bomb blast in their school. The movie called *The Cokeville Miracle* shares the story of how elementary school children saw angels and deceased ancestors protecting them from the bomb blast.

EXAMINE YOUR LIFE EXERCISE #3
God and Your Guides Watching Your Life Review

How do you feel about God and your guides watching your Life Review with you and why?

Which situations of your life would you be most proud about having God and your guides watch and why?

Which situations of your life would you most want God's and your guides' support on when you examine them?

Which situations of your life would you be most embarrassed about having God and your guides watch and why?

EXAMINE YOUR LIFE EXERCISE #4
Pausing and Fast-Forwarding Events of Your Life

Which situations of your life would you want to pause and zoom in on to really learn more about and why they happened as they did?

Which situations of your life would you want to fast forward through quickly and why?

EXAMINE YOUR LIFE EXERCISE #5
Most Impactful NDEr Quote

Which of the NDEr quotes from this chapter most impacted you and why? When you reflect on the quote in relation to your own life, how does it lead you to think and feel?

GO/ON!

2.
EXPERIENCE YOUR LIFE

"You never really understand a person until you consider things from his point of view—until you climb into his skin and walk around in it."

Atticus Finch, *To Kill A Mocking Bird*

Tom Sawyer's Life Review

"I know that I experienced a total Life Review . . . and the best way to describe it is to give you an example. When I was around eight years old my father told me to mow the lawn and cut the weeds in the yard. We had a cottage in the back and a double house in the front. Aunt Gay, my mother's sister, lived in the cottage out back. Aunt Gay is a very delightful person; she's a friend of mine as well as my aunt . . . She had described to me her plans for some wild flowers that grew on little vines in the backyard.

> 'Leave them alone now, Tom,' she said, 'and as soon as they blossom we'll make tiaras for all the girls, and flower necklaces for some of the guys.'

And then everybody could pitch in and she'd teach them how to weave such things. That was typical of her. We were looking forward to that.

However, my father told me to mow the lawn and cut the weeds. Now, I had several choices. I could explain to my father that Aunt Gay wanted the weeds left to grow in this particular area. If he said to cut them all, I could have explained to Aunt Gay that father had just told me to mow the lawn and said to cut that patch of weeds. I could ask if she wanted to make her request to my father. Or, I could methodically and deliberately go ahead and mow the yard and cut the weeds. I did that. Well, worse than that, I even came up with a name for the job. I called it 'Operation Chop-Chop.' I deliberately decided to be bad, to be malicious.

And I went ahead, feeling the authority that my father gave me when he told me to cut the grass and the weeds.

> I thought, 'Wow, I got away with it; I did it. And if Aunt Gay ever says

> anything, I'll just tell her father told me to do it. Or if father asks me I'll say, well that's what you told me to do.'

And I would be vindicated. It would be okay; it would be a perfect Operation Chop-Chop. End of story. My Aunt Gay never said a word to me; nothing was ever mentioned; I got away with it totally.

Guess what? I not only relived it in my Life Review, but I relived every exact thought and attitude; even the air temperature and things that I couldn't have possibly measured when I was eight years old. For example, I wasn't aware of how many mosquitoes were in the area. In the Life Review, I could have counted the mosquitoes. Everything was more accurate than could possibly be perceived in the reality of the original event.

I not only re-experienced my eight-year-old attitude and the kind of excitement and joy of getting away with something, but I was also observing this entire event as a thirty-three-year-old adult; with the wisdom and philosophy I was able to attain by that time. But it was more than that.

I also experienced it exactly as though I was Aunt Gay, several days later after the weeds had been cut, when she walked out the back door. I knew the series of thoughts that bounced back and forth in her mind.

> 'Oh my goodness, what has happened? Oh well, he must have forgotten. But he couldn't have forgotten, everyone was looking forward to, Oh no, knock it off. Tommy is, he's . . . He's never done anything like that. I love him so . . . Oh, come on, cut it out. Gee, it was so important. He had to know . . . he couldn't have known.'

Back and forth, back and forth, between thinking of the possibility, and saying to herself:

> 'Well, it is possible. No, Tommy isn't like that. It doesn't matter anyway, I love him. I'll never mention it. God forbid, if he did forget and I remind him, that will hurt his feelings. But I think that he did, though. Should I confront him with it and just ask him?'

Pattern after thought pattern. What I'm telling you is, I was in my Aunt Gay's body, I was in her eyes, I was in her emotions, I was in her unanswered questions. I experienced the disappointment, the humiliation. It was very devastating to me. It changed my attitude quite a bit as I experienced it.

I experienced things that cannot be perceived. I watched me mowing the lawn from straight above, anywhere from several hundred to a couple of thousand feet, as though I were a camera. I watched all of that. I was able to perceive and feel and know everything about my Aunt Gay regarding our relationship in that general time frame and regarding Operation Chop-Chop.

In addition to this, and what is probably more important, spiritually speaking, I was able to observe the scene, absolutely, positively, unconditionally. In other words, not with the horrendous emotional ill-feelings that my Aunt Gay experienced not knowing for sure, and yet being afraid to question for fear that she would inflict some kind of disease, or ill feelings on my part. God forbid, if I did it by accident and her reminder would hurt my feelings. And yet she experienced hurt in losing the flowering weeds, not being able to do the things for all the children she had promised, and constantly questioning whether I could have done it on purpose. I did experience that in this unconditional way, with this unconditional love that is only God's eyes, or the eyes of Jesus Christ, or the light of Jesus, or the light of Buddha enlightened, the spiritual entity.

It is that combination that is God unconditionally, not 'Boy, Tom, you sure did a good rip-off,' or 'There, Tom, now do you feel bad enough?' Or, 'You sure were bad.'

None of that, only, as in the eyes of God, simple, pure, scientific observation, complete, totally, non-attachment. No judgmental aspect whatever. This is simultaneous with the total devastation of what I created in my aunt's life. And the arrogance, the snide little thoughts, the bad feelings, and the excitement of what I created in my own life at that young age, that was one event.

I wish that I could tell you how it really felt and what the Life Review is like, but I'll never be able to do it accurately. I'm hoping to give you just a slight inkling of what is available to each and every one of you. Will you be totally devastated by the crap you've brought into other people's lives? Or will you be equally enlightened and uplifted by the love and joy that you have shared in other people's lives?"

The Intensive, Immersive, and Instructive Life Review

The Life Review is not something where we gather God and some angels together in Heaven, passively plop down on a cloud-like couch, grab a celestial soda, pop some buttery popcorn, and mindlessly watch our life events and escapades like we're binge-watching a series on Netflix.

Instead, as the Tom Sawyer example you just read highlights, a Life Review is a fully immersive, intricately detailed, totally comprehensive, emotionally intensive, and highly instructive process where we actually re-experience our life events and choices all over again—but with an entirely new and extra expanded level of perspective from multiple vantage points.

In addition to examining our life from birth until death, NDErs tell us we actually re-experience our whole life again during the "flash" of the Life Review. It isn't a passive watching of our life, but we actually fully re-experience our life by seeing all the sights, hearing all the sounds, tasting all the tastes, and feeling everything all over again.

> "I see the Life Review as—life! Physically, I wasn't there, but it felt like I was reliving my entire life. It felt like I went through it all, and did it exactly the same way, but understood differently." Neev

> "Far from being a mechanical process in which the experiencer is just a passive spectator during his or her Life Review, this experience offers many opportunities to become involved in one's life, to see it with new eyes, to learn from it, and, potentially, to grow from it." Dr. Ken Ring

See and Experience Our Life at Microscopic Levels of Detail

This time around in our Life Review we see and understand things at a microscopic level of detail that we would have never imagined possible during our human life. Our senses become so heightened we experience and tune into things during our Life Review we certainly missed when we experienced them the first time around during our human life. As NDEr Tom Sawyer said, he could have counted the number of mosquitos in the area and told you the exact air temperature too. NDEr Robert Bare said he could even taste the extra sweet flavor of Kool-Aid his friend's mom made for him as a boy in his Life Review.

> "I could feel, taste, smell, hear, and view each experience; and relive each and every event exactly as I remembered it in 'real life'. All of my life's feelings were re-lived exactly as they originally occurred." Andy Petro

> "When you have a panoramic Life Review, you literally relive your life in a 360-degree panorama. In astonishing detail, you see everything that has ever happened. For example, you can count the number of hairs in the nose of the doctor who delivered you at birth. You can even see how many leaves were on the tree in the front yard when you were six years old playing in the dirt. You literally relive it all." Dannion Brinkley

You probably don't want to count the number of nose hairs of the doctor who delivered you—but hopefully you get the picture between the nose hairs, mosquitos, and Kool-Aid of how intricately detailed and fully immersive your Life Review will be.

Step into Their Shoes and See Our Life from Everyone's Perspective

Probably one of the most mind-blowing and paradigm-shifting, if not paradigm-shattering, aspects of the Life Review is that we not only re-experience our life from our vantage point, but we also now get to see and feel our life from the unique perspectives of everyone with whom we interacted. In addition to seeing the world through our own eyes, we will see ourselves and the situations we encountered through the eyes of others too.

I realize this sounds utterly impossible, fantastical, and unbelievable as you read this—but remember, the heavenly realm is very different than earth as we discussed in an earlier chapter. Let's hear our NDEr friends explain it because it is so hard to comprehend, let alone fathom.

> "I saw all of the good and bad events from my childhood years and re-experienced the choices I made then. I was able to see everything significant that happened from all angles including the perspectives of the humans my choices affected. I felt all of my emotions and the emotions of the souls I had hurt as well as loved. Much of what I saw was surprising to me because there were more sides to the events than I was aware of when I was living my life. As I watched I thought to myself, I never realized, or I never knew. From all of this I learned that it matters deeply what choices I make." David Oakford

> "I'm gonna try to explain what my Life Review was like. A continuous bombardment of every single event that ever happened to you from birth. But wait there's more. Not only are you seeing every event, you are reliving it from different viewpoints. If you had an argument with your mom, you'll see it from her viewpoint. It's eye-opening to say the least. It's shocking." Chase Robert

In our Life Review, we not only experience the world from our own point of view as we interact with others in the 3D holographic movie of our life, but we also understand everything everyone else thought, felt, and experienced from their unique point of view.

Somehow, through the magic and miracle of the Life Review, we're able to essentially crawl into the heads and hearts of all of our family members, friends, co-workers, neighbors, and even mortal enemies and see ourselves and the world through their eyes. As we learn of and adopt their perspective, we also understand their individual motivations, fears, frustrations, personalities, and why they thought and acted the way they did in those situations. We understand others' entire psychological profile and how they viewed us in each and every interaction.

> "During a Life Review, many of us don't just experience our own feelings; but we also experience the feelings of everyone else, as though all other people participating in our lifetimes are joined. This gives us an immediate and powerful understanding of the effect that all our words, actions, and behaviors have had on those around us . . . Some of it felt good and some

"Oh the gift that God
could give us,
to see ourselves as
others see us."

ROBERT BURNS

of it felt awful. All of this translated into knowledge and I learned. Oh, how I learned!" Barbara Harris Whitfield

"At the same time, I saw the effects of my life on the people around me . . . I felt all that they felt and, through this, I understood the repercussions of everything I did, be it good or bad. The Life Review was the most beautiful thing I had ever seen, and at the same time, the most horrifying thing I was ever to experience." Neev

Many of us have been taught to empathize with and put ourselves in the shoes of others. The Life Review does exactly that and then some. It not only puts us in other people's shoes but into their bodies, minds, hearts, and souls. Being able to see life's perplexing and complex situations from multiple angles and realize the perspectives and motivations of all involved provides us with valuable insights to explain people's motives and ultimate behavior.

By being able to crawl inside other people's heads, we not only step into their shoes, but we actually become them and learn how our thoughts, words, and deeds impacted them.

"In this review, I realized that I was every single person I'd ever encountered or thought of. As I merged with and became them, I felt exactly what they experienced as a result of my loving or unloving thoughts and actions. I saw it all from their point of view, not only how my actions affected them, but then through them affected others they encountered, as the effects kept on going." David Oakford

Third-Person Perspective on Our Life

If seeing situations again through our own perspective and every other person's perspective with whom we ever interacted with isn't enough, many NDErs also tell us they simultaneously get to see their Life Review from a third-person perspective as well. Imagine watching the movie of our life as if there was an omnipresent invisible drone with a camera hovering over every moment of our life. This drone captured every word we said and action we took and provided us with an objective and omniscient viewpoint on every situation.

> "The review was everything that had ever happened to me . . . I saw it from three perspectives simultaneously. It was as though I was looking through my own eyes as I was experiencing it again as I first had. And then I was experiencing it through the eyes of everyone with whom I had ever interacted. And then it was this sort of omniscient viewpoint where I could see everything." David Beckman

> "I found myself reliving my life. I mean my WHOLE life, every bit of it, and it took no time at all . . . You could call it a 'Life Review' but it was more in-depth than that. It was multi-faceted. These were three facets. First, I experienced incidents from my life from my own point of view, second, from the point of view of whoever was with me, and third, from the point of view of a witness, a watcher of sorts, all simultaneously." Carol I.

> "Like, if you were going to have a Life Review, and we were going to have a play of it. I would be in the play, but I'd also be watching the play from the audience. And I would feel all the emotions, pain, and suffering of all of the characters around me in the play. And I'd feel it as an actor in the play, and I'd also experience it as the viewer of the play." Neev

Neev's description of the Life Review like experiencing a play really hits home in terms of the multiple perspectives from which we get to experience our life. We see and experience our entire life from our own viewpoint, from the viewpoints of all the people in our life, and as an objective observer watching our life play out. All of these different perspectives provided for us from virtually every viewpoint and angle, seen simultaneously, yield so much knowledge, depth, wisdom, and understanding. We get to see the world through the eyes and thoughts of thousands of people who interacted with us to definitively know how we impacted them and the world, both positively and negatively.

Our Life Review Shows Our Impact on Animals and Plants Too

However, it's not just our fellow human beings that our lives impact but animals and plants too. NDEr Carter Mills saw an incident in his Life Review when he was just eight years old where he killed a mother bird with his slingshot. Originally proud of the event, Carter then felt the pain of her three baby birds starving to death without her in his Life Review. Mills said, "It's not true that only humans have souls. Insects, animals, and plants have souls, too. Yes, I still eat meat, for in this realm species eat each other to survive, but I bless my food and say thanks for the gift life gives."

> "While watching/re-experiencing each moment, I found I was now able to experience each event through the emotions of all present at each time. I

watched my own poor mistakes and learned from every re-living. I watched myself as a child, bitten by a guinea pig and in shock, half launch it onto the sofa. I felt shame at this time. Because I felt the fear of the guinea pig. No one condemned me. I was asked only, what I had learned. I was comforted at this time. Consoled and reassured, I had learned so much. How big an impact my seemingly small actions had on a large scale. How my choices and behavior rippled through the lives of countless others. How the Love I showed spread like wildfire. How the way I mistreated others, deeply hurt and affected them and also how that pain, fear, and confusion would then impact the lives of others too." Rachel F.

"It was very apparent that every single thought, word, and action affects everything around the entire universe, and indeed us, including trees, plants, and animals too. I have been a long-term vegetarian since about eighteen years old and I know this was appreciated and is a good choice in life. Spiritually it seemed to show proof of respect for all life." Justin U.

"All forms of life—plants, rocks, animals, people—are interconnected; they come from the same source of Light. Everything is united by a transparent net, or web, and each thread shines with great radiance. Everything pulses with the same luminosity—a magnificent light of unparalleled brilliance." Josiane Antonette

---

"We are all interconnected in a web of kindness from which it is impossible to separate ourselves."

Geshe Kelsang Gyatso, Buddhist Monk

In addition to animals, we learn in our Life Review how we impact plants as well. Here is a heartwarming example of our influence on plants as experienced in Mohammed's Life Review.

"One example of my Life Review was when I was a little kid. We were traveling by car and stopped somewhere along the way. There was a river not far from the road and I was asked to go and bring some water in a bucket from that river. I went to fill up the bucket but on my way back, I felt that the bucket was way too heavy for me. I decided to empty some of the water to make the bucket lighter. Instead of emptying the water right there, I noticed a tree that was alone by itself in a dry patch of land. I took the effort to go out of my way to that tree and emptied some of the water at the tree base. I even waited there a few seconds to make sure the water is soaked in the soil and is absorbed. In my Life Review, I received such an applaud and joy for this simple act that it is unbelievable. It was like all the spirits in the universe were filled with joy from this simple act and were telling me, 'We are proud of you.' That simple act seemed to be one of the best things I had ever done in my life! This was strange to me, because I didn't think this little act was a big deal and thought I had done much more important and bigger things. However, it was shown to me that what I had done was extremely valuable because I had done it purely from the heart, with absolutely no expectation for my own gain." Mohammed Z.

While animals and plants may be pushing the believability envelope for some people in terms of the living things our actions and attitudes impact, Mohammed takes it a step further with our influence on insects and rocks with this additional example from his Life Review:

"Another example of my Life Review was when I was a 10-year-old boy. I had bullied and mercilessly beaten another boy who was also around my age. He felt tortured and deeply hurt. In my Life Review, I saw that scene again. The boy was crying in physical and deep emotional pain. As he was walking in the street crying and going back home, he radiated negative energy which affected everything around him and on the path. People and even birds, trees, and flies received this negative energy from him, which kept propagating throughout the Universe. Even rocks on the side of the street were affected by his pain. I saw that everything is alive and our way of grouping things in categories of 'alive' and 'not alive' is only from our limited physical point of view. In reality everything is alive. I felt all of the pain and hurt that I had inflicted upon him inside of myself. When this boy went home to his parents, I saw the impact that seeing him in that state had on his parents. I felt the feeling and pain it created in them and how it affected their behavior from that point forward. I saw that as a result of this action, his parents would be always more worried when their son was out of home or if he was a few minutes late." Mohammed Z.

"God sleeps in the rock, dreams in the plant, stirs in the animal, and awakens in man."

Ibn Arabi, Muslim Philosopher

Far beyond our fellow humans, our Life Review also shows us how our actions impact animals, insects, plants, and even rocks—basically everyone and everything in our environment. While this understanding may unnerve some people, especially when it comes to eating meat or even cutting the grass or pulling weeds, this next NDEr insight might help put it into perspective.

"I asked how will we survive without eating plants. They said we are expected to eat plants and animals, that we just need to have compassion, respect, and appreciation for them. Gracing our food before eating is probably the best for now. Plants and animals knowingly sacrifice themselves for humans, so be appreciative." Anonymous NDEr

While many NDErs become vegetarian following their NDEs, we don't necessarily need to follow suit or even feel bad the next time we eat a hamburger, pull a weed, or throw away a plastic bottle. NDErs just encourage us to be much more conscious of our impact on all living creatures and our environment. We should do our best to minimize our consumption and appreciate the animals and plants we do consume for our nourishment and not waste our food. We can honor them by consciously appreciating the life-sustaining nourishment they provide. Further, we can become an animal welfare advocate and get involved with organizations that plant trees and sustainable crops.

Our Effect on the Environment

Finally, some NDErs also see their impact on the environment in their Life Reviews. They see how the small decisions they made of even flicking a used gum wrapper out a car window added up to have a negative impact on the environment.

"[In my life review] I'm driving across this bridge with my windows down and I open up some gum, put it in my mouth, and I flick out the silver wrapper. I watch in slow motion this silver wrapper spiraling slowly all the way down into the river. I watch this gum wrapper go down the river being met by trash, Burger King, McDonald's, Wendy's [wrappers], needles, cat litter, you name it. All this pollution was being accompanied by my silver wrapper. And as this collected more and more trash going down the river I saw it going through lakes and I saw it passing an oil refinery. And I watch all the toxic energy, all this murky stuff come from the refinery and meet all this trash . . . And what I saw were children swimming in the river and the lakes. I could see these children who had died because of toxic waste. It made me realize that my one wrapper affects everyone. One action. I learned at that moment in life that my small action did affect someone, somewhere, somehow." Peter Anthony

The Life Review undeniably demonstrates that our choices in life have consequences, even though we may not see or realize them at the time. We realize our daily choices impact not only ourselves but others, animals, plants, and our environment. Because of this significant impact, we must understand and take full responsibility for the consequences of our choices.

"My Life Review showed me with complete clarity that every choice I made in attitude, thought, or action had an inescapable wanted or unwanted consequence. I alone was responsible for what I had done with my life." Dr. Joyce Brown

See Our Powerful and Unending Ripple Effect

It is amazing enough to learn that we will simultaneously see our life through the eyes, minds, and hearts of everyone with whom we interact throughout our lifetime. But this next part of the Life Review takes it to an even greater level.

Not only do we see the initial impact of our choices, words, and actions on others in our immediate surroundings, we get to see the extended and long-term Ripple Effect of our actions as they ripple out across different people over time and space. Like dropping a rock in a pond, our actions ripple out far beyond the first people we impact but continue on through the people they impact as well, ultimately impacting dozens, hundreds, and sometimes thousands of people with a single action.

"I went through a little bit of a Life Review — not so much looking at events in isolation but looking at the unseen Ripple Effects of those events, how an event had an impact not just one or two degrees removed but 16, 20, 25 degrees removed. This was another profound aspect of the experience. It made me truly understand that every action, every decision, every choice, every human interaction really does matter. You may not know it, and almost always you don't recognize the impact. But everything really, really does matter." Dr. Mary Neal

"I remembered many past events. There were two screens. The first was a replay of every moment of my life to this point and included what I was thinking and speaking. The second screen showed the Ripple Effect of both good and bad actions on my part and how it impacted other people's lives. This was very intense. During the Life Review, I was humbled and very excited at the good I had done and its Ripple Effect. Then I felt a period of shame and sadness for the selfish hurt I had inflicted on others and its Ripple Effects." Lee C.

"I saw that the love we express ripples out, creating an everlasting beauty that is often unbeknownst to us at the time. I saw this happen when I spoke a heartfelt word, thought a truly kind thought or gave undivided attention to someone. I recall simple gestures having the most impact, like a spontaneous and genuine smile. For example, I smiled at a woman I passed on the street and it turned her day around. She had been feeling disheartened about life, and my smile changed her interactions later that day with her children and others." David Oakford

"I experienced, in a sort of holographic or instantaneous way, how every action I had taken was like a stone cast into water causing ripples outward. If an action is loving, that action touches the first person for whom it was intended, then it touches another person, and then another, because it affects how that person interacts with people and so on. Every action has a reverberating effect on every single one of us on the face of this planet." Reinee Pasarow

Through the Life Review, we learn that our singular actions don't just directly impact the immediate people around us, but they ripple through others creating an expansive, exponential, and everlasting Ripple Effect on a much wider circle of people we often don't even realize.

Here's an example of how a simple, single action might ripple out across both time and space. Imagine if a manager at a company compliments a team member, making his day so much that he buys ice cream for the person in line behind him at lunch. That next person, surprised by the kind gesture of a free ice cream, thinks of his mother and gives her a call because she did the same kind of nice thing for others and it reminded him of her. The mother, inspired by her son's call, contributes $50 to the Boys and Girls Club in honor of her son because she is so proud of the man he's become and wants to help others become like him. The money the mom donates to the Boys and Girls Club helps a young girl have access to a computer she uses months later to reach out to a respected female doctor in the community who ends up mentoring her. Deeply inspired by her kind mentor, ten years later the young girl becomes a world-renowned doctor at a children's hospital and helps treat thousands of kids with cancer. One of those kids, who is miraculously cured from cancer by her loving care, gives her grandmother a huge hug—who just so happens to be the same woman who started this whole Ripple Effect over a decade earlier as a manager when she complimented her team member. This remarkable chain of events, started years earlier by her simple compliment, comes full circle and is revealed through the Life Review.

"My every action or reaction, I found, went out in time like unending circles that somehow came back to me. Anything I did or did not do for anyone else had an effect that came back to me." Dr. Joyce Brown

We come to understand that our lives often have a massive, unseen, and unrealized yet undeniable Ripple Effect. We realize our words and

"I alone cannot change the world, but I can cast a stone across the waters to create many ripples."

MOTHER TERESA

actions don't just impact us but ripple out to others. Our positivity, compassion, and love spread to others and inspires and encourages them to do the same. Unfortunately, our negativity, indifference, and hatred also infect others and they take out this negativity and anger on other people.

> "Everything we do, including the words we speak, our actions, our thoughts, has an effect on both ourselves and the world around us. We can liken these effects to energy radiating outward from our centers. Our words and actions do not affect just us, they travel outward and touch others, too. And the sphere of that impact can be quite large." Nancy Rynes

> "Now, in the Life Review, I was forced to see the death and destruction that had taken place in the world as a result of my actions. 'We are all a link in the great chain of humanity,' said the Being. 'What you do has an effect on the other links in that chain.' Many examples came to mind, but one in particular stands out. I saw myself unloading weapons in a Central American country . . . My task was simply to transfer these weapons from an airplane to our military interests in the area. When this transfer was complete, I got back on the airplane and left. But leaving wasn't so easy in my Life Review. I stayed with the weapons and watched as they were used in the job of killing, some of them murdering innocent people and some the not so innocent. All in all it was horrible to witness my results of my role in this war." Dannion Brinkley

Whether positive or negative, we have a bigger and farther-reaching impact than most of us realize until we see the full extent of it in our Life Review. It encourages us to ask the question, "What kind of ripples do we send out in the world?"

The Butterfly Effect

Through the Life Review, we can trace back the long chain of dominos that occurred for every moment in our life. Often called the Butterfly Effect, which states that small events can serve as critical catalysts for much bigger events elsewhere, we learn that small little actions by ourselves and others can create huge impacts on the other side of the state, country, and world.

> "You will be responsible for yourself, judging and reliving what you have done to everything and everybody in very far-reaching ways. You do have that effect on plants. You do have an effect on animals. You do have an effect on the universe. And in your Life Review you'll be the universe and experience yourself in what you call your lifetime and how it affects the universe. In your Life Review you'll be yourself absolutely, in every aspect

of time, in every event, in the overall scheme of things in your lifetime. Your life. When you waved a loving goodbye to a good friend the other day, did you affect the clouds up above? Did you actually affect them? Does a butterfly's wings in China affect the weather here? You better believe it does! You can learn all of that in a Life Review!" Tom Sawyer

> "I was shown everything that happened in the past and because of that I could see the Butterfly Effect. I could see the trickle effect. I could see why we made choices the way that we made them and how that affected it." Heidi Craig

> "I saw how I had wronged people and how they had often turned to others and committed a similar wrong. This chain continued from victim to victim, like a circle of dominoes, until it came back to the start—to me, the offender. The ripples went out, and they came back. I had offended far more people than I knew . . ." Betty Eadie

The little things we do have often unforeseen and far-reaching effects on others and we see and realize them all in our Life Review.

Unfortunately, the COVID-19 virus, which killed millions across the entire planet and crippled the world's economy, is probably one of the most memorable and salient examples of how something so small can quickly spread from person to person, state to state, and country to country. What started off with one person in Wuhan, China obviously transmitted across people and borders and ended up infecting hundreds of millions of people across the entire world in just a few months. Similarly, our small acts send out a Ripple Effect far larger and wider than we imagine.

> "I was shown incidents in my life where I was very mean to people or hurt people without realizing it due to self-absorption or distraction. Jesus showed me events where I was not loving towards others or careless and hateful and how it affected so many people besides just the one person. The review was so fast, in a rush, like I could see all of the incidents at once with such efficiency . . . The way things flow there is so perfect. When He showed me all of these things, He did not condemn me but just showed me all of the lost moments of love and how it had a domino effect on others." Katie W.

Seeing All the Dominos in the Chain

The Life Review reveals to us all the dominos that fall in a certain direction based on our actions. We see the event happen with the first domino falling but then get to see the chain reaction it creates with others and realize how it eventually causes all the dominos to fall in the chain even though they may be 300 or more dominos away from the original one.

"The walls came to life! 360 degrees of 'movies' all projected at once. I watched the domino effect of what harsh and unkind words and actions would do to people, how it would start with one person and spiral down to 300 people. I 'felt' the anger and sadness of everyone! I thought I was going to explode! I was emotionally shaken to the core." Anonymous NDEr

"Kind words are short and easy to speak but their echoes are truly endless."

Mother Teresa

NDErs tell us that we can see events that happen in our life and are able to trace back those events to the original domino that fell, even though it may be multiple generations further away from us in the past.

The Ripple Effect Through Generations

The Ripple Effect not only occurs across space and time but also across generations. As an example, I learned first-hand about the generational Ripple Effect of our life at my own father's funeral. As I greeted and chatted with various people who had come to pay their last respects to my dad, my eighth-grade football coach, Lari DeBruin, approached me to share his condolences.

Coach DeBruin had been an absolutely pivotal figure in my life. In seventh grade, I had been the reserve, third-string quarterback on our community's football team so I sat on the bench and didn't get on the field very much. Because all the same players came back to the eighth-grade team, I knew I had to find a different position if I wanted to play. During the first days of practice, I went over to the wide receivers' group hoping to find a new position where I could make my mark. Since tryouts occurred during those first few days, it was important to impress the coaches, especially the head coach, Lari DeBruin.

As I was in line waiting my turn, I noticed Coach DeBruin heading over to our receivers' group to observe. I could feel my heart racing and my palms sweating as I thought, "Oh boy, Coach DeBruin is watching. You can't screw up or you'll end up sitting the bench again this season like you did last season." As it was now my turn, I nervously sprinted out and executed my route. As I turned over my right shoulder, I saw a perfectly thrown pass from the first-string quarterback spiraling toward me. The ball hit me right in the hands, but because I was so nervous, I dropped it. Instantly I thought, "Oh no, Jeff, you really blew it! That was a perfectly thrown pass and you dropped it. Maybe Coach DeBruin was looking the other way and wasn't watching."

I hesitantly looked up at Coach DeBruin. Not only was he watching, but he motioned for me to come over to speak with him. Now I'm thinking, "Oh my goodness, they're making cuts soon and I wonder if he is going to cut me." Terrified, I jogged over to Coach DeBruin thinking my eighth-grade football career might be over before it even started. He put his arm around me and said, "Son, I don't think you have what it takes to be a receiver."

Those words tore through me like a knife. I thought, "Oh my gosh, my career is over. I've actually been cut from the team. What am I going to tell my dad? He is going to be so disappointed in me."

Coach DeBruin continued, "Son, are you listening to me? I don't think you have what it takes to be a receiver—but come on over here to the running backs' group. I'm going to make you our team's running back."

I thought, "Huh? Are you kidding me? I couldn't play quarterback last year and I just dropped the ball right in front of you this year. How are you going to make me into the team's running back?"

But Coach DeBruin saw something in me that I didn't see in myself. With his arm around me, he guided me over to the running backs group. Surprised but also tremendously relieved, I walked over to the running backs group with him. He patiently showed me how to hold my hands depending on which side the quarterback handed me the ball. Of course, I made a lot of mistakes at first, but Coach DeBruin supported and encouraged me every step of the way. I gained a lot of much-needed confidence from his coaching and ended up being the team's starting running back that year and leading the team in rushing.

While I wish I could tell you I went on and won the Heisman Trophy and played professional football, I honestly can't tell you that. But I can tell you without a shadow of a doubt that the difference Coach DeBruin made at a pivotal moment in my life as an eighth grader is something that absolutely changed the trajectory of my life. His confidence in me transformed me from a highly doubtful and inept young boy into someone who had confidence and ended up training thousands of coaches on the power of their leadership over a 30-year career because of the impact Coach DeBruin had on me. His small act of confidence in me decades ago was life-changing.

So, amidst the sadness of my father's funeral, I was delighted to see Coach DeBruin again after all these years. I sincerely thanked him for coming but what he said next absolutely floored me. He looked in my eyes and said, "Jeff, I don't think you know this but your dad was an influential person in my life. He was about 10 years ahead of me in school and he was the lead in the high school play, *Babes in Toyland.* He did such an amazing job in that play that he was a person who was a big inspiration to me in my life. He was so classy and professional and I admired that in him and wanted to be like him. I just wanted you to know that."

That surreal moment shockingly made me realize the generational power of the Ripple Effect. Coach DeBruin, the man who had had one of the biggest and most profound influences on my own life—had actually been influenced by my own father over three decades earlier. I realized then that the seemingly little things we say and do have powerful and long-lasting Ripple Effects across generations.

The Ripple Effect informs and reminds us that we all have the power to be a Coach DeBruin kind of person in anyone's life, someone who positively changes a person's life trajectory by our simple yet powerful belief in them—and we are called to do so. It's one of our primary purposes in life.

Seeing the Full Ripple Effect of Our Actions

In our Life Review, we see all the positive and negative generational Ripple Effects our life creates for others. While we just explored a positive example, unfortunately our words and actions can also negatively impact people's lives for the long-term as well. Here is an example from NDEr Rene Jorgensen:

> "The Life Review continued all the way down to third grade . . . I was teasing a smaller girl . . . I'm feeling how it feels for her to receive my actions that are very hurtful. And I am not only feeling her sorrow and her pain, but I am also sensing and understanding how my actions are impacting her future life. I'm now seeing, sensing, and feeling that she will become much more shy and introverted for the rest of her life because of my actions. But not only do I sense and feel that, I also feel the pain and sorrow in her parents because she's now going to turn out a more shy and inward person. So I'm really feeling the full consequences—not just how my actions are changing the life of this little girl, but I am also feeling . . . how my actions

> caused ripples far away, not just in her life, but in her parents' lives, in her whole family, also in everyone around her. So I get the full spectrum of the full consequences—all the links in the chain . . . spending a few minutes in a schoolyard teasing a girl." Rene Jorgensen

Stopping the Cycle of Negative Ripples Across Generations

Our words and deeds have the power to ripple across many generations. Unfortunately, this works for positive events like Coach DeBruin did for me as much as it does with negative events like abuse, bullying, alcoholism, etc. In fact, NDErs can often trace the abuse they may have experienced from their own father, to how their father was abused by his father, and so on going back multiple generations. NDEr Dr. Rajiv Parti explains in his excellent book, *Dying to Wake Up,* how he saw in his NDE the abuse he received from his father went back multiple generations and unfortunately was a cycle he continued with his own son.

> "He [Rajiv's father] was the same yet different. He looked like a person who was enlightened by love. He looked like a person who had gazed into the eyes of God. Universal knowledge granted us in the Afterlife allowed me to see and feel him in this new way. I looked into his eyes, and my hard heart melted in love. I saw a man who was truly at peace . . . For the first time, I knew his father had abused him as he had abused us. Visions of his anguish as a child came into my mind as I felt his pain at being brutally beaten as well. 'Anger isn't usually about an event,' said my father. 'It's passed on from father to son. If you know that; you can stop it. You can choose not to be angry.' I knew that behind him was a chain of ancestors, each of whom had been filled with anger by their fathers . . . But now I felt empathy from my father. 'Don't pass the anger to your sons,' he communicated. I looked with shame at my father, who returned the look with love and kindness. [I thought] 'I have become the worst of my father as he was the worst of his.' That thought came to me in a flash and with it came a stream of moments in which I had chosen anger over rationale behavior." Rajiv Parti

When Dr. Parti fully recognized the cycle of abuse that had plagued his family for generations, the realization motivated him to stop the abuse rather than continuing the negative Ripple Effect and perpetrating it on future generations. He sincerely apologized to his own sons for his behavior and vowed to stop the psychologically abusive behavior from continuing and impacting future generations. Here is the letter he wrote to his deceased father to forgive him and stop the family's generations-long history of abuse.

"Dear Father,

When I saw you during my near-death experience, you revealed much to me about why you behaved so abusively toward me during my childhood. I had not known about your unhappy youth, but now I see and feel what you suffered as if I shared it with you. Harshness was your defense, your shield against unloving abusive parents . . . Your desire to hide your pain hardened your heart. You sometimes mocked and swore at me. If I cried, you would laugh at me and say that strong boys do not cry. I had to harden my own heart against you, often hating you as you hated your own father . . . I understand that you treated me as your father treated you because you knew of no other way to love me . . . I forgive you for every cruel word and every raised hand. I forgive you for the abuse and thank you for your love, unexpressed though it often was. You wisely told me during my NDE that anger was a choice. I now choose that the anger that plagued our family shall stop with me.

With Love and Forgiveness,

Rajiv"

The Ripple Effect of our actions and those of generations before us can have long-lasting effects. Think about the challenges you experience in your life. How might they have originated from generations before you? And more importantly, how can you be the person who takes full responsibility to recognize the issues and stop them moving forward?

The Life Review allows us to experience our life from so many vantage points—even those of our ancestors who came before us whose positive and negative actions from decades ago still ripple through us and our family today.

"If we do not transform our pain, we will most assuredly transmit it—usually to those closest to us: our family, our neighbors, our co-workers, and, invariably, the most vulnerable, our children."

Father Richard Rohr, Christian Author

Even Our Thoughts Have an Impact

Finally, as we conclude our Experience Your Life chapter, we learn that in addition to our words and actions having an impact on people, plants, and our planet across generations, NDErs tell us that even the thoughts we think impact others too.

> "God showed me, He said, 'A thought has a certain measure of energy to it, and a word has even more, and an action has even more than that. But it all starts with a thought.' Because what you think about is what you talk about is what you end up doing. And so you've got to control your thoughts. And so He showed me these negative thoughts that I had had about people—and they were deserved. Let me tell you, they were some jerky people. He showed me though, He said, 'When you spend your energy on this and you're thinking these negative thoughts, it hurts you because the energy you put out there impacts you.' He showed me that when you have a negative thought about a person, that energy goes out there and it attaches itself to that person and you contribute to the jerk that that person is because now you've attached more of that energy to them . . . So if I think something negative about you, that thought attaches itself to your spirit and it makes you more of the person that I'm thinking you are." Penny Wittbrodt

> "I was shown my life from birth to unconsciousness. I saw myself on the wrong side. I was not as good as I thought I was and was ashamed of myself. But the Being of Love didn't judge me. He just supported me and gave me love. I saw not only the ACTIONS I had done, but also the THOUGHTS I had sent out. And the thoughts meant more than the actions. That surprised me. I hadn't thought it would be like that. It was scary. It's very good to do good deeds towards others, but the feelings and thoughts you send to them count more. For instance, it is bad to smile politely at someone while sending negative thoughts to them." Anni S.

> "A book was opened in front of me which contained everything I had ever said, done, experienced—good and bad. It was like a record of my life. Even my thoughts! It was confronting. Yes, I learned that life was just a schoolroom, just a learning place. We are here to learn and better ourselves but not materially! We are souls with bodies, not bodies with souls. We are here to learn." Annie

> "When I sent out a thought like when I'm driving in my car and somebody cuts me off and I'm like, 'Oh you #@$%!' That thought is energy and that energy is directed toward that person. And that person is going to feel that thought and they're going to react to that. And the next person they encounter, because of that reaction, they might give a negative reaction to that. I was able to see that everything's connected." Heidi Craig

It's not just our words and actions that impact the world, but it all starts with a thought. We may think our thoughts don't have any effect if we just keep them to ourselves, yet we learn that they too eventually influence our own words and actions and ultimately get transmitted to others in a small yet significant way. We are encouraged to watch our thoughts because they soon become our actions and destiny.

"Watch your thoughts, they become your words;
watch your words, they become your actions;
watch your actions, they become your habits;
watch your habits, they become your character;
watch your character, it becomes your destiny."

Lao Tzu, Chinese Philosopher

Experience Your Life Summary

We learned in this chapter that we will get to relive our life in microscopic detail and notice so many things we hadn't the first time around. We also learned that we will not only review our life from our own perspective, but get to see ourselves and our life from everyone's perspective with whom we ever interacted. And finally, we get to see the long-term Ripple Effect of our behavior and all the dominos that fall because of our actions. But what we will learn in our next chapter becomes one of the most instructive and unforgettable parts of the Life Review . . . turn the page to discover more.

EXPERIENCE YOUR LIFE
PRACTICAL REFLECTIONS AND EXERCISES

EXPERIENCE YOUR LIFE EXERCISE #1
Seeing Through Other's Eyes

NDErs tell us we will get to see our life through the eyes of others.

Through whose eyes would you most like to see your life from and why?

Through whose eyes would you least like to see your life from and why?

EXPERIENCE YOUR LIFE EXERCISE #2
Trajectory Changers

Who positively changed your life's trajectory and how?

Who negatively influenced your life's trajectory and how?

Whose life trajectory have you positively impacted and how?

Whose life trajectory have you negatively influenced and how?

EXPERIENCE YOUR LIFE EXERCISE #3
Thanking Your Coach DeBruins

Hopefully we all have "Coach DeBruin" figures in our life—people who our lives would have taken a different course without them. If you haven't already, I encourage you to thank the Coach DeBruin figures in your life—the people who positively and profoundly changed the trajectory of your life and may not have realized it at the time. Let them know of your immense appreciation for their gift—and that you wouldn't be the same person without them. (Author's Note: I had coffee with Coach DeBruin in our hometown in Wisconsin as I was writing this book and thanked him again for the immense influence he had on my life decades ago.)

EXPERIENCE YOUR LIFE EXERCISE #4
Generational Ripple Effects

What are the positive generational Ripple Effects that have occurred in your family?

How can you continue them?

What challenging behaviors, trauma, or abuse might still be rippling and cycling through your family in terms of alcoholism, drug use, gambling, physical abuse, emotional abuse, sexual abuse, etc.?

Where did it all start with the first domino?

More importantly, how can you stop the cycle of problems within your generation so it doesn't adversely affect future generations?

EXPERIENCE YOUR LIFE EXERCISE #5
Forgiveness Letter

Like NDEr Dr. Rajiv Parti did with his father, write a letter to someone you would like to forgive. Express your feelings and offer your forgiveness. Writing the letter is a great way to recognize and release the hurt and resentment you've been carrying. It will be up to you to decide whether it is productive to send it to the person. For some of you, the letter should be addressed and written to yourself to forgive yourself for something you've said, done, or not done. Many times forgiving ourselves is even harder than forgiving others.

EXPERIENCE YOUR LIFE EXERCISE #6
How You've Treated Animals and Plants

Which life situations would you be proud of in terms of how you treated animals?

Which life situations would you be proud of in terms of how you treated plants?

Which life situations would you be concerned about in terms of how you treated animals?

Which life situations would you be concerned about in terms of how you treated plants?

EXPERIENCE YOUR LIFE EXERCISE #7
Be an Advocate for Animals and the Environment

Be an advocate for animals this week: take a dog for a walk, volunteer for or contribute to an animal rescue organization, explore the products you buy to see if they use animal testing, plan one or more less meals with meat this week, move bugs outside instead of killing them, etc.

Be an advocate for the environment this week: reduce, reuse, and recycle, conserve water, plant a garden/tree, use less chemicals and insecticides, bike instead of drive, check and improve your home's energy efficiency, use cloth bags, buy local, choose reusable over single use, etc.

EXPERIENCE YOUR LIFE EXERCISE #8
Most Impactful NDEr Quote

Which of the NDEr quotes from this chapter most impacted you and why? When you reflect on the quote in relation to your own life, how does it lead you to think and feel?

EXPERIENCE YOUR LIFE EXERCISE #9

Shamanic Rock Exercise

NDEr Jeff Olsen told me that shamans developed this powerful exercise to help people see multiple perspectives on situations. Find four large rocks, preferably of increasing height, that you can stand on. Set them out in a circle. The first and lowest rock represents your personal perspective on a situation, challenge, or conflict you're having with someone. Physically stand on the rock and fully state your personal perspective on the situation. Be sure to describe your viewpoint, internal motivations, and the exact emotions you are feeling about the situation. After you've completely stated your perspective, move to rock #2. The second slightly higher rock represents the other person's perspective on the situation, likely a person with whom you have a conflict. Do your best to breathe in their essence and try to become them. From their perspective, describe their unique and valid viewpoint, internal motivations, and emotions on the situation or conflict. Even though you personally may not agree with them, really try to see, feel, and express the situation from their perspective. After you have fully stated and experienced the situation from their perspective, move to the third rock. Rock #3 is the objective, third person perspective. Take a deep breath and adopt this independent, dispassionate, fact-based perspective. Stand on the third rock and now look at this situation as if you are an unbiased, unemotional, totally objective observer. State what you see now from this third perspective and how you would view the situation or conflict as an outsider. Finally, move to Rock #4, which ideally is the biggest and tallest rock. Rock #4 represents the Divine's perspective on the situation. Take a deep breath and attempt to see the situation how God would see it. Experience and state how you think the Creator would look at this same situation from the vantage point of unconditional love and total acceptance. For most people, by the time you finish with Rock #4, the formerly emotionally-charged conflict gets reframed, often subsides, and likely solved because you can see it from multiple valuable viewpoints and put it in its proper perspective.

3.

EMPATHIZE WITH OTHERS

"How you make others feel about themselves, says a lot about you."

Boonaa Mohammed, Muslim Author

Roland Webb's Life Review

"I saw myself at five years old [in my Life Review]. I was in the neighborhood where I grew up in Washington, D.C. I was with my brothers and sisters and my neighborhood friend, whose name was Hydie. Hydie was maybe a year younger than us.

We lived in an apartment building at the time. On the bottom floor of the apartment building, there was a beehive on the windowsill. I said, 'Hey Hydie! Pick up that stick and whack that beehive and we're gonna run and see if we can beat the bees.' So Hydie, listening to me, I don't know why, picks up the stick and whacks the beehive and we all took off running.

The apartment building had a really dark green door. Everyone got into the apartment building and the last one to approach the door was Hydie. I had a devious thought in my mind: 'I'm going to hold the door and not let Hydie in, and see what happens to Hydie.'

All those bees from that beehive stung the daylights out of Hydie. Every single bee sting I felt. I felt every sting, the burning sensation, and the swelling.

His mother came out of the apartment building scared and frightened. I felt all her fear, all her fright, and all her rage. His father came out, trying to figure out what happened.

I felt it all—it rippled. I felt every single thing. All the bees, how angry they were. I felt it all, every aspect. I felt everything."

If Roland Webb's Life Review doesn't sting you at least a little bit and get you to reconsider your devious acts, I'm not sure what will. It's not shared to terrify or torture us, although it may create a haunting buzz the next time you're tempted to do something unkind, rather it is shared to inform us that not only will we experience our life through the eyes of everyone with whom we interact, we will also physically and emotionally feel what they felt when they were with us.

> "You literally become every person you ever encountered. You will experience what it felt like to be that person, and you will feel the direct results of the interactions between you." Dannion Brinkley

> "With every interaction, I got to feel what it was like to be on the receiving end of whatever I was dishing out. Whenever I gave someone pleasure, I felt it too; and whenever I caused someone pain, I felt that too." David Beckman

> "One occasion I relived affected me deeply. I was in the eighth grade and was with my friends at school leading them on in verbally abusing another one of our friends. It was cruel behavior and I was drenched in it. I got to be me and experience that secret little thrill you get when you are cleverly mean to someone. I got to experience the admiration, tinged with fear, of the girls who were going along with me, and lastly, I also experienced the humiliation and pain of the one we were tormenting. I got to not just see her but to BE her, including her being huddled next to the lockers, alone and crying, after the rest of us had left. I found myself full of remorse, first, over what I had done, and then over the fact that I was dead and couldn't make up for it. My mind and my heart were crying out, 'I'm sorry! I'm so, so sorry!'" Carol I.

Precisely perceiving and fully feeling what others felt when they interacted with us is one of the most intensive and instructive parts of the Life Review because we intimately experience exactly what it was like to be with us. We feel the identical impact of our own words and actions on others as though we said them and did them to ourselves.

> "By reviewing my past, I was brought to new places of discovery within myself . . . When I was five years old I teased Tammy Fowler, another five-year-old girl, to the point of tears. I was now in a unique position to feel what Tammy felt. Her frustration, her tears, and her feelings of separateness were now my feelings. I felt a tremendous amount of compassion for this child. I was Tammy and needed love, nurturing, and forgiveness." Laurelynn Martin

> "The primary thing I took from the experience that really changed who I am now as a person was due to the Life Review. To feel the pain that I

caused the other person, not from my own perspective but from theirs, to feel what I made them feel with no 'ego' to protect me and defend me from that shadow was really hard." Jennifer Tielking

"While I was in the presence of this Light I was shown a review of my life and all the events that brought me to that point. I was fascinated as I watched my life unfold, that I was aware not only of my own emotions, but also the feelings of those around me as well as those whose lives we touched. I experienced their pain or pleasure and understood what motivated their actions toward others and me." Sandra Rogers

Life Reviews generate total empathy and complete understanding for others because we deeply feel what it's like to be on the receiving end of our own words and actions. We directly experience what we did to others and exactly how it made them feel physically, psychologically, emotionally, and spiritually—which is the heart of empathy. In essence, we become them in our Life Review, we feel their exact emotions and experience how we made them feel as they interacted with us. Fundamentally, a Life Review equals absolute empathy for others.

"Not only did I review my life from my own personal viewpoint, but also from the perspective of others with whom I had connected at various times and places. Now I knew precisely what people were thinking and feeling about me. Every time I hurt someone's feelings, I felt their pain. Now I felt the results of all my hurtful words and deeds; I could literally sense their every thought and feeling in response to me, which felt downright awful. On the other side of the fence, every time I was kind, or whenever I had helped people or brought them happiness, I felt their joy and appreciation. For the first time, I truly understood how I had affected others and also how they had affected me. What an eye-opener that was!" Malcolm Miller

"I felt everything. Every little kindness. Every subtle dig, each moment of carelessness, the wasted potentials, the comfort passed on to others, the secret joys, impatience, self-pity, a genuine smile to a lonely person at the right moment . . .. Ripples from a tossed pebble, I experienced how everyone experienced my actions and intentions, and how everyone they affected felt." Cami Renfrow

"In my Life Review, I was forced to look at all the pain that I had caused through my negative actions. The review was a flashback, like a movie, playing out all of the scenes in my life when I had caused suffering to others. I saw myself being angry and hurting my mother. Then there was a flashback of hurting an ex-girlfriend. I saw myself teasing a younger classmate so ruthlessly she was scarred for the rest of her life. All my negative reactions played out right in front of my eyes, only this time I saw and felt the full effect these actions had on the people I had hurt. My Life Review

> showed me the effects of my anger, selfishness, and cruelty, everything that I had been ignorant about before. In the review, I was forced to experience the pain that I had given to others. The pain of recognizing my culpability was indescribable, and I was totally overpowered by a deep regret and remorse." Rene Jorgensen

We Feel the Physical and Emotional Pain Our Choices Cause Others

Like the bee sting example with which we started this chapter, NDEr Tom Sawyer re-experienced a brutal fistfight he had with another man and felt what it was like to have his own fist hit him in the face multiple times as well as the humiliation of the event.

> "I hit that man 32 times. I saw what an enraged Tom Sawyer not only looked like but felt like. I experienced seeing Tom Sawyer's fist come directly into my face. I felt my teeth going through my lower lip. In other words, I was in that man's eyes. I was in that man's body. I experienced the physical pain, the degradation, the embarrassment, the humiliation, and the helplessness in being knocked back like that. I broke his nose and really made a mess of his face. I almost killed that man. He didn't have time to bring his hands up, he fell straight backwards hitting his head on the street. I experienced everything of that inter-relationship between Tom Sawyer and that man that day." Tom Sawyer

Our Life Review doesn't have us feel this physical pain to torture us but to directly teach us how our actions impact others—literally in this case with a fist. While the physical feeling is obviously unpleasant, especially if it is a violent fistfight, the emotional pain caused by our words and actions is often an infinitely more intensive and instructive part of the Life Review. Tom continues:

> "In the Life Review, I came to know the man's chronological age: he was 46 years old. I knew that he was in a drunken state and that the rationale behind his desire to drink to oblivion was that he was in a severe state of bereavement for his deceased wife. He turned to alcohol as an escape mechanism for dealing with her death. I experienced unbelievable things about that man that are of a very personal, confidential, and private nature." Tom Sawyer

In reviewing the fistfight, not only did Tom directly feel himself the physical pain he caused the man, he also fully felt and completely comprehended the man's emotional state of bereavement. He learned that not only had he hit a man, but even worse, hit a man when he was emotionally down in the depths of despair of alcohol abuse from the loss of his wife. Ouch!

Be Kind: Everyone is Fighting A Battle You Know Nothing About

In all likelihood, if Tom knew this man's whole story and what he was going through, the last thing he would have done was punch him in the face—which Tom ultimately saw, felt, and realized in his Life Review. Had he acted instead from compassion and understood the man's emotional backstory and fragile state, he would have tried to help the man fight his inner battles rather than compounding the problem by adding on an outer physical battle as well.

Without needing to have an NDE and Life Review, Tom Sawyer's painful lesson reminds us that we too need to consider the private, internal battles our friends, family members, and even strangers face when interacting with them. Instead of fighting with them verbally, emotionally, psychologically, or God forbid physically, perhaps we can take the time to listen to them, understand the pain and fear they're experiencing, and lend an open hand instead of a closed fist—or a closed heart.

NDEr Marion Rome witnessed a time in her Life Review when she was extremely upset with a grocery store cashier over a minor issue and angrily notified the store manager about it. Her Life Review revealed the cashier's difficult backstory and Marion felt the woman's pain and realized she almost cost the cashier her job over a trivial matter.

> "What I knew now—in that amazingly loving Light—was that that woman nearly lost her job because of me that day . . . During my NDE, I learned that that woman, on the other hand, was caring for a very, very sick and mentally disabled child. I was seeing her looking after her kid and I could feel all of her emotional pain and fear as she thought she really couldn't afford to lose one of her two jobs. I knew absolutely all the thoughts that had passed through her mind when this incident happened. I felt the tears and the sadness my own words had caused her. I felt her distress in such an intense way. I have never, ever felt so much pain in my entire life . . . I knew everything about her very tough earthly life, how she died from cancer leaving her son an orphan and how my reaction to a 'non-problem' that day affected her in a very big way." Marion Rome

Through her Life Review, Marion learned the full picture of the struggles the cashier experienced and felt horribly for how she turned a molehill into a mountain for the woman. Mercifully, we don't just feel the pain and misery our choices, words, and deeds created for others but their positive emotions as well. Here's another Life Review episode Marion Rome felt as she relays it in her fabulous book, *Beyond Sight*:

> "I was viewing an occurrence that had happened in the earthly life just a few weeks before my NDE, in a practically empty train station. I was walking up an escalator that was out of order when I saw an old and frail lady trying hard to make her way to the top. I was carrying numerous shopping bags as well as my own large handbag and a huge backpack. That woman looked exhausted . . . I told her to stop there, that I would help her . . . As my soul was witnessing the whole scene I felt her smile . . . I FELT it in an incredible and magical way. I felt like I was hugged by it. Her smile was pure joy, tremendous happiness, and relief. It screamed: 'Thank you so much for helping me. That is so kind of you, you really have no idea.' What I was made extremely aware of during my NDE was the simple fact that I had taken time for her filled her with enormous joy . . . In that amazing afterlife, her joy was now my joy, too. My entire being was filled with every bit of it in such an intensified way and it is a sensation I'd give anything to feel again." Marion Rome

> "I could see my whole life as if I was watching it in a movie theater. I just slid into the experiences. I began to feel everything I had caused others to feel. If I had said a mean thing and thought, 'Oh, they'll get over it,' now I felt what they felt . . . I did experience being nice to an elderly woman and helping her cross the street. I could feel how this event rippled through her life. She was so grateful for this kindness and passed it on to others. I got to feel the repercussions of the time I went into a bank and was rude to a female bank teller. I experienced how she went home and was mean to her kid. She kicked the dog in anger and slammed the door. I realized my action had triggered this." Christopher Sassano

Focus More on the Feelings and Less on the Events

While the Life Review replays all the events of our life, the focus of it is much more on the feelings our thoughts, words, and actions led others to experience than the actual events themselves. How we made others feel is the real key of the Life Review as we feel those exact emotions ourselves often in a much greater sense.

> "I saw, relived, remembered things that had happened in my life: not only what actually took place but also the emotions involved . . . Going through what happened to us [his brother], my focus was not on what we actually did to each other. The emphasis was all the time on our exchange of emotions. And because of the love and understanding radiating from the Being of Light, I found the courage to see for myself, and with open eyes and without defenses, what in my actions had caused him pain." Goran Grip

"Then I saw my life pass by in a kind of retrospective. And it seemed like a movie. From that moment all the way back until my birth I could see all the emotionally significant or very moving moments I had experienced in my life. In particular, all those moments involving love. When others and I were emotionally touching each other in some way; those kinds of situations . . . In that moment, not only did I recognize his genuine feelings for me, I also had an immediate understanding as to why he was completely different with me at other times. This moment came with a lot of additional information. I was able to perceive the entire range of his emotions, not just mine. I felt as if I was emotionally the same people both at the same time. This enhanced perception continued with other people in my life. My perception encompassed both my feelings and those of the other person in their respective situations . . ." Manuala Fazzi

"I felt their pain, the pain I had unwittingly caused and the pain I had freely and often purposefully given to some persons, particularly the ones I loved—my mother, my father, my sisters, my brother, my friends, but my classmates, acquaintances, and strangers, too. They were all there—everyone and every instance. I witnessed and suffered every instance of pain." Peter Panagore

We'll Feel What It Was Like to Be Our Own Spouse . . .

One of the most enlightening, impactful, and transformational aspects of the Life Review is the opportunity to really feel what it was like to be in a relationship with us for as short as a single interaction or as long as an entire lifetime. It doesn't matter if the person is our own beloved child or a random stranger, we feel precisely what others felt when they interacted with us.

Of course most of us consider our most intimate, treasured, and long-term relationships when it comes to considering how we treated people such as our spouse(s), children, parents, siblings, friends, neighbors, etc. From our knowledge of the Life Review and the millions of NDErs who have experienced them, we know:

We will experience and feel what it is like to be our own spouse . . .
We will experience and feel what it is like to be our own child . . .
We will experience and feel what it is like to be our own parent . . .
We will experience and feel what it is like to be our own sibling . . .
We will experience and feel what it is like to be our own friend . . .
We will experience and feel what it is like to be our own neighbor . . .
We will experience and feel what it is like to be our own co-worker . . .

*"The truth will set you free,
but first it will make
you miserable."*

JAMES GARFIELD

When I sincerely reflected on the gravity of this, I had to admit it threw me for a loop for at least a week. Unfortunately, it pained me to consider many of them. Sadly, but necessarily, it brought me to a deeper level of reflection, awareness, and understanding. Honestly, there were many times and ways I realized I would not have wanted to be my spouse, child, parent, sibling, friend, neighbor, or co-worker—and these difficult yet revealing realizations highly motivated me to make some necessary improvements.

> "Watching and re-experiencing all those events of my life changed everything. It was an opportunity to see and feel all the love I had shared, and more importantly, all the pain I had caused. I was able to simultaneously re-experience not only my own feelings and thoughts, but those of all the other people I had ever interacted with. Seeing myself through their eyes was a humbling experience." Anonymous NDEr

> "Something that is very hard to talk about; I watched a video of my life . . . I watched myself from the day I was born, from birth all the way until I was 28 years old . . . I watched good things that I had done but I also watched bad things that I did. One thing that I noticed that really hurt was how I treated my wife at the time that I died. I wasn't very good to her. It was all about me. It was not about my family. It wasn't about my wife. It was all about me and how I could get ahead and how much money I could make. And I realized that what I was doing was wrong. It wasn't one of the better things that I watched but it was something that was real. This was an experience that really changed my life." Scott Drummond

Discovering My Mom's Diary After Her Death

I got a surprising, sad, and sobering glimpse of what it was like to be my own son when cleaning out my mom's house after she passed away and discovering her diary. Fortunately, I had a loving relationship with my mom throughout my life and I was definitely a "Mama's Boy." But, although there were numerous positive passages describing happy and proud times, there was a painful passage in my mom's diary that still haunts me today. Although it is embarrassing for me to include in this book, I share it with you to help all of us reflect on these vital questions.

For some context, my mom lived in Wisconsin and we lived in North Carolina so she would come out and visit for a week a couple of times of year. She wrote in her diary during one of her visits, "I sit here most of the day and read while everyone is busy and no one pays any attention to me. I'm not sure why I am even here."

Ouch! Talk about a painful shot directly to the heart and soul. Of course I felt horrible when I read it and still regret it to this day. Unfortunately, during most of her visit, I realized I was so focused on my work and the trivial busy things in life that I neglected my own mother during the few times I got to see and spend time with her each year. Reading her sad but true passage hit me like a ton of bricks because I now fully understood and empathized with her sad feelings that I created. It made me realize I had not been a good son to her on that visit—and it also made me wonder about other times when I had likely acted in the same way toward her and other loved ones.

Did I intentionally set out to be a callous son that week? Of course not! But reading her diary and getting a rare glimpse into her real thoughts and feelings, like a Life Review does and then some, gave me a painful but instructive view of myself on how I had been as a son. It enlightened and motivated me to be more present and attentive to family members and friends in the future.

In essence, the Life Review allows us to see everyone's private diary when it comes to their real, unvarnished, inner thoughts about us. Reading my mom's diary gave me a mini-Life Review of how she felt forgotten that week. I definitely realized I could have done so much better as a son.

> "I then went through a Life Review. It was all about my relationships with others in this review. During this, I felt what they felt in my relationship with them. I felt their love or their pain or their hurt, by things I had done or said to them. Their hurt or pain made me cringe and I found myself thinking, 'Oooh, I could have done better there.' But most of what I felt was love, so it was not too bad." Jean R.

In addition to family members, we often have the opportunity to be helpful to others in our neighborhood, workplace, church, or community. In fact, God and our guardian angels may even work behind the scenes of our life to orchestrate opportunities where we can assist others—if we have the courage, compassion, and commitment to act on them.

> "I saw a woman whom I had been asked by our local church leader to visit periodically. I was just to check up on her and see if she needed any help. I knew the woman quite well but was afraid of her constant pessimism and negativity. She was locally renowned for her bitterness. I didn't think I could handle the depressing influence she would have on me, so I never went to see her. Not once. I saw now that the opportunity to visit her had

been orchestrated by Higher Powers, that I had been just the person she needed at that time. She didn't know it, and I didn't know it, but I had let her down. Now I lived her sadness and felt her disappointment and knew I was a cause of it. I had fallen through on a special mission to her, a responsibility that would have strengthened me over time. I had retreated from an opportunity for growth, both for me and for her, because I was not caring enough to fight through my petty fears and laziness. But the reasons didn't matter; I could see that, even now, she was living in sadness and bitterness, living through it just as I now experienced it, and there was nothing I could do to go back and help." RaNelle Wallace

The Golden Rule

Ultimately, the Life Review confirms the validity and power of the Golden Rule. When we realize what we do to others, we actually do to ourselves, we live with much more awareness of our actions and hopefully become much more kind. We stop and think, "How would I want to feel in this situation?" and speak and act accordingly.

Essentially, most religions boil down to the Golden Rule of treating others as we would like to be treated—with love, kindness, compassion, understanding, patience, and forgiveness.

- **Christianity—**"In everything, do unto others what you would have them do to you. For this sums up the law and the prophets." Matthew 7:12
- **Buddhism—**"Do not offend others as you would not want to be offended." Udanavarga 5:18
- **Islam—**"None of you are true believers until you love for your brother what you love for yourself." Prophet Muhammad
- **Judaism—**"What is hateful to you, do not do to your neighbor. This is the whole Torah; all the rest is commentary." Hillel, Talmud, Shabbat 31a
- **Confucianism—**Tzu-kung asked, "Is there one word which can serve as the guiding principle for conduct throughout life?" Confucius said, "It is the word altruism (shu). Do not do to others what you do not want them to do to you." Analects 15:23
- **Sikhism—**"I am a stranger to no one; and no one is a stranger to me. Indeed, I am a friend to all." Guru Granth Sahib, pg. 1299

- **Taoism**—"Regard your neighbor's gain as your own gain and your neighbor's loss as your own loss." T'ai Shang Kan Ying P'ien, 213–218
- **Jainism**—"One should treat all creatures in the world as one would like to be treated." Mahavira, Sutrakritanga

Through the Life Review, we learn the Golden Rule isn't just some nice platitude. We discover it is indeed 100% true, across all of the major religions of the world. With the wisdom of the Life Review, we realize the Golden Rule is not just an intellectual knowing but an emotional and physical knowing which makes it much tougher to deny or forget. What we do to others, we do to ourselves.

> "The Life Review is where you learn that 'do unto others as you would have them do unto you' is not just a philosophy, but a law." Dannion Brinkley

> "I saw that whenever I had done something good to anyone or anything, that I had done it to myself. And whenever I had hurt someone, I had done it to myself." Mohammed Z.

> "What we do to others, we do to ourselves. To hurt another is to hurt ourselves; to judge another is to judge ourselves; to hate another is to hate ourselves; and to love another is to love ourselves." Helen S.

> "The Golden Rule is the only rule that matters in the Life Review." Cami Renfrow

Karma: What We Put Out We Receive Back

The Life Review is the ultimate example of karma. Everything we put out in the world during our lifetime does actually come back to us—in full force at the end of our life in our Life Review.

> "I felt the positive and negative energy I gave to the people I met. Almost like karma, if I had committed a good deed to a person happiness would return to me. If I caused someone pain, their pain would return to me." Philip S.

> "The one overarching rule of the game is called karma. If you pat somebody in the back, we get a pat on the back later. If we kick somebody in the butt, we get kicked in the butt later." Duane Smith

> "I was shown all my life experiences, and I WAS the person whom I had hurt or helped so that I felt what they felt when I had erroneously acted against or helped them . . . Hard to explain, seems easiest for me to call it karma." Ruth

When we love others, we experience that same love back ourselves. When we give generously to others, we feel that same generosity ourselves. When we hurt others, we feel that same pain ourselves. What we do to others boomerangs back to us.

> "I then began to see my whole life unfolding before me as if a film being projected on a screen, from babyhood to adult life. It was so real! I was looking at myself, but better than a 3D movie as I was also capable of sensing the feelings of the persons I had interacted with through the years. I could feel the good and bad emotions I made them go through. I was also capable of seeing that the better I made them feel and the better the emotions they had because of me would give me some credits (karma) and that the bad ones would take some of it back—just like in a bank account, but here it was like a karma account to my knowledge." Roger C.

> "I was given my Life Review. I was shown my life; everything I had ever said and done was shown to me . . . It was after the Life Review that I heard a male voice say, 'What you put out into the universe will come back to you.'" Sharon Milliman

> "The messages of the scenes I viewed became clear to me: forgiveness reaps forgiveness, mercy reaps mercy, love reaps love, violence reaps violence." Dr. Joyce Brown

---

"When a bird is alive, it eats ants. When the bird is dead, ants eat it. One tree can be made into a million matchsticks. But only one match is needed to burn a million trees. Time and circumstance can change at any time. Don't devalue or hurt anyone in this life. You may be powerful today but time is more powerful than you. So be good and do good."

Anonymous

We Understand the Emotional Backstory and Baggage of People

The Life Review not only has us feel the feelings of those we helped and hurt, it also provides us with the complete emotional backstory of why people act the way they do by helping us understand why they are the way they are. We realize the pains and problems they perpetrate on us are often symptoms of a deeper unresolved trauma they experienced themselves, sometimes years and decades before.

> "This Life Review began. He showed me my life because my life had been marked by extreme experiences; a lot of grief, loneliness, losses, and several phases where I wished my own death. He showed me the

experiences I had had in my life starting from my birth and ending at the moment I arrived in hospital. He explained the connections to me. The crazy thing I noticed was that every time I relived the situation, I seemed to experience everything at the same time. For example, I had a conversation with my father; I could sense the feelings of my father and I knew why he was reacting. I could feel my own feelings and everything at once. And this increased even more because I was shown if I or my father had made a different decision at that moment, something would have happened differently. I could perceive this as well. It was so multidimensional. It was like holograms that opened up and you were able to zoom in, as if with a microscope, and capture everything simultaneously. If I tried to describe it briefly, I'd say I completely comprehended my Life Review." Anke Everitz

"In that other realm the picture was finally complete. I got all the answers, or remembered all the answers. And, yes, there was significant insight into others who I was in relationship with at the time, in particular, my stepmother. I was shown, or could see, her whole life, her struggles, her fears, and all that had made her into who she was. And I could finally see her abusiveness was not about me being a 'bad' kid. It was ALL because of her fears, her earthly amnesia, and her struggles, insecurity, etc. I saw that she had been abused growing up. And in the end, I could only feel great compassion and admiration for her . . . We are all blind and scared while we are here. We do our best, and it's all understood and our mistakes are forgiven once we have our expanded spiritual awareness back." Amphianda Baskett

The Life Review essentially affords us with a complete psychological profile and life history of each person in every interaction. We understand their perspective on the situation, their motivations, their mental and emotional state at the time, their ulterior motives, etc. It's like having x-ray vision into their mind, heart, and soul (as well as our own) as we clearly realize and understand what motivated their actions and why they did what they did. We see into their psyches and understand their personality types as if we can read all the results of their DiSC profile, Myers-Briggs Type Indicator, Enneagram number, etc. We somehow understand people at their deepest core due to the knowledge afforded to us through the Life Review.

"I was able to feel exactly what others around me had felt during my life. I understood how everything I did, said, and thought, had touched others around me in one way or another. I was able to enter the minds and emotional centers of many who had been around me, and understand where they were coming from in their own thinking. I could see how their own personal views and life experiences had shaped their lives. I felt their struggling and their fears, their own desperate need for love and approval, their confusion, and more than anything, I could feel how child-like everyone was." Amy Call

"I saw my father leaving us when I was three years old, and I realized his decision pained him too. I understood why he left and why I became so sad and angry about it." David Oakford

"You have total knowledge. You have the ability to be a psychologist, a psychiatrist, a psychoanalyst, and much more." Tom Sawyer

With this expansive and complete knowledge of ourselves and others, we finally understand the crazy and complex relationships and situations that confound and perplex us now as humans. In the Life Review, we transcend our human ego and see things from a much higher, deeper, and expanded perspective. It all makes sense and comes together in the Life Review and fully answers all of our questions.

See Our Parents as Real People

We get to see our parents as real and fallible human beings with their own set of challenges, fears, issues, etc., in our Life Review. Instead of only viewing them as the larger-than-life, invincible superheroes we often make them out to be if they treated us lovingly, we see that they too, like us, experienced their own set of worries, cultural biases, and ego-driven behavior as parents and adults. NDEr Tom Sawyer experienced his mother's biased feelings about him and her financial concerns about his father when he was only two months old in his Life Review.

"Let me tell you about one incident when I was a couple of months old, seeing my mother's eyes. I was not able to sit up properly and she was dressing me in this little suit and just being the mother that she was, having her blond, blue-eyed boy on the receiving blanket on the rug . . . I was not only viewing the experience in the capacity of a two-month-old child, I was seeing out of my mother's eyes. She is looking at and living in the capacity of a mother. But she is also a biased, prejudiced person. And she extra-loved the fact that she got her blue-eyed, blond-haired boy, instead of an equally divine, beautiful, lovely dark-haired, brown-eyed boy . . . So she's dressing me in a little blazer . . . at the same time she is concentrating on, psychologically and emotionally, what Tom (which was my father's nickname) will think. She's thinking, 'God forbid that Tom finds out that I spent this much money on these new clothes.' Since we were very poor, she's thinking she shouldn't have spent the money for a little baby." Tom Sawyer

Obviously, a two-month-old baby would never notice or even be privy to these parental issues as an infant, but in the Life Review we glean the complete backstory of others, which helps us see the bigger picture of everyone involved and understand their underlying motivations.

If our parents treated us in unloving ways when we grew up, we see and feel the origins of the various traumas, difficulties, and abuses they experienced during their lifetime.

> "When I had my NDE, it had been exactly seven years since I had spoken to my mother . . . I hated her with a passion. I could not spend even one minute in the same room as her. Yet, in that amazing world, I felt instant forgiveness for all the horrendous things she had done to me. I know now why she had caused me so much pain and torment. She herself was a very tortured and suffering soul and, in the ego-centered physical world, inflicting pain on others was the way she could feel her own [pain] to a lesser degree. I could feel her pain, enormous distress, her fears, and I knew that it was all of that that led her to treat me so badly, just like her dad treated her poorly in her childhood . . . My way of responding to her aggressive behavior has now completely changed. I used to fight back, return her insults, retaliate . . . I now simply couldn't fight back anymore. Not after the eternal and real forgiveness I experienced and felt for her in that magical world, without my ego in the way preventing me from doing so . . . Without my NDE, I would probably have had to see a therapist for a lifetime in order to figure out her abusive behavior. I now don't do any form of psychotherapy. I have all the answers I need." Marion Rome

We also have the ability to see in our Life Review that sometimes our parents disciplined us because they loved us and discover it pained them as much as it did us to do so. Even though we may not have understood, enjoyed, or approved of their discipline methods at the time (or now), we learn of their inner intent in our Life Review.

> "Another portion of my Life Review came to mind that showed me how love can come in many forms. I had lied to my mother about something, and I could feel the sharp sting of the belt that she brought down on my rear end as she impressed upon me the importance of telling her the truth. The whipping hurt me both physically and emotionally. The amazing thing, however, was how much it hurt my mother. In my Life Review, I could feel the pain she felt as she spanked me. I could also tell she was spanking me out of love so that I would grow up to become a better person." Dannion Brinkley

Understand Why "Hurt People" Hurt People

With this deep and comprehensive knowledge and x-ray vision into the hearts, minds, and souls of others courtesy of the Life Review, we especially understand why some people might hurt us. We discover and completely comprehend the phrase "hurt people, hurt people." We realize the people who hurt us often acted out of their own psychological issues, internal pains, and past traumas they couldn't process in their life. From this new and expanded vantage point, unfortunately but somewhat understandably, we learn it was easier for them to drag us into their drama and act out their pain and unresolved trauma on us rather than work through their issues and rise above them.

> "Recognize that when someone has done something hurtful to you, it's usually a sign that they're suffering themselves. If you stay invested in other people's pain, you'll carry it around with you as if it were really yours—when, of course, it isn't. Take the opportunity to transcend the petty, destructive, and unconscious things that we humans can sometimes do, usually in an effort to enhance or 'protect' ourselves, and instead try to see them as opportunities to deal with someone's pain (maybe your own?) with generosity and compassion." Robert Kopecky

> "In Heaven, we get the privilege of seeing another person's heart as God would see it, so we can understand how someone might react differently than we would to a particular situation. In one scene, I observed someone very standoffish. After looking into their heart, I saw how they had been injured spiritually and acted harshly towards others out of fear. This knowledge made it easier to understand that not every action from another was about me or towards me. Sometimes it was just about them." Casper

> "In the Life Review, we understand why everyone chooses to act as they do; usually negative people have pain, hurt, rejection that causes them to act out that hurt in relationships. They don't know that, it's in their unconscious mind; but if we could know their pain we would be much more compassionate." Robert Farnsworth

---

"If you don't heal from what hurt you,
you'll bleed on people who didn't cut you."

Anonymous

Understanding Sets Up Empathy

When we understand the complete picture, it sets us up to potentially empathize with those who hurt us. Of course it doesn't make their harmful, hurtful, or heinous behavior right or justifiable in any way—it just allows us to understand why it happened and realize the origins of it. When we see the root cause of the behavior and how it runs far deeper than us, it makes it easier to understand the other person's pain and potentially forgive them.

> "At different stages of the Life Review, I saw instances of selfish people deliberately abusing me, but instead of feeling resentment towards them, I felt a sense of compassion for them. Not once did I feel anger or hostility towards anybody who had hurt or inconvenienced me. Instead, I only wanted them to understand love." Malcolm Miller

> "We relived thirty-two years of my life. I could hear myself saying, 'No wonder, no wonder.' I now believe my 'no wonders' meant 'No wonder you are the way you are now. Look what was done to you when you were a little girl.' My mother had been dependent on prescription drugs, angry and abusive, and my father wasn't home much of the time and did little to intervene. I saw all this again, but I did not see it in little bits and pieces, the way I had remembered it as an adult. I saw and experienced it just as I had lived it at the time it first happened. Not only was I me, I was also my mother, my dad, and my brother. We were all one. Just as I had felt everything my grandmother had felt, I now felt my mother's pain and neglect from her childhood. She wasn't trying to be mean. She didn't know how to be loving or kind. She didn't know how to love. She didn't understand what life is really all about. And she was still angry from her own childhood, angry because they were poor and because her father was sick almost every day until he died when she was eleven. And then she was angry because he had left her. She didn't know what to do with her anger so she gave it to my brother and me. Her anger boiled up all the time and then she physically abused us or she made us listen to all her resentments. Her list went back to her early childhood. Everyone had hurt her. I don't think that she, through her numbness and drugged state, understood how she was doing the same thing to us. Everything came flooding back, including my father's helplessness and confusion at stopping the insanity. I could hear myself saying, 'No wonder, no wonder.' And then the benevolent Energy that was holding me held me tighter and with even more love. We continued watching my mother in pain, always seeing doctors and always receiving prescription pain killers, sleeping pills, and tranquilizers. My only feeling during this time was loneliness. I saw myself down on my knees by the side of my bed, praying for a doctor to help my mother. I saw how I had given up 'myself' in order to survive. I forgot that I was a child. I became my mother's mother. I suddenly knew that my mother had had the same thing happen to her in her childhood. She took care of her father, and as a child she gave herself up to take care of him. As children, she and I both became anything and everything others needed. As my Life Review continued, I also saw my mother's Soul, how painful her life was, how lost she was. And I saw my father and how he put blinders on himself to avoid his grief over my mother's pain and to survive. In my Life Review, I saw that they were good people caught in helplessness. I saw their beauty, their

humanity and their needs that had gone unattended to in their own childhoods. I loved them and understood them. We may have been trapped, but we were still Souls connected in our dance of life by an Energy source that had created us . . . As my Life Review continued, I got married and had my own children and saw that I was on the edge of repeating the cycle that I had experienced as a child. I was on prescription drugs. I was in the hospital. I was becoming like my mother. And at the same time, this Loving Energy we call God was holding me and let me into Its experience of all this. I felt God's memories of these scenes through God's eyes, just as I had through my grandmother's eyes. As my life unfolded, I witnessed how severely I had treated myself because that was the behavior shown and taught to me as a child. I realized that the only big mistake I had made in my life was that I had never learned to love myself. And then I was back here, in this reality." Barbara Harris Whitfield

After seeing and feeling the exact origins of and repeated cycles of mistreatment, abuse, criticism, judgment, etc., NDErs are often shown they are the ones who can stop it. They are the ones who can make the changes and stop the violence perpetrated on their own family, friends, and future generations. Feeling what others feel enlightens us about the situation, the people involved, and ourselves.

Empathize with Others Summary

A Life Review not only shows us our life through other people's perspective, it also provides us with the remarkable opportunity to actually feel what others felt in their interactions with us. We experience the exact emotions they felt from our words and actions as if we said and did them to ourselves. Feeling what they felt allows us to fully empathize with them and highlights the importance of the Golden Rule and karma. With this heartfelt and first-hand knowledge, in our next chapter we'll focus on all the ways a Life Review helps us effectively evaluate our life.

EMPATHIZE WITH OTHERS
PRACTICAL REFLECTIONS AND EXERCISES

EMPATHIZE WITH OTHERS EXERCISE #1
Feeling the Joy or Sting of Your Actions or Words

When you read the NDEr Roland Webb story about the stinging bees, which similar situation in your life came to mind when you physically or emotionally hurt someone and why?

EMPATHIZE WITH OTHERS EXERCISE #2
Be Kind: Everyone is Fighting Battles

Which situations have you later discovered that people were fighting private battles you knew nothing about that might have better explained their difficult words and/or behavior?

How did learning about these challenging battles help you better understand their situation and potentially cut them some slack?

How might you proactively empathize and realize that people may be fighting some tough battles you know little about before you make their life tougher or get upset with them?

EMPATHIZE WITH OTHERS EXERCISE #3
Put Yourself in the Others' Shoes

Put yourself in the shoes of a homeless person, a refugee, an incarcerated person, or a persecuted person because of their skin color or religious beliefs, etc. This week see yourself in others who struggle and do something to ease their pain. Look them in the eyes, ask them their name and where they're from, acknowledge their humanity and worth, and listen to their story. Offer to help in whatever way you can, either financially or just listening. If you don't have many homeless people or refugees in your area, make a meal or bake some cookies for a shut-in, someone who works multiple jobs, or someone who was recently laid off.

EMPATHIZE WITH OTHERS EXERCISE #4
What Would It Feel Like If I Was My Spouse, Friend, Child, Etc.

Because we will eventually feel the things our spouses, parents, children, siblings, friends, neighbors, and co-workers felt when they are with us, it is highly advisable to ask and answer these critical questions NOW, rather than waiting until the end of our life:

How would I feel if I was married to me?

How would I feel if I was parented by me?

How would I feel if I was my own child?

How would I feel if I was my own sister/brother?

How would I feel if I was friends with me?

How would I feel if I was my own neighbor?

How would I feel if I was supervised by or worked with me?

These penetrating questions are some of the most crucial ones you can ask yourself and are the crux of the Life Review and the ultimate purpose of this book. Rather than waiting to see and FEEL the answers in your Life Review when you physically die, it is much better to ask, reflect on, and honestly answer these questions NOW! Consider these crucial questions now while we still have time to act on them. Moving forward, we have the rest of our lifetime, be that a day or several decades, to determine our answers to these questions, and be a positive and loving force in these important people's lives. Don't go any further in this book—or your life—until you really reflect upon and answer these questions. Yes, they may cause some regret and put you in a funk for a couple of days or weeks like they did for me. But hopefully they motivate you, as they did me, to make some necessary improvements.

EMPATHIZE WITH OTHERS EXERCISE #5
Reading Someone's Revealing Diary

Whose private diary do you think it would feel good for you to read after they died (or now) to understand their thoughts and feelings when they were with you and why?

Whose diary would it be challenging for you to read after they died (or now) to understand their thoughts and feelings when they were with you and why?

Which people in your life do you wish would better understand how you feel when you are with them?

How might you be able to help them understand how you usually feel when you're around them?

EMPATHIZE WITH OTHERS EXERCISE #6
Mirror Exercise

Find a large size mirror and stand in front of it. Think of a loving situation when you said or did something kind or helpful for someone else. Say those words again and repeat those actions and tune in to what it may have felt like for the other person. Really consider what it would be like to be on the receiving end of those words or actions as you say or do them to yourself. Hear it how they heard it and feel what they felt when you said those things. Promise yourself to say more of these kind words moving forward.

Now, think of an unloving situation in your life when you said or did some hurtful things to someone else. Say those words again and repeat those actions and tune in to what it may have felt like for the other person. Really consider what it would be like to be on the receiving end of those words or actions as you say or do them to yourself. Hear it how they heard it and feel what they felt when you said those things. With these feelings in mind, be much more thoughtful and kind moving forward.

EMPATHIZE WITH OTHERS EXERCISE #7
Most Impactful NDEr Quote

Which of the NDEr quotes from this chapter most impacted you and why? When you reflect on the quote in relation to your own life, how does it lead you to think and feel?

4.
EVALUATE YOUR LIFE

"To what degree did you learn to love?"
God's Question to NDEr Jeff Olsen

Dannion Brinkley's Life Review

"Guess what? When you have your panoramic Life Review, you are the judger . . . You do the judging. If you doubt me, believe this: you are the toughest judge you will ever have.

The concept that we are our own judges is a difficult one for most people to grasp. In the Western world, many have come to believe that God will preside over our eternal fate, sitting like a judge on the bench, deciding if we are good enough to join Him in heaven or are so bad that we warrant an eternity in hell . . .

I found that I sat in judgment of myself. I did not receive a stern rebuke from the Being of Light, which initiated my Life Review.

Instead I felt the love and joy that a wise grandfather might radiate to a grandchild who has not yet gained the wisdom of long life.

'You are the difference that God makes,' the Being of Light communicated to me. 'And that difference is love.'

The Being was then quiet. With gentle and loving support to back me up, I was allowed a period of reflection on my own life, the life I had just witnessed from all possible sides.

I took important questions away with me: Had I given as much love as I had taken? Did I practice random acts of kindness? Was I responsible for making people feel good just for the sake of feeling good? These are the things on which I reflected.

The Being of Light provided the forum for my judgment by allowing me to have a Life Review. I judged myself, a far more painful process considering that you really cannot lie to yourself . . .

The Being of Light stood by and kindly told me the meaning of life: 'Humans are powerful spiritual beings meant to create good on the earth,' He said.

'This good isn't usually accomplished in bold actions, but in singular acts of kindness between people.'

The Being told me that it was the 'little things that count' because they show who you truly are. I realize now that small acts of kindness are spontaneous acts, almost like reflexes. When you buy a homeless person a meal or offer assistance to a friend in need, you do it with no agenda. Help like that truly comes from the bottom of your heart. Help like that is true love."

As we examine, experience, and empathize with those our life influenced and impacted in our Life Review, we will also have the opportunity to evaluate our life. We will get to see, feel, understand, and reflect deeply on the millions of choices we made, words we said, and actions we did and didn't take throughout our lifetime. After clearly seeing the impact we made on the world and fully feeling the multiplicative Ripple Effects our life decisions and actions had on others, animals, and the environment, we will have the chance to honestly assess and thoroughly evaluate our life.

Standing Spiritually Naked Before God—All is Laid Bare

NDErs tell us that everything we do in our life is laid totally bare for us to analyze and evaluate in our Life Review. It's as if we stand spiritually naked before God and the angels as we account for the precious gift of life. The dense spiritual veil that kept us from even noticing the Other Side and all its glory lifts from over our eyes, the floodlights come on (remember the illuminated warehouse analogy?), and everything we did in our life comes to light in our Life Review—and comes before the Light.

> "When we die, we will realize that we have been living behind a veil our whole lives. The veil will be lifted and the floodlights will shine on us. Everything in life is really veiled spirit. We are literally on display our whole lives. Every thought, word, and deed has been recorded since birth and will be fully exposed. Everything we have ever done in secret will be brought out into the light for review in front of God and all the heavenly hosts." Daniel Rosenblit

> "In this process of ruthlessly honest self-reflection, nothing went unnoticed. Nothing was able to be hidden. Nothing. Not one single thing. This Life Review was like going through everything with a fine-tooth comb,

looking under every rock, leaving no stone unturned, seeing into each crevice with a Divine Light that revealed every hidden place. And through the entire process, it was all looked at and discerned through the lens of Love." David Oakford

"I heard the Voice of the Almighty deep within my soul . . . The Voice knew me fully and completely and there was no part of me that was unknown. I was revealed, fully revealed, in all my beauty and hideousness. Nothing could be hidden; nothing of me was hidden. I had no choice in the matter. I was fully and completely known." Peter Panagore

Our Life Review reveals our whole life to us; warts, wonders, wounds, and all. It's all there for us to see with Heaven's figurative floodlights shining upon every crack and crevice of our life, illuminating everything we ever thought, said, and did during our lifetime. As much as some of us might have been successful hiding behind our masks and defense mechanisms, making excuses or blaming others for our problems, and/or conning, manipulating, and lying to ourselves and others during our lifetime on earth, we can't hide any of our "bad" actions or sneaky motives because they are all there for us and those watching in Heaven to see and feel.

"I felt totally exposed and transparent before God. You can wear masks before other people but you can't wear a mask before God." Ian McCormack

"God showed me when I had generously done things without thinking about it beforehand, and when I had done unloving things. I even saw myself stealing sweets in a shop, thinking to myself, 'Whew, nobody saw me!' Indeed, somebody saw me. Yes, God saw me!" Leonard

"All of my life's actions were seen and known. I couldn't hide them or cover them and my carefully erected walls of excuses that had shielded me from accepting responsibility melted around me. All that was left was just me and the Being of Love and Light." Dr. Joyce Brown

"The truth judges us. In the light of God, there is no deception." Howard Storm

In Heaven, our entire life is a complete open book with total transparency and undeniable truth. All of our actions, and especially our heart's true intent behind every one of them, are fully exposed and analyzed. Sorry, there is just no pulling the wool over God's or our guardian angel's eyes since they have been with us our entire life and have seen deeply into our heart and soul. As our life plays out in our Life Review, we must examine, tell, own, and embrace the whole truth and nothing but the truth about our life—so help us God.

"God put his hand on my head. He was able to see everything and feel everything that I had done in my life. He saw if I was sorry for the bad things I had done, how I felt in my heart at the time I had done things, how I felt afterwards, and whether or not I apologized or made the bad things right. He also saw all of the good I had done in my life and whether or not I was truly good or if I was doing good things to get something, and how I truly felt at the time." William R.

"It was both painful and exquisitely beautiful. It was like viewing a film, filled with precise detail. Every single thought, word, deed, decision, and action was brought forth and re-experienced and re-examined. It was self-evaluation, with total transparency and honesty. Throughout, I was never judged by any of these divine beings. They simply held me in Love, with complete compassion and acceptance." David Oakford

Reviewed with Total Support and Unconditional Love

While we might be harshly judgmental of ourselves, we need to always keep in mind our Life Review takes place in an environment of total and unconditional love and acceptance. Our heavenly companions, God and our guardian angels, compliment us when we act with love and support and teach us when we don't.

"I had a kind of Life Review. I never felt chastised at all, even though I know I've been very cruel at times and have hurt many people. I've lost my temper in horrible ways and I have had great trouble with forgiveness, and yet, I felt only Love and understanding through the entire Life Review. What it felt like to me was that I was being given the opportunity and gift of being able to stand back and more fully understand and love myself." Amy Call

"I had deep respect and reverence for these beings. I felt that they loved me completely and without any judgment. In psychology there's a term to describe this called 'unconditional positive regard.' I felt completely sure that they had this feeling for me. This surety felt like a warm glow of light around me." Katherine I.

"Even though I had been an atheist for years, I felt God's love. This love was holding me. It felt incredible. There are no words in the English language, or maybe in this reality, to explain the kind of love God emanates. God was totally accepting of everything we—God and I—viewed in my life . . . No matter how I judged myself in each interaction, being held by God was the bigger interaction. God interjected love into everything, every feeling, every bit of information about absolutely everything that went on, so that everything was alright." Barbara Harris Whitfield

The Life Review is Designed to Teach Us, Not Torture Us

Of course we may feel mortified at times as we witness things in our life we're extremely embarrassed about, disgusted by, or horrified over, but NDErs tell us that God and our guides hold nothing against us. There is no reason to dread or fear our Life Review. We're lovingly shown the whole truth of our life so we can acknowledge it, reflect on it, learn from it, and most importantly, benefit and grow from it. God and our guardian angels show us both our loving and unloving decisions and behaviors to help us learn from them rather than to torment us. The Life Review is designed to teach us, not torture us.

> "The Life Review is not punishment or torture and the only reason to fear it would be if you are afraid to confront truth and afraid to grow more loving. The word 'sin' is the farthest thing from what I experienced during my Life Review . . . I felt nothing but unconditional love and understanding from those helping me review my life. It was no feeling of judgment, just an internal feeling of, 'I know I can do better than that!'" Karen Thomas

> "When I die I know for certain that I'll witness and feel the effects of my actions again. But I'm not dreading it in any way whatsoever. To the contrary, I'm looking forward to my death with great anticipation. One might suspect that a comprehensive Life Review is a difficult thing through which to endure, but witnessing my entire life unfolding before my eyes was in no way unsettling." Malcolm Miller

> "The entire Life's Review would have been emotionally destructive, and would have left me a psychotic person, if it hadn't been for the fact that my friend [the Being of Light], and my friend's friends [angels], were loving me during the unfolding of my life. I could feel that love. Every time I got a little upset they turned the Life's Review off for a while, and they just loved me. Their love was tangible. You could feel it on your body, you could feel it inside you; their love went right through you. I wish I could explain it to you, but I can't. The therapy was their love, because my Life's Review kept tearing me down. It was pitiful to watch, just pitiful. I couldn't believe it. And the thing is, it got worse as it went on. My stupidity and selfishness as a teenager only magnified as I became an adult—all under the veneer of being a good husband, a good father, and a good citizen. The hypocrisy of it all was nauseating. But through it all was their love." Howard Storm

Mistakes are a Normal and Natural Part of Being Human

God and our guardian angels all understand we are fallible human beings who make tons of mistakes and are prone to do some downright despicable things throughout the course of our lifetime. Because we've been pre-set with the default factory-setting as "human" for our time on earth, they know it naturally means we will many times make mistakes, act from our ego, hold grudges, take things personally, be selfish, seek revenge, and have a high propensity to lie, cheat, and steal to get our own way. These many human faults, foibles, and fallibilities make us human and ultimately provide great fodder for the many lessons we learn during our time on earth.

> "It was also clear to me that my brokenness was simply a part of being a human being. To cause pain to another was, or so it appeared to me, the natural order of life on earth. I was not special; I was not unique in that regard. I had just been a human and did what all human beings do to each other. We hurt each other." Peter Panagore

> "Mistakes are an acceptable part of being human. We are here to make all the mistakes we want because it is through our mistakes that we learn. As long as we try to do what we know to be right, we will be on the right path. If we make a mistake, we should fully recognize it as a mistake, then put it behind us and simply try not to make the same mistake again. The important thing is to try our best, keep our standards of goodness and truth, and not compromise them to win people's approval. God loves us just the way we are, mistakes and all." Howard Storm

> "We all have weaknesses and are not perfect nor are we expected to be perfect. Our imperfections lead to mistakes which teach us how to live and love and how to do no harm. Our defects of character and shortcomings are our teachers. And God made us with imperfections to become with. If he had made us perfect then and maybe only then would we be judged. We do the best we can." Ken Kemkaran

It seems the many mistakes and screwups we make are a normal and natural part of life's curriculum on earth to help us learn. Even though we may be disturbed, demoralized, and embarrassed by our mistakes, those on the Other Side don't even view them as mistakes but as valuable lessons. The mistakes allow us to learn lessons on how love and its companion virtues of kindness, patience, empathy, and forgiveness are always the best answer for every situation, challenge, and predicament.

> "No matter what age we are, we are like children, learning our life's lessons and making mistakes in the process. When we went to school and made mistakes on our tests, did we suffer needlessly from guilty feelings? Probably not. We were given the correct answers and we learned from those mistakes. We moved on to our next lessons. The Light sees us as children making mistakes while we learn our lessons." Nancy Clark

> "All of my experiences now took on a new meaning. I realized that no real mistakes had been made in my life. Each experience was a tool for me

to grow by. Every unhappy experience had allowed me to obtain greater understanding about myself, until I learned to avoid those experiences . . . Some experiences were sad and some were joyful, but all were calculated to bring me to higher levels of knowledge . . . I saw my sins and shortcomings in a multi-dimensional light. Yes, they were grievous to me and others, but they were tools for me to learn by, to correct my thinking and behavior." Betty Eadie

See Alternatives That Would Show Love

As we review our life, we all have numerous situations we wish we could do over again. Like in golf, we wish we could get a mulligan, not have the situation count against us, and try it over again. We all wish we could turn back time, take back words, declare a "Do Over", and try again with more forethought, concern, compassion, patience, empathy, and love.

Interestingly, NDErs tell us that not only did they get to see and experience the things they did during their lifetime, they also saw the different choices they could have made that would have brought more love, peace, understanding, and kindness to the event. They saw what they could have said and done in the situation—not to beat them up over it—but to gently and helpfully show them how they could approach similar situations more lovingly moving forward in a positive way.

"I relived every instance of my existence, every emotion and thought. I saw why I was the way I was; I re-experienced the way I had dealt with people and they with me. I saw where I could have done better. I felt emotions I was ashamed of, yet I realized there were things I had done well and felt good about. As we looked at different scenes, I would respond, 'Yes, I see how I could have done it another way, a better way.'" Valvita Jones

"For most of the episodes we went through, the Being offered me an alternative way to act; not what I should have done, which would have been moralizing, but what I could have done—an open invitation that made me feel completely free to accept or not accept His suggestions. I felt totally free and respected. Needless to say, His suggestions were all for a more loving and understanding attitude." Goran Grip

"As I looked I began to see my whole life go before me. At the age of seven my life story was not extensive, but everything was projected on to that screen, and I knew it was a summary of my life. I was shown key moments during my brief period on Earth — what I had done, followed by what I should have done. Sometimes it was what I had said, followed by what I should have said. I didn't feel condemned, but I knew that what I was witnessing was true — that what was being said or shown was not something that I could argue against because it was fair and right. I could hear a voice explaining things to me, but I did not see anyone or anything, other than this huge screen." Susan Finlay

Our Life Review not only shows us how we reacted to life's various people and events, but how we could have more consciously and compassionately responded that would have brought more love into the situations. The intent is not to judge us but to gently teach us how to love bigger, better, bolder, and more unconditionally whenever possible.

"He was asking me, 'What different choices could you have made? What are you learning from this?' Not yelling at me and saying, 'How could you do that!?' or, 'You're going to Hell!' This was clearly not the punishing God I had been taught to believe in. The hardest part of this was realizing He had already forgiven me." Mary Beth Willi

"The Light was talking to me with the voice of love and compassion, 'Why did you treat yourself that way? You didn't deserve to be treated that way. Not even by yourself.' I was then shown hundreds of solutions that could have solved my problem, literally dozens and dozens of solutions all at once." Marion Rome

"In the Life Review, you see on a big monitor your life that has passed. I was shown basically from the time my mom and dad conceived me. I saw and felt emotion and events. And very often I was shown an event in my life and the voice of God, the voice of the Being of Light, said, 'Was that a loving thing to do?' It wasn't a judgment. It was a question against perfect love and against the event I had just seen again. How could I answer, 'Yes it was?'" Jack Bybee

God Doesn't Judge Us

What shocks many people through this whole Life Review process is that God doesn't judge us. Despite many religions threatening their followers with a harsh and punitive Judgment Day, ominous Day of Reckoning, or daunting weighing of our soul when God will throw the book at us and decide our soul's fate of going to Heaven or hell for all of eternity, NDErs adamantly and repeatedly tell us God doesn't judge us in the least bit. Why?

"I had spent a lifetime of fear of judgment and now, standing with God, I had been known completely and found faultless. I knew God regarded me as perfect. God loved me because love is the totality of God. God loves without limit. Finally it all made sense. God could only love me because

God is only love, nothing other than love. The only reality is God; there cannot be another and GOD IS LOVE." Linda Stewart

God is unconditional love and loves everyone and everything unconditionally. There are absolutely no conditions on God's love—it is 100% freely, fully, and indiscriminately shared no matter what words we say, choices we make, or actions we take. God's love is infinitely unconditional, which is completely and totally judgment free. He does not judge us in any way for how we conduct our life.

"I was delivered into the hands of God, and I remember waiting and thinking, I haven't been judged yet. I was imperfect! Shouldn't God judge me? Isn't that what I deserve? On earth, I had been judged by people for making mistakes, not being skinny enough or not wearing the right clothes, just being different from everyone else. I waited to be judged by God. I was sure it was coming. But as I waited to be judged the most unexpected thing happened. God, once again, began to fill me with unconditional love. As love flowed through me, it washed away any thoughts and feelings of judgment and disappointment. I never felt judged but I should have been judged. Yet he did not judge me. He loved me!" Erica McKenzie, RN

"The Being was not judging me in any way during the Life Review, even though I saw a lot of shortcomings in my life. It simply showed my life the way it had been to me, loved me unconditionally, which gave me the strength I needed to see it all the way it was without any blinders, and let me decide for myself what was positive, negative, and what I needed to do about that." Lisa M.

"He does not judge me. In fact, this is what hit me the most. God does not judge, He just loves us with unconditional love, this love is indescribable, it is not like what we feel on earth, this is rather a force-of-love." Leonard

---

"You judge by human standards; I pass judgment on no one."

John 8:15

God Doesn't Sentence Us to Hell

Because God doesn't judge us, He also doesn't send us to hell for all of eternity. Of course God not banishing us to hell for our "sins" and misdeeds also contradicts what many religions teach and pastors preach. In essence, hell is a judgmental and vindictive concept based on not obeying certain rules established by some religions. These strict rules and stern commandments threaten us to believe and act in certain ways or an angry, judgmental, and vengeful God will not love us, favor us, or allow us into Heaven. These stringent and often arbitrary conditions are man-made conceptions of God's desires and demands and are not compatible with the unconditionally loving God NDErs experience in Heaven.

> "What I experienced was so different than what I was expecting because I was born into a Roman Catholic family. Within the religion itself there's sin, judgment involved, and there's hell. I saw none of that and I felt none of that. It was so far from my reality." Daniel Giroux

> "Many sacred texts claim that you must serve God otherwise you'll face the consequences of going to 'hell.' What is 'God' for the most widespread religions? He is an entity capable of sending you for eternity to a lake of smoke and fire if you don't obey His rules. In other words, a superior force who loves you conditionally. Well, this has nothing to do with the unconditional love I felt during my NDE . . . There wasn't even an ounce of 'hell' as so many religions describe it. Hell was rather all the hurt I caused to others and that I felt in a way beyond description—and even in this case, I was completely forgiven by the love of the entire universe." Marion Rome

The "hell" we may experience during our Life Review is learning how our choices caused others physical, emotional, and psychological stress, agony, and trauma. Experiencing and feeling the pain we caused others can seem like going through hell as we'll feel all the angst, disappointment, sadness, fear, frustration, and hopelessness we doled out to our friends, family members, co-workers, neighbors, and strangers.

> "Mine was not a review, but a reliving. For me, it was a total reliving of every thought I had ever thought, every word I had ever spoken, and every deed I had ever done; plus, the effect of each thought, word, and deed on everyone and anyone who had ever come within my environment or sphere of influence, whether I knew them or not. No detail was left out. No slip of the tongue or slur was missed. No mistake or accident went unaccounted for. If there is such a thing as hell, as far as I am concerned this was hell." PMH Atwater

> "I do not believe in hell . . . I think we may have to face our wrongdoings towards others for a while—that may feel like hell, but I do not believe it is a permanent state." Riki E.

God Allows Us to Evaluate Our Life

God unconditionally loves and trusts us enough to evaluate our own life. In the brilliant light of truth and with the supportive backdrop of unconditional love, God provides us with the opportunity to examine all of our life's choices, see them from multiple perspectives, feel how our thoughts, words, and actions felt to others, and then decide for ourselves how well we did in unconditionally loving ourselves and others during our time on earth.

> "Every detail of twenty years of living was there to be looked at. The good, the bad, the high points, the run-of-the-mill. And with this all-inclusive view came a question. It was implicit in every scene and, like the scenes themselves, seemed to proceed from the living Light beside me. What did you do with your life? It was obviously not a question in the sense that He was seeking information, for what I had done with my life was in plain view . . . Hadn't I ever gone beyond my own immediate interests, done anything other people would recognize as valuable? He was not asking about accomplishments and awards. The question, like everything else proceeding from Him, had to do with love. 'How much have you loved with your life? Have you loved others as I am loving you? Totally? Unconditionally?'" Dr. George Ritchie

> "I heard the voice of the Being of Light of God for the first time. I was asked three questions: 'What have you done with the life just passed? Whom have you loved and been loved by? What have you learned?'" Jack Bybee

> "I was shown a movie of my life from start until then, it was so fast and yet so precise. I was asked if I would change anything which I answered 'Yes of course.' He also asked me questions too! Like, was I happy with my life? To which I replied that I was. I was left with a feeling inside as to how much good I'd given and how much bad I'd given." Linda G.

We Evaluate Ourselves

Surprisingly to many, we are the only ones who evaluate our life and ultimately judge ourselves. That's right, NDErs tell us time and time again God doesn't judge us, the angels don't judge us, even our deceased ancestors don't judge us; we judge ourselves.

> "No one great deity judges us in the end. It is we who must judge our own performances. This is truly a daunting prospect when watching your life play out in front of you; aware of the contents of each scene, unable to change them, yet knowing what's coming next. In that all-knowing space, I understood that it was me, myself, to whom I must be accountable." Dr. Mary Helen Hensley

Having the amazing opportunity to see our life from birth to death from a plethora of perspectives and understand our inner motives at the clearest and deepest levels, we evaluate how well we lived and loved during our time on earth. We see exactly how and when and why we spoke and acted with love, truth, and integrity, and how and when and why we didn't. Through the power of the penetrating Life Review, the quality of our life and the depth of our love becomes self-evident to us and an undeniable and unforgettable truth.

> "I did find out about the so-called 'Judgment Day' I feared so much as a child. We judge ourselves and that at first was a big relief but our life is still our job. My past flashed before me, out of my control. I learned that the feared 'Judgment Day' shouldn't be feared at all. I found out during my Life Review that we actually judge ourselves." Glenda H.

> "Even at the end of it, no one is going to judge you but yourself. You will be accountable for everything you've done here. But not accountable like you are going to be punished. It is not going to happen like that. You are going to be accountable [because] you will understand and see what you did and what you should have done. And you, from the love of who you are; the immense love that you are, you will want to do something about it and you will not allow it to not be corrected and fixed by yourself . . ." Julie Aubier

> "In our Life Reviews, it's not God that's judging us, it's not the ascended masters, it's not our loved ones, it's us. We're not judging ourselves harshly or negatively or mean. We're just looking at it as, 'Oh, wow! So because of that action I caused that.' We're looking at it with compassion and with love so that we can learn and we can grow. But it's us—we are the ones reviewing our own life. We're not really judging it, we're having to process it to learn from it." Heidi Craig

We Evaluate Ourselves from a Higher Perspective

Fortunately, as we transition to Heaven, not only do we shed our earthly body but our human ego along with it. Instead of solely viewing ourselves from a biased, defensive, and insecure perspective with all of our human baggage, we also evaluate our life from a higher more heavenly perspective which is much more mature, objective, and spiritually evolved. As we move from earth to Heaven, we see and evaluate our life through a bigger, broader, and empathetic lens than the myopic, subjective, and selfish one we typically use as humans.

> "The universe simply presented me with a broadened understanding of myself, and all of it was aimed at easing my transition over to the Other Side. Throughout the Life Review, not only did I identify with my physical self, but also with my much larger and truer identity—my eternal soul." Malcolm Miller

"The Life Review allowed me to examine my life without having my ego involved. This lack of ego involvement, and the increased empathy, enabled me to make a totally honest appraisal of all the aspects of my life. In some ways the effects of this review were similar to psychotherapy. Instead of taking several years, though, it only took seconds or perhaps minutes. Still, it was an extremely effective form of transformation. By examining my life from a distance, I was able to make significant changes in who I was and what I valued." Dannion Brinkley

The Life Review provides us with a different and more enlightened perspective on life and our fellow human beings we would do well to incorporate more often into our life while on our earthly journey. When we evaluate our life, we see how moving from our typical Human Perspective to our Higher Perspective is a practical and effective way to bring Heaven down to earth.

- *Human Perspective*—We view the world and others from a fearful, individualistic, judgmental, competitive, and vengeful mindset. We see people solely as selfish human beings who primarily look out for themselves. Put simply, living life from the Human Perspective means being leery of others and living a "dog eat dog" kind of existence.
- *Higher Perspective*—We view the world and our fellow souls from a loving, interconnected, accepting, cooperative, and forgiving mindset. We see people as fellow spiritual beings having a common human experience complete with challenges and mistakes. Put simply, living life from a Higher Perspective means consciously and compassionately taking the high road.

"My mission, I have come to understand, is to overcome the egoic challenges that all humans face. With humor and humility, we're here to turn fear, anger, selfish greed and gloating pride into love and compassion for all life." Louisa Peck

How often do we live and love from our Human Perspective vs. our Higher Perspective?

"We're taught that there are bad people and good people, monsters and angels. And yet the truth of the matter is that monsters and angels live in every single one of us."

Jacqueline Novogratz, Author

Our Intent is Key in Evaluation vs. Our Actual Actions

As we evaluate and judge ourselves, we learn that our words and actions matter less than our intent behind them. We discover our heart's intent is what really matters in each and every situation. Even though we may be able to fool others, God always knows what is in our hearts.

For example, if we served at a soup kitchen primarily for the photo opportunity to post it on social media so our friends would think we were a good person, unfortunately we get zero credit for it. We served mostly for selfish reasons rather than to help others. We see and have to account for the real motives behind all of our words and actions in our Life Review, not just the outward acts.

> "What was important were the choices I made. And what was more important than the choices I made, were my motivations and intent, and really the state of my heart in doing any single action . . ." Reinee Pasarow

> "Choice making is a serious challenge, one that requires great patience and wisdom from us. It also requires a clear vision of our intent. Sparkling clarity is vital if we are to use the power of choice in a manner that guarantees the greatest good of all concerned. Whether our intent is the salvation of the world like the valiant efforts of a Mother Teresa, or just personal happiness, during the panoramic life review, we will see clearly the real intentions of our choices . . . The reason we do something is far more important than the act itself. The intention motivating us to take action determines the spiritual effectiveness of that action . . . When the intention is pure, not meant to be harmful in any way, the result of an action will always be measured before the action is." Dannion Brinkley

> "In my Life Review, intent was definitely part of it. I recall one of my reviews when I was in the 5th grade. I was playing king of the hill and was shown the part where they warned me that I would break a friend's arm if I pushed her down the hill. So I was made aware of the repercussions of my actions and proceeded anyway. I recall at the time, I knew I would hurt her. I heard that warning. Well, in my review I faced my actions and felt the emotions of disappointment in myself." Yvonne Mergner

3 PRIMARY WAYS WE EVALUATE OUR LIFE

As we review our earthly life from Heaven, we evaluate it in three primary ways:

1. How well did we love others and ourselves unconditionally?
2. How well did we live our life fully and fearlessly?
3. How well did we fulfill our life's purposes?

Let's explore each of these critical questions in greater depth as we presently and proactively contemplate them for ourselves rather than waiting until the end of our life.

1. How well did we unconditionally love others and ourselves?

Our Life Review clearly lays out how well we loved others throughout our lifetime. We examine our millions of interactions with others, be they friends, family members, co-workers, neighbors, acquaintances, or mortal enemies, and evaluate how well we treated them with love, compassion, kindness, generosity, patience, forgiveness, etc. (Yes, we are even asked to be kind to and forgive the people we despise the most.) By feeling precisely what all these people felt when they were with us, we analyze and assess if our actions brought more love into their lives and world in general—or less love.

> "The most important criterion for judging my Life Review was this: How well had I used my life to love myself and others . . . It boils down to this. Every moment of every day while we exist on earth, we are given two choices, to either react from a loving or unloving way. Our purpose on earth is to learn this lesson." Nancy Clark

> "The Light then told me, 'You are here to learn how to love and to gain knowledge.' When I was told this, all the implications of the word love and knowledge were imparted to me. With the word 'love', it wasn't just about physical love but the love of nature, accepting all people as the same, everything that pertained to love. I was being told this is why you are here on earth to learn how to love and accept each other." Barbara S.

> "I was greeted by acquaintances, friends, my grandparents, my father's best friend, as well as a school chum from seventh grade . . . For the first time I saw the depth of the impression we make on one another's lives . . . As they greeted me, I inexplicably seemed to understand the highest purpose of our earthly connection. It was love. I saw each person for who he or she was apart from the descriptions I had previously used to define each of them. As they taught me love, I realized what an important role we play in the development of one another's personality . . . I also knew that I had never felt so remembered, recognized, understood, or loved . . . The highest purpose of our earthly connections is love." LynnClaire Dennis

Unconditional Love is the Standard of Measurement

NDErs tell us that in the realm of Heaven, the high standard of unconditional love is what we use to assess our behavior on earth. We observe our actions and measure them up against what we could have done had

3 WAYS WE EVALUATE OUR LIFE

1. Did we love others and ourselves unconditionally?
2. Did we live our life fully and fearlessly?
3. Did we fulfill our life's purposes?

JEFF JANSSEN

we acted with unconditional love in the situation. Obviously, this is a super high standard but it helps us see what could have been done in the situation.

> "I got a Life Review without any judgement whatsoever but my own life seen against a backdrop of pure unconditional love, which made everything that was NOT love in my life stand out like blobs of ink against a white paper. It was entirely up to me what to do with it and how to assess it, and I measured my own actions against the perfect unconditional love I was shown." Lisa Meyler

> "I realized that the only standard by which one can judge one's life and choices was by this same pure, selfless, limitless, incomprehensible love. From this heightened point of consciousness, I reviewed my life, along with the life of every other human being that I had ever effected in any way through my actions." Reinee Pasarow

> "All of a sudden . . . my life passed before me . . . What occurred was every emotion I had ever felt in my life, I felt. And my eyes were showing me the basis of how that emotion had affected my life. What my life had done so far to affect other people's lives using the feeling of pure love that was surrounding me as the point of comparison . . . Looking at yourself from the point of how much love you have spread to other people is devastatin'." Darryl

"I Could Have Done Better"

With unconditional love as the standard, it is easy to see why many NDErs think as they watch their Life Review—"*I could have done better.*" They see numerous times where they could have responded from a Higher Perspective with love, empathy, kindness, patience, and forgiveness—but didn't and instead came from a Human Perspective of ego, selfishness, greed, spite, etc.

> "I remember in high school my sister was sharing a locker next to me and it was my birthday. And my sister and I were very close. All my football buddies were around me and she was saying, 'Aren't you gonna say how much you love me and how much you care for me and that I'm your best friend?' I'm watching this moment, embarrassed, because she's doing all this in front of my friends. And I'm watching this as though, not in a perspective of judgment and sadness, but awareness, watching my sister say all these things. And I can hear my thoughts in my head watching this moment in my life saying [to myself], 'Oh just go away. My friends are watching.' And I didn't say anything and I just walked away. That was the night my sister was killed by a drunk driver. What I learned was those moments when we go through life that we don't share with people how much

we love them, how much we care for them . . . There was no judgment, there was no angel saying, 'See what you did.' There wasn't any of that. What was there was in my heart, 'You could have done better, Peter.'" Peter Anthony

"After the Life Review, I was taken before more beings which seemed to be wiser than the two who brought me to my Life Review. I communicated with them about my decisions during my Life Review and areas where I could improve . . . The conclusion of these conversations was that it wasn't so much a decision of doing the 'wrong' thing in situations, or making unwise choices, but that the times of greatest challenge for me were times in which I could have acted but chose inaction. It was concluded that when I returned to earth, I must choose action and use my experiences and feelings to guide these actions so that they be an act of love . . . What I got out of this experience before leaving was that I must choose action instead of inaction. I must behave in a way that would help bring more awareness and love to the world." Katherine I.

"I have no idea how long it was, my ENTIRE life played out in the most vivid color, detail, and understanding. There was no fear or anything of that sort during this other than I was a bit surprised to know that I could have done much better in life . . . I realized that connection really matters because every human action reverberates and is felt by others. I felt I could have done better but there was no sense of judgment only realization." Barry

"I began to do the Life Review . . . As I began to see these things I got excited to come back and I thought, "Ok, I can do this better, I could do this differently." Isabella Johnson

So many NDErs experience their Life Review and deeply know and readily admit they can do better—and sincerely want to do better. Seeing the loving way they could have responded differently instead of the indifferent, callous, or hurtful way they many times did teaches them how love would have been the better response. When they come back to human life, many NDErs are much more conscious of choosing unconditional love than letting the automatic default response of their human ego unconsciously pick their actions. (And hopefully we all will be too by learning and applying their powerful lessons.)

"God asked me, He said, 'Let me ask you one question. Have you ever loved another person the way you have been loved here?' The love I had received in that time was so overpowering—I had never felt anything like it so I answered God honestly. I said, 'No, it is impossible, I am just a human, you are God.' He gave me the illusion of a sweet protective chuckle. He then said, 'Mary, you can do better.'" Mary Jo Rapini

"They showed me how God had given us the opportunity to learn love by having children and raising them to be loving. In my Life Review, I had to turn away numerous times when I saw myself treating my children in unloving ways. The most unloving thing that I did was to be at times too obsessed with my concerns that I was indifferent to their needs. I am sorry for those occasions that I was impatient or cruel to my daughter and son. The most disturbing behaviors I witnessed in my Life Review were the times when I cared more about my career as an artist and college professor than about their need to be loved. The emotional abandonment of my children was devastating to review. It was horrifying to see how I had become so much like my father, putting my status and success above all else." Howard Storm

Seeing the many times and ways they withheld love motivates many NDErs to be that much more loving to everyone and everything when they return to life. They seek to share love and do so whenever possible. I find it refreshing and enlightening when I attend NDE conferences just how loving, accepting, and kind many NDErs are because they know from their Life Reviews the value and impact of acting with love.

How well did we unconditionally love ourselves?

While observing and feeling how we treat others is obviously important, the Life Review also reveals how we treat ourselves. So many of us don't fully love ourselves, which makes it tough to love others. We beat up ourselves with internal criticism, poor self-esteem, unfounded fears, limiting beliefs, and just don't treat ourselves well. We live our life fearful of what other's think of us, do things solely to please them, and fail to live a life that is true to ourselves. NDErs learn the unconditional love they are encouraged to give to others, they also need to extend to themselves.

"In this Life Review, I realized that during my life, I cut off myself from this spiritual quality more and more; that I tried to function more and more and adapt to society. But I became more and more unhappy. Eventually, I stopped asking myself what makes me actually happy, who am I, how would I like to live my life. I did everything to please the outside world. This was emphasized in several situations. Again, there was a situation where I thought, that's so sad, that's such a shame, and how wasted this life is . . ." Anke Everitz

"Until my NDE, I didn't love myself . . . I didn't realize that loving ourselves is actually the most important thing we can do, and that it's the key to living a blissful life . . . I saw myself through the eyes of God, and I realized that far from being unloved and unlovable, I was actually a beautiful child

> of the universe who was loved unconditionally, simply because I exist." Anita Moorjani
>
> "Rarely did the people whose thoughts I was picking up focus on what great and powerful spiritual beings they were. Few took credit for their greatness. I began to realize that people have almost a need to feel guilty, wrong, or inferior, and that this need seems to overwhelm any consideration that they are spiritual beings. Instead they see themselves as being trapped in a reality that is controlled and manipulated by everybody else." Dannion Brinkley

(If you struggle to love yourself, I highly recommend NDEr Anita Moorjani's book, *Dying to Be Me,* for ideas on learning to love yourself.)

2. How well did we live our life fully and fearlessly?

We also evaluate our life in terms of how fully and fearlessly we lived it. We assess if we took full advantage of this amazing life we've been given and squeezed every ounce of fun and learning out of it. Or regretfully, did we die with our music still trapped inside us?

> "The being, whom I'll call a spirit guide, although it could've been an angel, asked me a question. 'If this marked the end of my life, would I be satisfied with how it went?' All I had said and done, and specifically how I responded to what was said and done to me? I answered honestly, as I could sense that was what the being wanted to hear. So I told it, or communicated with it, my thoughts flowing out from the center of my being to its center, that no, I would honestly have to say I would not be satisfied . . . I had held back. Not said what I wanted to, not done the things I wanted, out of fear. Fear of being rejected, fear of something unknown. Fear of loss." Kim A.

Too many people let unfounded fears hold them hostage and keep them from living full and fulfilling lives. They settle for an anesthetized life rather than living life all out with a "Carpe Diem" attitude. They settle for careers that are below their talents and abilities. They settle for relationships that don't honor and bring out the best in them. Instead of treating life as a grand and glorious adventure, they stay locked in their self-imposed comfort zone and always play it safe in their careers, their relationships, and their aspirations. When most people look back on their life either from their death bed or their Life Review, many times they regret the things they didn't do or take advantage of instead of the ones they did.

> "We have everything inside of us or at our disposal to live loving, beauty-filled, glorious, full lives. The only thing really standing in our way is

ourselves. Our own preconceived ideas and fears limit us. Many of us fall into the trap of thinking 'small,' of not believing that we have the capacity to live the full lives that our hearts crave. Instead we settle for a life on autopilot, one that is much less fulfilling than our hearts long for us to live. Our ideas of what life should be like, how this should work out, how people should be—these all limit us and keep us from living our lives to the fullest." Nancy Rynes

3. How well did we fulfill our life's purposes?

A final way we evaluate our life in our Life Review is how well we lived out our life's purposes. NDErs adamantly tell us we each have at least one if not several sacred purposes to fulfill doing our precious time on earth. In fact, many choose to come back to human life from the boundless bliss and beauty of Heaven because either they realized they had not yet fulfilled their sacred life's purpose—or God sent them back to ensure they completed their purpose before getting to stay in the Afterlife.

> "I was floored at how important we all are to God—especially how important I was to God. I didn't think He knew I even existed. All the years I was beating myself up and His question to me was, 'Why would I go through all the trouble to make you just the way you are if I wanted you to try and be like someone else?' No one else could do the job I came here to do the way He wanted me to do it! That is why it is so important that we not be so judgmental of each other. Some of us are here to teach, some to learn, and some to do both." Mary Beth Willi

We all have a few important purposes to achieve during our lifetime. These special purposes reveal themselves over the course of our life and usually correspond to different phases of our life's journey like parenting our kids, helping a friend through a difficult time, assisting our elderly parents, and sharing our gifts and talents through our profession or volunteering.

Making the world a better place is one of our primary purposes. We're born with unique talents that when developed and applied, make a positive contribution to others, animals, and/or the environment. It is up to us to discover these gifts and talents during our lifetime, develop them so they can do the most good, and deploy them so they can help others.

> "You have a specific purpose. You're going to see people that I'll never see. You're going to touch lives that I'll never touch. You're on your own mission. And no one else can fulfill your duties but you. That's what's so

beautiful about you being you. You are special. But there is a fulfillment there that you've got to find—for your sake, His sake, for the world's sake. You were put here for a reason—to help." Oliver John Calvert

"The Light communicated telepathically to me the words, 'No, you cannot stay. I have work for you on earth. You are to become a communicator, to help people understand there is life after death. Help them become aware of their true nature, and help them to learn to live their lives expressing unconditional love for one another.'" Nancy Clark

We also have another purpose during our time on earth which focuses on learning, developing, and evolving as a soul. Whether it is learning various virtues like unconditional love, patience, forgiveness, or empathy, we come here to develop and refine our soul by experiencing challenges that call forth these qualities to endure and overcome them.

Essentially, we come on this earthly journey because human life offers a kind of "Spiritual Obstacle Course" and teaches us things, often through hardships, adversities, and tragedies, that we just can't experience and learn in the perfection and bliss of heaven. Thus, we come here to this Soul School, Soul Summer Camp, or Soul Boot Camp to learn how to love unconditionally and develop our souls with the "help" of challenging people and less than perfect circumstances.

"I was about to review every event, thought, emotion, and experience of my life. I became aware that the purpose of the review was for me to evaluate my life in terms of my intended mission as a human, to review my life in a manner that permitted me to focus on the areas that provided the most important experiences in terms of my spiritual growth and development." Ned Dougherty

"I was told that it wasn't my time, that I'd been granted a visit 'back home', but that I had to fulfill my purpose and do the work I myself had chosen to do on earth. The Being of Light reminded me that my purpose was to learn more about love, compassion, and how to express them on earth, and that my work was to help other people in any way I could. I had chosen this myself. And it told me that I would be back in the world of light in no time." Lisa M.

"I was transported to this dark city street. All around me was a city like here on Earth such as New York or a big city of that nature. I was standing on the city block. It was all dark looking—like night time with a full moon out. Then God asked me, 'What do you see?' I looked and I saw a homeless man laying on the street slightly sitting up against the building. Then, one at a time, there were three people that passed by him walking on the sidewalk he was laying on—a lady and two men. When the first man walked by I felt everything he was feeling and I could hear what he was thinking in my own head like it was my own thoughts and feelings. He was disgusted by the homeless man. He hated the degeneration of society. It sickened him and he felt like that person should get a job. The next person to walk by was a woman. As it was with the man, I felt all of the emotions and could hear the thoughts she was thinking like they were my own thoughts. She was afraid and scared that the homeless man would hurt or rob her. The last was a man who walked by and was angry at the homeless man because he owned property in the area and he felt that these low lifes were making his property values go down. Then God said to me, 'Now I am going to show you the truth of it.' I turned and watched the homeless man and all of a sudden, from the top of his forehead to the middle of him, he began to split apart revealing a huge, beautiful, brilliant, bright light. His flesh just tore straight down the middle in half and fell away and I saw his spirit as he truly was. I knew who he was by reputation. He was a huge spirit in heaven 'in terms we can better understand' like a celebrity that we would chase after to get their autograph. Everyone in heaven wanted to be like this soul. This was one of God's finest!!!! And was given this task here on Earth because it took the very best to teach in this manner and to sustain the suffering that went with it. It was explained to me like this, 'How can compassion be taught if there is nothing to feel compassion about?' The pain and suffering which happens to us here on Earth is allowed because of its purpose and the importance for learning. When all the people who walked by this homeless man finally died, they will see this act again in their 'Life Review.' All of us will have a Life Review. Only this time we will know the truth and feel the emotions and hear the thoughts of these 'special spirits' and see ourselves for the truth of who we really are and learn from it . . . like a report card. We have chosen this path of learning . . . we are victims and victimizers . . . sometimes both on this Earthly plane. But in reality, we are all learning or teaching. It was explained to me that we must believe in consequences (cause and effect) so that we can learn faster and understand more. We needed to believe in the pain, hardship, and suffering to look inside and to understand and choose to love and care for the right reasons and to look for the truth in ourselves and others above all else. A handicapped person is a very high teacher. People who suffer greatly come down here to teach the rest of us." Darlene Holman

Darlene's powerful NDE reminds us that not everyone and everything are as they appear from the outside. What might look like an obstacle may actually be an opportunity divinely provided for us to grow our soul. Our Life Review provides us with the perfect forum to evaluate how well we achieved our dual purposes of sharing our gifts and developing our souls while we are here on earth.

> "The Life Review is NOT about making us feel guilty. The purpose of the Life Review is to review the success of our mission to earth." Karen Schaeffer

Did We Attain Our Spiritual Development Goals?

We discover through evaluating our life that we had numerous choices we could have made during our time on earth to attain our spiritual development goals. Even though our ego wanted us to look out only for ourselves, we could have risen above it, viewed the situation from a higher, more heavenly perspective, and thought of others. Even though our human heart may have been hurt in an interaction with a friend, we get to see the situation from a much higher perspective in our Life Review and understand that the friend really acted out of their own pain—rather than trying to personally do something against us.

> "The panoramic Life Review's sole purpose is to act as an impartial tool to help us measure the spiritual growth that took place in the life we are leaving. It determines which threshold of consciousness we are prepared to crossover as we reenter Heaven." Dannion Brinkley

> "Everything that I was re-experiencing during my Life Review totally related to my goals for my life experience and where I was meeting those goals or missing obvious opportunities . . ." Karen Thomas

> "I was drawn to a massive screen lit up displaying three moving scrolls. I felt an incredible sense of peace and wellbeing. On the far-left hand side of the screen was my life scrolled in scenes the way it had been planned. Standing there I 'knew' that I had planned my life that way. Nothing I had read on earth had given me that information but in the moment I 'knew' it. The center column contained the life experiences I had during my twenty-six years of my life. On the far-right hand side of the screen were the objectives of the experiences and what I should have learned from them. My head moved swiftly from one side of the screen to the other. I noticed that the inscription at the end of each entry on the right-hand side of the screen ended with the words: 'objective not accomplished.' It was a compassionate assessment of my life as I had planned it, as well as the way in which I had lived it." Dr. Norma Edwards

Our Life Review provides us with our own helpful report card as we grade ourselves on how well we loved others, how well we loved ourselves, how well we lived fully and fearlessly, and how well we found and fulfilled our life's purpose.

Gift of Life was "Wasted"

NDErs implore us not to look back on our life and come to the gut-wrenching and disheartening feeling that we wasted it, like some of them felt they did. They didn't recognize the amazing gift of their life—until seeing it all over again as they observed all the thousands of choices and opportunities they had all laid out before them and realizing they had squandered the precious gift of life they had been given. They realized they had so much they could have contributed—but didn't.

> "In that moment I realized I had wasted a human life. I had not completed my mission or my purpose . . . I pleaded with the Light, which I called God (I was raised Catholic and the Light felt like God), 'Please don't let me die—you know I have not finished my work in this lifetime! Please let me go back!' My body started to slow down and I was now fully embraced by this warm, loving, all-knowing Light. I stopped in the midst of this great Light . . .. held in the arms of God, if you will. Then I received a message from the Light: 'Make something of your life.'" William

> "When I had finished going through my life and settled down for a moment I felt a loving Being in front of me . . . I could sense a very strong and loving aura of somebody. And this Somebody was communicating with me in thoughts: 'So, now you've seen it one more time. How would you assess your life?' It was friendly, not judgmental. And of course I was honest and responded with my honest opinion, 'Well I haven't really made the most of those 20 years. I wasted this gift of life.'" Bo Katzman

---

"Let's say you're living life without the thought of death, and the Angel of Death comes to you and says, 'Come, it's time to go.' You say, 'But no, you're supposed to give me a warning so I can decide what I want to do with my last week. I'm supposed to get one more week.' Do you know what Death will say to you? He'll say, 'My God! I gave you 52 weeks this past year alone. And look at all the other weeks I've given you. Why would you need one more? What did you do with all of those?' If asked that, what are you going to say? How will you answer? 'I wasn't paying attention . . . I didn't think it mattered.' That's a pretty amazing thing to say about your life."

Michael A. Singer, Author of *The Untethered Soul*

---

4. Evaluate Your Life

Do you honestly feel like you have made something of your precious life?

Have you shared your gifts to make the world a better place?

Have you developed and grown your soul?

Have you done what you came here to do?

God isn't asking us if we've made a million dollars, have lots of friends, followers, and likes on social media, or earned educational degrees. Instead, God wants us to honestly consider: Have we served others, made a positive contribution to the world based on our unique talents and gifts, developed our capacity to love unconditionally, and done what we really came here to do? Have we made something of our life by finding and fulfilling our purpose rather than wasting it?

> "I came to earth to accomplish a mission. All of a sudden, I realized that I had not accomplished this mission. My joy and serenity turned into anguish: I had failed to accomplish this mission. I never felt so sad. Sad is not the word, I felt anguish, I felt like a failure. Nothing else I had accomplished while in this life mattered to me, I was a failure. The Being of Light, sensing my anguish, asked me, 'Would you like to stay or would you like to go back?' I immediately replied (with thought, as our communication was by thought). 'I must go back; I have not accomplished my mission.' In that moment, I sensed I was going backward into a tunnel and I found myself back in my body." Chantal L.

> "An unknown voice inquired, 'What have you done with your life?' Sadly, I heard myself say, 'Nothing. I have wasted the entire forty-seven years.'" Casper

When NDErs realize how much they wasted their life, they often beg God to go back so they can fulfill their purpose and better appreciate and act on the amazing gift of human life.

Ways of Wasting Our Life

Sadly, there are many ways we can "waste" our life when we get caught up in the tempting ways of the world. Some people realized they wasted too much of their time on their own hedonistic and selfish pursuits like mindlessly and excessively binge-watching TV, Netflix, and/or YouTube videos, playing video games all day long, or overindulging in eating, alcohol, sex, and/or drugs rather than selflessly helping others.

> "I felt as though I had squandered and wasted my life feeling sorry for myself when in actuality there was so much in my life that I had not appreciated and that my purpose was to help others instead of being engrossed

in myself. Make the most of your time and do not squander it on trivial things. I still struggle with this occasionally." Vido

"I realized I had led a very selfish life, rarely reaching out to help anyone. Almost never had I smiled as an act of brotherly love or just handed somebody a dollar because he was down and needed a boost. No, my life had been for me and me alone. I hadn't given a damn about my fellow humans." Dannion Brinkley

"The Holy One showed me that throughout my entire life, my ego had occupied the center-stage of my life. I had lived solely for gratifying myself. I was motivated by self-interest in everything that I did; though, I had never consciously thought about this before. The foundation of my life was myself and all of my actions were performed to obtain some type of reward for myself; either tangible or intangible. Either I wanted money, sex, a pat on the back, a wink, a smile, someone to think well of me, etc. Thus, all of my acts had been polluted by selfish motives in varying degrees." Daniel Rosenblit

---

"To get a human body is a rare thing—make full use of it . . . one should not waste this chance. Every second in human life is very valuable. If you don't value this, then you will have nothing in hand and you will weep in the end. Because you're human, God has given you power to think and decide what is good and bad."

Swami Brahmananda Saraswati

Others evaluated their life and realized they spent so much of their time furiously climbing the ladder of career success—only to realize it was up against the wrong wall. They spent all their time on earning money, garnering promotions, buying designer clothes, building big houses, driving luxury cars, going on exotic vacations, putting their kids through elite schools, etc., only to discover in their Life Review that the stuff society deems as successful doesn't count for anything in Heaven. They regret all the time and money they spent trying to get the world to see them as successful while neglecting what Spirit sees as successful and significant.

"All my life I thought that hard work was what counted. My life was devoted to building a monument to my ego. My family, my sculptures, my painting, my house, my gardens, my little fame, my illusions of power, were all an extension of my ego. All of those things were gone now, and what did they matter? All those things that I had lived for were lost to me, and they didn't mean a thing." Howard Storm

> "It is not about the jobs, material success, education, awards, beauty, talent, or family background—those things which we believe here would define you. None of the things we think of as success or failure in the earth plane are of importance . . . How well have you demonstrated love and kindness to all who surround you? Especially the ones that don't have those power props I listed in that first sentence . . . What have you done within the constraints of your life and talents and energy to make this world a better place? A use of your talent or time and energy volunteering in a way that gives people pleasure, laughter, hope, healing; and or supporting the plants and animals in a way that makes them thrive. Those are the things that get focused on. Take the love and kindness that has been given to you and pay it forward." Jody VanderYacht

Some evaluated their life and saw they never found nor fulfilled their purpose. Many times it was right under their nose all along but they never took the simple steps to discover, develop, and do it. They had the powerful seeds of service and significance within them but they didn't bother to plant them, cultivate them, nurture them, water them, harvest them, and share them, either because of their own sheer laziness, they didn't think their life mattered, or they let their fears hold them hostage. In their Life Review, they saw hundreds of simple and easy ways they could have helped others by sharing their special gifts and unique talents, but let them go to waste and squandered their valuable opportunities to contribute. A Life Review helps us see not only when and how we acted, but when and how we could have done something, but didn't.

> "I could have done more with my time on earth than I did . . . Time was to be used wisely and however it was spent, it could not be called back . . . I understood that each person has a definite purpose for living and only so much earth time to fulfill that purpose . . . I was filled with anguish for not having used my time on earth more productively . . . I knew that every day I lived on earth I had exchanged a day of my life's time for whatever I had chosen to do that day. Many days I had squandered my fortune of time and now I saw what I had thrown away. I had wasted precious time . . . Being in the presence of this Personage of Love and Light made me wish I had used every minute I had on earth planting love so I could reap the blessings." Dr. Joyce Brown

Whatever the reason for wasting their life, all of these insights from NDErs are highly instructive to us now and we should heed their helpful advice starting today. Hopefully they inspire us not to have these same regrets about wasting our life and motivate us to act and speak differently no matter how much time we might have left.

"This is the beginning of a new day. You have been given this day to use as you will. You can waste it or use it for good. What you do today is important because you are exchanging a day of your life for it. When tomorrow comes, this day will be gone forever; in its place is something that you have left behind . . . let it be something good."

Anonymous

Like them, we don't want to look back on our precious gift of life and come to the regretful and agonizing conclusion that we wasted it and grade ourselves with D's and F's on our Life's Report Card. No matter how many days, years, or decades we might have squandered to this point, we still have an opportunity to use our unique gifts for good and make the world a better place while developing ourselves in the process. As the Turkish proverb says, "No matter how far you may have gone down the wrong road, turn back." Turn back and do what you came here to do.

"I was shown scenes from my life, scenes where I didn't act properly, where I was mean, and many times when I stood by and did nothing as others did nasty things. By now I thought that I was dead. I realized that I was a coward, and that I had wasted my life . . . I think Hell is a moment of ultimate clarity when all of your life is laid out before you in stark realism. The wasted opportunities, the selfishness, the greed and unhappiness, all become clear and apparent for the first time. Hell for me was true realization of all that I had wasted, a life squandered . . . Realizing that my life was a waste and that I was not a nice person, this experience has significantly altered my life and my choices as I have sought purpose, and to make myself a better person." Colin F.

"I felt a powerful Being, God-like, at my immediate side . . . I was told to go back, do important work, and use my previously wasted life to do good for others. I felt a hard return to my body. Recovery was slow at first, but I became well after two months and then set about doing amazing things with my life. I have made it my life's work to inform all others I meet about my NDE and do only good deeds for all." Archie M.

"I felt like I had wasted my life on trivial pursuits of material success, hedonism, and social esteem. All of these things were understood to be of no value and completely meaningless. Those things really did not matter. It was as though they never occurred. They were inconsequential. A great feeling of sadness overcame me at this point. My life was insignificant." James G.

Our Life is Part of a Master Plan that Impacts Others

As we look back on and get a big picture view of our entire lifetime and all the choices in it, as well as how they interweave with others, we see that our life is part of one big master plan. When we experience our Life Review, we fully understand how important our seemingly small yet significant role is within it. We need to realize that our family, friends, neighbors, co-workers, churches, schools, and communities really need our gifts. People need our time and talents to help them in their life, as we need theirs. People's lives will be significantly different if we choose to withhold our gifts and squander our talents. (I shudder to think how my life would have turned out if Lari DeBruin didn't coach me and the other kids in our small community back in eighth grade.) Our work, contributions, and love are desperately needed and a crucial part of God's plan.

> "God then told me, 'You can stay, but I want you to go back because you are a part of my plan.' I asked, 'What do you mean I am a part of your plan?' It was then shown what my part of God's plan was and how each of us affect all those around us. I was shown that there is a reaction to all our interactions, like a domino-effect of good or bad. I was made to understand that if I stayed there, that God would have to change millions of events in order to make his plan work because I would not be there to make it happen. I told God, 'I will go back for you if it is a part of your plan' (which I had a complete understanding of at the time)." William R.

> "When I came into the light, there was a Being of Light . . . The Being told me I was HOME but that I needed to go back because He had some work for me to do. He said I would not understand the meaning of the work until I went back. He showed me what it was like to have a peaceful world and that we can attain that peaceful world if we have faith and help one another. He said I would come back here and help with this work. In time, I would remember who I really am and what my purpose is on earth. After my work was complete I would come back home. I agreed to come back and help." Karen B.

> "When I wondered why a specific event had happened, God gave an explanation. I learned that things really do happen for a reason, because it is His plan for us . . ." Erica McKenzie, RN

As we evaluate our life, we realize our human life does have a critical purpose for others, for ourselves, for our planet, and for God. Our life truly does matter in many ways to someone and something and Spirit. It is up to us to live accordingly.

"I saw that everything we do makes a difference. The impact we have on one another is profound. And all of it is registered telepathically somewhere in our minds, so that we carry within ourselves the consequences for our thoughts, words, and deeds. We have a responsibility, and we hold ourselves accountable for all of it." David Oakford

Further, when we don't find and fulfill our life's purpose, it also has an adverse Ripple Effect on others being able to live out their purpose. Essentially, if the domino of our essential purpose doesn't fall when it is supposed to or in the correct direction, there are others who won't be impacted and they too won't be able to share their purpose.

"I also became aware that we are all much more powerful than we have been led to believe. I realized that I hadn't completed my purpose yet. And that my purpose was linked to my husband's purpose, Danny's purpose. And that if I didn't come back, he wouldn't be able to complete his purpose either. So with all of that understanding, I chose to come back." Anita Moorjani

"We were connected to each other in vital ways. If one of us were to fail in his or her mission, all of us would be hurt in some way. If one succeeded, we all would benefit. It was as if we were part of a puzzle with millions of pieces. It was put together perfectly, but if one piece were removed, we all would be lacking and would not be content until that piece was found and returned to its rightful place. We needed each other." RaNelle Wallace

"When my NDE come to an end, I understood how what we do in this life might injure others and how we will be held accountable. Theoretically, if being cruel made another person fail to complete whatever job they were sent here to do, we will have to complete that task for them." Casper

Thus, our sacred purpose is not only important for our own life and fulfillment, but others as well. If we don't complete our primary reasons for coming to earth, we may also prevent others from living out their life's purpose and impacting the people they need to help. It reminds us that everyone and everything is interconnected and matters in some way.

"As I came into the Light, I was filled with an indescribable love and peace. I did not speak with my mouth but telepathically. I was shown my life on earth, the beginning to now, and I was shown the impact I had on others I connected to. I could feel their feelings and experiences in how I treated them. I was filled with total knowledge and understood everything . . . God wanted me to go back and told me my purpose was not finished on this earth, I would have children. I wanted to do God's will. I told God I wanted to stay but in my heart to do His will was stronger. This experience changed me forever. I always had faith. Today I can say absolutely God is real, Jesus is real, and love is all that matters!" Frances W.

With the help of the Life Review, we realize that every breath is precious, every day is a gift, every relationship is a blessing, and every interaction is a special opportunity to share love, hope, and kindness.

Evaluate Your Life Summary

Contrary to what many believe, NDErs consistently tell us no one in Heaven judges us or our life. We judge ourselves. Based on seeing and feeling the impact our life had on everyone and everything through the Life Review, we assess how well we unconditionally loved ourselves and others, how well we lived our life fully and fearlessly, and how well we shared our gifts and talents to make the world a better place and develop spiritually.

> "In the final analysis of our lives, we will judge ourselves according to the difference we made in every event that transpired and for every person who crossed our path." Dannion Brinkley

EVALUATE YOUR LIFE
PRACTICAL REFLECTIONS AND EXERCISES

EVALUATE YOUR LIFE EXERCISE #1
How will your life be judged?

What is your belief on how your life will be evaluated or judged?

How have these beliefs been influenced by your religion or spiritual beliefs?

Do you believe we are the only ones who evaluate ourselves? Why or why not?

EVALUATE YOUR LIFE EXERCISE #2
Your Life's Do Overs

In what situations of your life would you love to get a "Do Over"?

How would you have done things differently that would have brought more love to the situation?

EVALUTE YOUR LIFE EXERCISE #3
Our Life Review Report Card

Like we will do in Heaven, we can take a moment now to consciously, compassionately, and constructively evaluate our life.

Like in Heaven, the intent of the grade should be to inform and inspire us rather than scare or depress us. I have put a positive spin on the usual grading scale so we can grade ourselves in the proper context. Remember, we grade ourselves rather than worrying about how God or our guides might grade us. They love us unconditionally whether we give ourselves A's or F's or somewhere in between.

Life Review Grading Scale

A = Awesome, B = Bravo, C = Currently Improving, D = Developing this Area, F = Future Strength

1. How well do you unconditionally love others and yourself? *Grade_____*

2. How well do you live your life fully and fearlessly? *Grade_____*

3. How well have you found and fulfilled your life's purpose? *Grade_____*

Essentially, rather than waiting to evaluate ourselves when we do our Life Review in Heaven, why not do it now while we still have precious time left in our life? Grading ourselves now provides us with real-time, valuable feedback to see where we may want to continue on the track we're on and where we may want to make some changes. Better to assess ourselves and make these changes now while we still have time left than to have regrets and feel like we wasted our life and opportunities when looking back on them in our Life Review.

EVALUTE YOUR LIFE EXERCISE #4
Salvaging Your Life and Sharing Your Gifts

In what ways do you feel like you may have "wasted" your life to this point?

In what ways might you feel like you have wasted your God-given gifts and talents?

How can you better use what time is left of your life to take full advantage of the life you have been given?

How can you live fully and fearlessly?

EVALUATE YOUR LIFE EXERCISE #5
1 Week Left to Live Exercise

Imagine if you only had one week left to live. This next week is all you have left of your life.

What would you do and say in the next seven days?

What is still left undone in your life?

What regrets would you have if your life ended in the next seven days?

Who would you want to make amends with?

How can you go about fulfilling your life's purpose with your remaining time left?

What specific actions will you take this week in light of these reflections?

EVALUATE YOUR LIFE EXERCISE #6
Most Impactful NDEr Quote

Which of the NDEr quotes from this chapter most impacted you and why? When you reflect on the quote in relation to your own life, how does it lead you to think and feel?

5.
ENLIGHTEN YOURSELF

"The mind, once stretched by a new idea, never returns to its original dimensions."

Oliver Wendell Holmes

Romy's Life Review

"I saw my whole life unfolding. I was watching millions of the pictures of my life's events, like a movie broken down into picture frames. All the little deeds, thoughts, and moments upon moments, even the ones I forgot ever happened, they were all there. It was such a fascinating sight. The most curious thing was that the pictures were not connected to one another; they had a gap between them that looked like a string of light. It looked like they were threaded upon this string of light.

My main feelings were equanimity, awe, and curiosity. There was a strong quality of inquiry and inquisitiveness as I was examining everything. Every time a question came to me, the answer was immediately revealed. This unfolding of pictures and gaps developed and progressed continuously, presenting a constant delicate consequential line, in perfect order, a chain of events, yet somehow they were all happening at once. The past, the present, and the future were all happening at once. It was inspiring to witness the order and sense that all these little pictures seemed to have in 'the big picture'.

I felt a lot of compassion. I was all forgiven. In fact, there was nothing to forgive. I could see that my life had 'perfect order' to it. In some way it was like watching a mathematical equation, or sum, that makes perfect sense. Such event and such event create this kind of result. It was a simple portrayal of natural cause and effect, with a gentle understanding. There was no judgment, only innocence.

As I was watching this linear unfolding of pictures, I realized that just by looking and focusing on a specific picture, 'zooming in' on it, I could also 'enter' that scene and then come back out of it, 'zoom out' and return to my place of observation.

I looked back at my childhood. I could enter pictures there. From each picture, moment or thought, there was always the possibility to access that light that separated between it and the next picture. I could also see all the thoughts I had all my life. Their 'pictures' were as strong as the pictures that depicted action or words. I was amazed to see that our thoughts are that strong, so real. It looked as though they were also threaded on a string of light . . .

As I looked, I felt very peaceful. I could see how the last moment of my life was a result of everything that had ever happened to me, before. I could see my life was a perfect manifestation of just what it was, who I was. There was complete acceptance, even of those moments that I remembered as less pleasant."

"I saw how my life had touched all the people in it—it was sort of like a tapestry and I saw how I affected everyone's lives around me."

Anita Moorjani, Author of *Dying to Be Me*

The Goal of the Life Review is Education and Enlightenment

We have to ask ourselves, why would the Universe go through all the trouble to:

- record everything we've ever thought, said, and did from birth to death
- play it all back to us when we physically die so we can re-examine our life
- show us the perspective of every person with whom we've ever interacted
- allow us to feel exactly how everyone else felt in our interactions with them
- provide us with the complete backstory of others and what motivated them
- gather God and our guardian angels to guide us through our Life Review
- nonjudgmentally support us through the intensive and instructive process

- share what we could have said and done to bring more love to the situation

With so much time, energy, and effort invested in recording and replaying our comprehensive Life Review, the obvious and only real logical conclusion is this: the Universe seeks to educate and enlighten us by allowing us to come to our own realizations and conclusions about the meaning of life and value of love. It presents us with our own life's experiences as undeniable evidence to learn what really matters and to realize there are Universal Truths we can live and love by.

Ultimately, we experience a Life Review for the unforgettable lessons we learn about love. There is no more immersive or intensive way to learn about the value and power of love than by reviewing all of our choices during our lifetime and feeling directly ourselves how they actually impacted others. By experiencing these lessons first-hand in our Life Review, we understand them at such a personal, piercing, and powerful level because we do them to ourselves. The Life Review imprints these indelible lessons about how to love others and ourselves on our heart, mind, and soul as we feel their full impact and see their long-lasting Ripple Effects.

Earth is like a Boarding School, Summer Camp, or Boot Camp for the Soul

One primary goal of the Life Review is to educate and enlighten us about what really matters—and how much everything we do matters to someone or something. Many NDErs are told in Heaven that life on earth is much like attending a boarding school, summer camp, or boot camp for our soul. We come here primarily to learn how to more fully, consistently, and unconditionally love ourselves and others. It's like we enroll in various classes, activities, and challenges in the school of life designed to teach us love, kindness, patience, forgiveness, etc. Some of earth's classes and challenges are obviously much tougher than others.

> "I was told that the earth is like a big school, a place where you can apply spiritual lessons you have learned and test yourself to see whether you can 'live' what you already know you should do. Basically the earth is a place where you can walk the walk and live the way it should be done. It was made clear to me that some people come to the earth to work on one or more aspects of themselves, while others come to also help the world as a whole . . . We're under continual pressure to make decisions that have a spiritual base. We may be taught on the 'Other Side' what we are

'supposed to do,' but can we live it under the pressures of the earth? From what I saw and heard on the Other Side, everything is about relationships and taking care of each other. We aren't expected to be perfect, but we are expected to learn. All of our experiences in a lifetime follow some sort of pattern, and we often learn the same lessons, but in a different way and under various circumstances. This is how we know what we are here to learn." Jean R.

"Earth life, I found, is designed as a university, a school where we learn from our choices and our mortal experiences. I recognized that my most painful experiences taught me the most. It was enlightening to understand the bigger eternal picture—to know that I was not a victim of circumstances . . . I learned that being charitable, patient, and forgiving toward others are some of the most important character traits to be acquired—learned in the school of life." Dr. Joyce Brown

"The fear of dying subsided and I am not afraid anymore because where I was felt like my real home and this reality on Earth is just some sort of school to learn life lessons." Glenda H.

Others, like NDEr Dr. Mary Neal and bestselling author of *To Heaven and Back*, liken our time on earth to going away to summer camp for a week, a month, or an entire summer. We leave our heavenly home for a temporary adventure at "Earth Camp" that is filled with family, friends, and fun as well as frustrations, fears, and failures, but we eventually get to go back home to Heaven when camp is over.

"When I grew up, I loved my home. I loved everything about it . . . When I was home I felt comfortable and content. I felt safe and secure and loved. And I never wanted to leave. But then one day, I went off to summer camp. Now, I knew I'd be challenged. I was a little nervous, had never been away from home, didn't know what to expect. I assumed that I would learn and grow and maybe become a better me. And I did and it was great. I learned to swim and sail and waterski. I learned about kindness and humility. I made friends . . . But, of course, it wasn't all good. The beds were hard and I really didn't like the food. My sandals were stolen one day and I was pretty angry; but I actually felt compassion for the girl when I learned of her plight and I ended up giving her most of my clothes. And I hated, hated, hated the time I spent in the nurse's cabin after being stung by a bee. But I was able to find humor in all of this because I knew that my time at camp was temporary, and before long, I would be going back to my comfortable and familiar home. Sure enough, the camp bus came and took me home. And my friends were sad and they cried a little bit. But really? I was looking forward to going to my home, and sleeping in my own bed, and I knew my family would be waiting for me. And they would be overjoyed by my return. The point I'm making with this story is that it was the existence and

> reality of my childhood home and the knowledge that I would be going back there again that brought a context to my time at camp that allowed me to experience it as a great adventure. And since 1999 [her NDE], that's exactly how I experience my life here on earth." Dr. Mary Neal

Mary's summer camp analogy is a fantastic way to look at our lifetime on earth; as a temporary, exciting, and sometimes excruciating adventure complete with all the joys and pains that help us learn so much, but we eventually get to return to our true Home in Heaven. Our time on earth is like a summer camp for the soul—sometimes a great experience, other times a horrendous experience, but often a balanced blend of both depending on how we look at things in the moment and afterwards.

> "Then, I was Home. Earth and this life were a bad summer camp, in comparison, and I knew I wanted to stay. I didn't want to go back to camp. That's all I knew . . . I was 'sitting in God's lap', wrapped in the warmest embrace, and immediately involved in a 'conversation'. We communicated telepathically. I don't know how else to describe it. I didn't want to come back. That was my focus. I was Home, I liked being Home, just let me be Home. God was holding me tighter (in the best of ways), and showing me the life to which I must return. My field of vision was akin to being inside a TV screen watching a movie." V.

Finally, some NDErs talk about our time on earth like a more arduous and intensive boot camp for the soul. Ask any parent who has had a child pass away and they will definitely tell you that life during these horrific times is way more torturous than trying to make it through a hellish Navy SEAL boot camp. Their hearts shatter into a billion pieces when their child passes and they experience life's toughest crucible. However, so many of the dozens of grieving parents I know eventually come out of the ordeal as so much stronger, kinder, and wiser souls.

> "Earth is a boot camp and school for soul's spiritual education, and as such, it's tough. Nevertheless, I knew that I had to return and finish whatever mission I had to do here." Karen Brannon

> "It's kind of like life is a school, or a trip, or boot camp, that a spirit signs up for, in a way, to further their knowledge." Mary H.

Humans Seen as Heroes in Heaven

Whether our lifetime seems more like attending a boarding school, a cushy or challenging summer camp, or a hellish boot camp, NDErs tell us that God and our guides appreciate and honor our tremendous courage and commitment to go on this human journey as they watch our Life Review with us in Heaven. They admire and appreciate us for being so willing to learn more about loving ourselves and others and developing our souls away from the bliss, beauty, and perfection of Heaven. They don't look to condemn us for our mistakes, but instead joyously celebrate us as courageous heroes, as if we've just completed a grueling Ironman Triathlon, for taking our earthly journey and experiencing and learning the difficult lessons the hard way through experiencing the heart-pounding, gut-wrenching, mind-expanding, and soul-stretching ups and downs of human life.

> "In Heaven, we are considered heroes just because we were valiant enough to leap fearlessly into the great adventure called life. Leaving the spiritual kingdom in order to be born in the physical domain requires immense fortitude and unshakable faith . . . The spirits say that everyone who is here should hold himself in high esteem." Dannion Brinkley

> "The souls were so proud of me and were trying to touch me. They knew I had a difficult time here and they were proud of me." Leni D.

Life Review Helps Us See from a Higher Perspective

The mind-blowing movie of our life allows us to see ourselves, others, and our life from totally different vantage points of all we interacted with throughout our life; a unique perspective on our life that is impossible to gain otherwise. Through this new and massively broadened perspective, we can't help but expand our view of ourselves, others, and our world.

A Life Review not only awakens us to the fact that death is not the end of our life and existence, but it awakens us to a whole new reality and teaches us a whole new way of living and loving; a powerful way of doing life differently. Each of us has a certain way we currently think about life, death, God, Heaven, etc. Our particular viewpoint, worldview, paradigm, or perspective often comes from what we were taught by our parents, teachers, society, religion, culture, the media, etc. Our worldview largely determines how we approach our life, think about death, handle adversity, and determine what is right and wrong among many other things. Whatever our perspective may have been before experiencing or learning about the Life Review, it is likely at least slightly if not significantly different afterwards.

A Life Review both enlightens us and in-LIGHT-ens us. The term "enlightenment" perfectly encapsulates this new outlook because it essentially means to bring loving and brilliant light into our thoughts and actions and encourages us to embody, reflect, and shine the love of the LIGHT into the sometimes depressing darkness of the human world.

The Life Review completely shatters our paradigms and dramatically shifts, expands, and deepens our previous perspectives of how we viewed ourselves, others, the world around us, our life's purpose, the meaning of life, and so many other groundbreaking ideas. NDErs are never the same after having a Life Review—and hopefully we are never the same after learning about them. A Life Review spiritually cracks us open, alters our perspectives, and awakens us to a new way of living and loving.

> "Enlightenment comes when a person realizes that love is everywhere and is the only thing that matters. Yet most don't reach that realization until they leave the earth. The ones who come back remember the purpose and presence of love in everything. And they remember it the rest of their lives." Archangel Michael to Dr. Rajiv Parti

New Awakenings and Enlightenments

Experiencing a Life Review, or reading about them and absorbing and applying their profound and powerful lessons, creates a series of mental, emotional, and spiritual awakenings. We become enlightened in whole new ways that it often takes some time for us to process these ideas, understand what they really mean, accept them into our reality, assimilate them into our life, and regularly act on them. For many NDErs, the process can take several years to fully integrate the experience—we should expect the same as we wrap our brains, hearts, and souls around these profound ideas, especially if they are newer to us and different than what we might have been taught previously.

Depending on your religious upbringing, spiritual path, or current beliefs, the enlightenments brought about and reinforced by the Life Review may range from the more mundane, basic, and superficial for some people to seeming absolutely sacrilegious and heretical for others. I'm just sharing the consensus of what millions of NDErs have experienced on their otherworldly and enlightening journeys to the Other Side. Take them for whatever they are worth for wherever you might be on your journey.

Here are some of the major enlightenments we come to experience and espouse as we understand the sheer power and brilliance of the Life Review. To make them easier to understand and apply, they're grouped into five main sections:

- Enlightenments about Life After Death
- Enlightenments about God
- Enlightenments about Earth
- Enlightenments about Others
- Enlightenments about Ourselves

THE LIFE REVIEW ENLIGHTENS US ABOUT LIFE AFTER DEATH

NDErs give us a rare and enlightening glimpse into what the heavenly realm will be like for us when it is our turn to go once we've fulfilled our life's purposes on earth. Not only are these enlightenments helpful to those who are curious about the mysteries of the Afterlife, these special insights about Heaven also provide tremendous comfort to those who have had loved ones pass away. NDErs assure us the spirit of our "deceased" loved ones lives on and is in a glorious place of peace, love, and light and will re-unite with us when it is our time. Here are some of the major enlightenments we can learn about Heaven by studying Life Reviews.

Life and consciousness continue after bodily death: If you've made it this far in the book, this one might seem rather obvious and basic but still it is worth mentioning as there are an estimated 450-500 million people around the world who deny, doubt, or disbelieve it: our consciousness undoubtedly continues past physical death.

> "This huge spirit comes . . . I asked her, 'Am I dead?' And she said, 'Oh no, no. You're not dead. There is no death. You're either alive in your body, or you're out of your body and you're super alive on the spirit side.'" Penny Wittbrodt

> "I was asked, 'Do you want to continue this life, or die?' I thought, 'What's death?' The Light began to show me. I knew without a doubt that death was not an ending, but a wonderful opening to my real life. I would be more knowledgeable and live in unconditional completeness and love. I remember feeling almost unworthy of such an indescribable, unconditional love. I was in awe of how much love was enveloping me." Judy G.

"If you expected to die when you die you will be disappointed. The only thing dying does is help you release, slough off and discard the 'jacket' you once wore (commonly referred to as the body) . . . When you die you lose your body. That is all there is to it. Nothing else is lost . . ." PMH Atwater

What if we lived our life knowing there is so much more to our existence than our physical lifetime here on earth? What if we realized we don't die?

Death is nothing to fear: Further, NDErs assure us that actual physical death is nothing we should fear in any way for ourselves or others. It is one of the most beautiful experiences they have ever had as they feel the love and peace "that passeth all understanding." Many say death is simply like passing from one room to another.

"The best way I can describe the transition from being 'alive' on the physical plane and the passage to the Other Side is like passing from one 'room' to another. You do not cease to be or lose consciousness; your consciousness simply shifts from one vantage point to another." Juliet Nightingale

"I remember thinking, knowing, I am taking my last breath. I had such a feeling of peace; I can only describe it as a peace that passes all understanding. Shortly after that moment, I remember a Light so bright and glorious . . . I knew I had died and my soul was telepathically communicating with God." Brenda I.

"I am no longer the least bit afraid to die. I know that I would not want to suffer, but I know that the actual dying process is nothing like I thought it would be, and that it was probably the most beautiful and peaceful experience I have ever had." Craig

What if we lived our life without the fear of death for ourselves and others and realized it will be a beautiful and joyous experience when it is our time to go Home?

There is an Afterlife: Based on millions of NDEs, there is obviously some kind of Afterlife we go to after physical death. While we may not understand the complete details about this vast, expansive, and otherworldly realm, we can be assured another realm exists beyond what we experience here during our physical lifetime on planet earth.

"I now realized and understood that there was life after death; I have died and left my body, yet I still exist. I tried to understand where I was. I was in a transition. All I could notice different from before, besides not having a body, was that the air, or the space, was of a slightly different consistency and shade. I reflected on how this whole transition between life and death, is very smooth and calm. It became clear to me that death is the continuation of life, and not the opposite of it. It was ongoing. I felt vibrant like a child, very curious to see what was next, looking at everything with new eyes." Romy

"I asked if this was Heaven and was told, 'Yes, if that is what you want to call the Afterlife.' I responded, 'I do not believe in Heaven (per say) or an Afterlife.' I was told I was wrong. I had been in so much pain and was so ill but not in this place. The euphoria, peace, and serenity were incomprehensible." Rose D.

What if we lived this life with the assurance that our spirit never actually dies but our consciousness continues on in the Afterlife? Would death be any less scary and worrisome for ourselves and our loved ones if we lived with this understanding?

THE LIFE REVIEW ENLIGHTENS US ABOUT GOD

Although impossible to capture the ineffable essence, breadth, depth, intelligence, humor, magnificence, and love of the Divine, the Life Review provides us with some critical insights into Her unconditionally loving nature and how She will receive us when we come home to Heaven.

"Many people have asked me what I believe in, how my NDE changed my life. All I can say is that I now believe in the God of the universe. Unlike many other people, however, I have never called God the Light, because God is beyond our comprehension. God, I believe, is even more than the Light, because God is also darkness. God is everything that exists, everything—and that is beyond our ability to comprehend at all. So I don't believe in the God of the Jews, or the Christians, or the Hindus, or in any one religion's idea of what God is or is not. It is all the same God, and that God showed me that the universe in which we live is a beautiful and marvelous mystery that is connected together forever and for always." George Rodonaia

There is a God: Whether God appears as a brilliantly bright loving Light, Spiritual Being, religious figure, or an indescribable Force of Love, millions of NDErs from all around the world tell us they unequivocally KNOW God exists, not just believe She exists. Why? Because during their NDEs they met Her, telepathically talked with Her, learned from Her, and felt Her unforgettable, universal, and unconditional love.

"I knew immediately I was in the presence of God. I have always referred to God as a him, and I guess I always will. But the being on my right was not a him or a her; it was just God . . . There was no distinct form, certainly no face or body, just a blinding profusion of brightness. I wasn't so much meeting God as I was recognizing Him. I already knew Him, and He knew me. I'd spent my life doubting His existence and disbelieving His love for me, but in that instant I knew God had always, always been there—right there with me . . . This was the Creator of the universe, and I was in His presence! The sheer ecstasy of it! The beauty of it, the joy and the grace, the way my spirit soared and my heart burst—how I wish I had the words to convey just how miraculous this was." Crystal McVea

"I became aware that the God I was experiencing was not just a life force, or some impersonal consciousness, but God . . . had a sense of humor! He and I both laughed at the thought of me questioning His existence. It seemed to me the absolutely funniest thought in the world, and we laughed at the thought of it. I realized that I was the shadow, and He was the reality. The very idea that I would question His existence was a source of laughter for God and me." John K.

"I knew that this love that I was feeling was the love of the Higher Power, or what I had been raised to call God. And how I was experiencing God was not at all like I had been taught God was supposed to be like. It was not like an old man with a long white beard sitting on a throne judging me whether I was good or bad. No, that was not what I was experiencing. I was experiencing God, or the Higher Power, to be like this immense, vast, omni-present, stretching throughout and permeating all of creation, like a force field of LOVE. An infinite intelligence that was like underlying, inter-penetrating all of everything, all of creation." Yvonne Kason

(For more on what NDErs say about their experience of God, check out Dr. Jeffrey Long's excellent book titled *God and the Afterlife*.)

How would our life be different if we absolutely *KNEW* there was a God who didn't judge us or needed us to behave in some prescribed way to please Her by obsessively obeying Her rules and commandments? Instead, She unconditionally loved, adored, and accepted us no matter what? Would we treat ourselves or others any differently if we lived with this understanding?

There are guardian angels/spiritual guides who help us: In addition to God, NDErs tell us spiritual beings greet us, guide us, comfort us, question us, and support us in Heaven (and on earth). Whether you want to call them guardian angels, spirit guides, Beings of Light, or a Council of Elders (it doesn't matter to them), these wise and loving heavenly guides deeply understand human life with its many trials and tribulations and emanate tremendous compassion and concern for us. It seems they have been with us since the very start of our earthly journey (and likely beforehand) and know us better than we know ourselves. They guide us along our human life but must always honor and allow our free will.

> "I realized I wasn't alone. There was someone, whom I can only describe as a Loving Being of Light, traveling beside me . . . at the speed of light! We communicated mentally. This was someone I have always known and I knew that as soon as I sensed the presence of this being. Yet I cannot now tell you now who it was. I didn't have the sense that it was any familiar religious figure or deceased relative, but rather a special friend who is always with me wherever I am; perhaps, my guardian angel. This Being told me telepathically that I had a choice about going back. I thought, no, no, no, I want this to go on forever! This Being showed me around on the Other Side where I saw many other light beings going about their lives. The only communication I remembered is that it wasn't my time to go, I had more work to do in this life, and if I chose to go back, I would be given access to knowledge that would help me with my mission." Diane Goble

> "I saw the earth with its billions of people on it. I saw them scrambling for existence, making mistakes, experiencing kindness, finding love, grieving for death, and saw angels hovering above them. The angels knew the people by name and watched over them closely. They cheered when good was done and were saddened by our mistakes. They hovered about to help and give direction and protection. I saw that we could literally call down thousands of angels in our aid if we ask in faith . . . We are all precious and carefully watched over. Their love never fails us." Betty Eadie

> "There are angels all around us and we each have 'personal' angels who watch over us all day. They help us, nudge us, and guide us in all sorts of little ways that we usually don't notice. Sometimes they push us forward and sometimes they pull us backward. Always, they want very much for us to follow the path that has been laid out for us by God." Dr. Mary Neal

How would our human life be different if we knew there was a special spiritual guide or guardian angel dedicated to each of us through absolutely every millisecond of our life to guide, support, assist, and encourage us through life's many ups and downs; that we are never ever alone? Shouldn't we ask for this being's guidance and try to tune in more to that faint, loving inner voice that always has our spiritual growth and best interest in mind? NDErs learn that our angels are always there to guide and support us—just ask and tune in to that inner voice.

God and the angels/guides love us unconditionally: This point cannot be stressed enough!!! Despite our multitude of human faults and failings, God and our angels/guides love us unconditionally!!! NO. MATTER. WHAT. There is nothing, zip, zilch, nada we can do as humans that would cause God to stop loving us. We are loved universally, wholly, eternally, and unconditionally.

> "Immediately, a strong but gentle voice spoke to me from the Light, a voice heard not with my ears but with my mind. The Being of Light said, 'Carry, I love you exactly the way you are.' The funny thing was that when I heard that voice I recognized it. Somehow, I 'knew' this Being. He was like the best friend I always wanted and wished for but did not know it. But, upon hearing his voice, I knew Him immediately. When the Being of Light first said this, I felt like the most loved human being of all time, the most favorite of all human beings in the universe, past, present or future, yet at the same time I knew this Being loved everyone equally and just as infinitely as I felt right then. The Being delighted in me and was completely focused on me. I was the center of its attention yet somehow I knew everyone was at the 'center' of its attention. When the Being said those words to me, I knew it saw me as I was, faults and all, not just at that moment, but for all the moments of my life. I felt no shame, no judgment; in fact, it was so liberating to be known so perfectly, to be so wonderfully accepted. Yet, at the same time, not judged or condemned in the slightest way . . . I somehow knew this being was God." Carry G.

> "The Light also knows everything that I've ever done and will do but loves me unconditionally. The Light loves me because I'm Andy—a piece of the Light. There is no fear, no judgment, punishment, blame, or shame. No ledger of good and bad deeds. Only warmth, peace, joy, happiness, forgiveness, and love in the Light. I'm one with the unconditionally loving Light." Andy Petro

What if we lived our lives knowing that God and our guides unconditionally love and fully accept us exactly as we are?

God and the guides do not judge us: As we discussed and detailed in the Evaluate Your Life chapter, God and the guides do not judge us for what we do on earth. We judge our own life based on how well we loved ourselves and others, lived fully and fearlessly, and fulfilled our primary life's purposes of making the world a better place and developing our soul.

> "I clearly remember turning to my left towards my spirit guides feeling very embarrassed and ashamed with myself based on my Life Review.

I was afraid they would also be ashamed of me but was surprised that they hadn't judged me at all. I knew at that moment that my guides knew everything about me, every thought I ever had, and they still loved me completely and unconditionally with no judgment." Brett D.

"Why are we never taught that there's no judgment? Believing we will be judged in the Afterlife really alters the way we live life here—and often not in a positive way. This belief keeps us in fear of what will happen to us on the Other Side, so instead of doing good for the sake of love and goodness itself, we can easily find ourselves acting out of fear of being punished after we die. And fear is not love . . . I wish I had not been taught to fear the Afterlife because I was somehow going to be judged and punished." Anita Moorjani

What if we lived our life not in fear of God judging us but trying to extend this same healing unconditional love out into the world? What if instead of worrying about sinning and displeasing God we instead focused our time and energy on loving our neighbor and taking care of our planet?

God does not send us to hell: Because God doesn't judge us, NDErs tell us She also does not send us to hell. In fact, most NDErs don't even believe in the existence of hell because it was not anything they experienced and so completely opposite of the heavenly love, bliss, and beauty they experienced. However, in full disclosure, a super small percentage (2% to 5% in most studies) of people report distressing or hellish NDEs. But the "hell" they experience is a temporary, self-imposed choice that offers them a valuable period of reflection before seeing and moving toward the Light.

"Hell is a state of being. It is a state of being separated from the loving grace of God by our choices. His love is constant. His grace is constant. But we choose. If we want to be separated from that, that's our choice. He doesn't put us in hell, we put ourselves there . . . It can be a pretty dark place, but it's not a permanent place and we can get out of it. All we need to do is ask and that Light will be right there." Sharon Milliman

"The hell I suffered was to see, hear, feel, understand, and embody all of the pain I had ever caused during my earthly life to anyone I had known, from their point of view. I had carried their pain with me and brought their pain with me into the afterlife. How unexpected. It was a record, a file, a folder, a book of life somehow written and recorded in my soul. God had not done this to me. God had not caused my hell. I saw that immediately. I had done it to myself. I had woven it on my own. I had burned each wrong action on to my own DVD, and yet it was also clear to me that my brokenness was simply a part of being a human being." Peter Panagore

Would our lives be any different if we spent less time worrying about being sentenced to hell for eternity (or possibly purgatory for a time for the Catholics) and invested more of our precious time trying to bring the love of Heaven down to earth?

These significant enlightenments about the existence of an unconditionally loving God and our dedicated team of spiritual guides who fully reveal themselves to us in Heaven, don't judge us, nor banish us to hell for all of eternity, should allay many of the debilitating fears that may haunt us throughout our life. Life Reviews show us that God is neither vindictive nor vengeful. Instead, She is unconditionally loving and infinitely forgiving. These essential enlightenments should provide us with tremendous peace, comfort, and confidence as we go about our daily life.

THE LIFE REVIEW ENLIGHTENS US ABOUT THE EARTH

Life Reviews also provide tremendous insights into the purpose of the earthly realm and the lifetime we spend here, which sometimes seems interminably long to most of us going through challenges and ordeals, but is likened to a blink of eye from the heavenly perspective.

We are amazing spiritual beings who go to earth for a human experience and soul-developing adventure: When they leave their bodies upon their death and realize they still exist, NDErs learn they are really magnificent spiritual beings whose essence and consciousness far transcend the confines of the physical body as well as earth time and space. They learn that our souls temporarily take on a limiting brain and confining body for our time on earth, much like a deep-sea diver dons a diving suit or an astronaut wears a spacesuit. They learn we are so much more than what we physically appear, like magical genies being squeezed into a confining lamp. They realize we are really eternal powerful spiritual beings having a temporary human experience.

"We are each amazing and powerful people buried there behind our fears and insecurities . . . Every person on Earth has amazing power and creativity. At our cores, we are shining beings of light, love, and energy who are living as humans in this time and place. Inside each one of us is a spiritual spark, a light-filled being capable of almost anything." Nancy Rynes

*"We are not human beings having
a spiritual experience.
We are spiritual beings having
a human experience."*

PIERRE TEILHARD DE CHARDIN

"We are not just human. We are Spirit. We were Spirit before we came into this lifetime. We are all struggling Spirits now, trying to get 'being human' right. And when we leave here, we will be pure Spirit again." Barbara Harris Whitfield

"The body is temporary, but a wonderful gift to use to transport us through this physical life. I do far less grumbling about our miraculous bodies now. Even so, the particular bodies are not needed as we continue on." Judy G.

What if we saw ourselves as powerful spiritual beings who temporarily left our heavenly home for an amazing adventure on earth cloaked in a human body? What if instead of obsessing over how our bodies look by spending thousands of dollars on clothes, makeup, plastic surgery, etc., we saw them simply as the functional covering for our souls for our time here on earth?

Earth purposely has duality and drama so we can experience opposites: On earth we experience difficult challenges we just can't in the bliss and perfection of Heaven. On earth we can experience both joy and pain, wealth and poverty, justice and injustice, love and hate, light and dark, lack and abundance, hopelessness and happiness, triumphs and tragedies. All of these opposites provide our soul with amazing opportunities to have experiences and learn.

"We came here for one thing. And that was to learn about ourselves. That's it . . . We came down here to experience opposition. We came down here to feel the opposite. For example, we would never know what great health felt like if you'd never been sick. You would never know what a wonderful day in Hawaii would be like if you didn't live in a winter environment. You'd go to Hawaii in the middle of the winter and you're going 'Yeah, this is awesome!' and the guy on the beach that's local is like 'What's your big deal, man? It's this way every day.' So it's the opposition that defines us. It's the space between these things that creates form. All of these things need each other. We need opposition to even know who we are." Ryan Rampton

"I learned that the bullying I received on the playground helped me to learn to stand up for myself. I learned that the denial of the job I wanted taught me to work harder. I learned that the breakup from the girl that I thought was 'the one' taught me that I needed to work on myself before I was able to give to another . . . I realized that all the 'bad' things that happened were actually necessary and beneficial for my soul's growth." Stephen Weber

"In order to enrich our highest form of energy—or our souls—and grow to be more perfect, or in other words to mature to a higher level of perfection

> we must first experience many facets of imperfection. The only way for us to accomplish this feat however is by gaining knowledge of what it is like to be imperfect, and all of the various aspects involved. Now, in this case, the only means of experiencing imperfection is to choose to incarnate and come to an imperfect world . . . We choose to visit a living mechanical world that was designed and created imperfect purposely for the evolution of the soul, essence, spirit energy or whatever term you prefer. In a paradoxical sort of way you could say that anger, hatred, greed, jealousy as well as all other forms of human suffering were designed to exist in this world exclusively for our benefit because they do not exist back home. Physical life is nothing more than an experience of a multitude of things that do not exist on the other side simply for the evolution and maturation of the soul. In essence, life is a learning, teaching, and growing experience." Steve B.

What if instead of cursing the duality and drama of the physical world, we accepted, embraced, and valued it for the necessary resistance it provides to develop and strengthen our souls?

Earth is like a boarding school, summer camp, or boot camp: We temporarily leave the bliss and beauty of Heaven and come to earth to experience a variety of lessons on love. Some of these classes and lessons are fun and easy and some are super hard like a boot camp for the soul. All of them are designed to stretch us and our souls by gaining more experience and wisdom about ourselves, others, and the meaning of life.

> "Where I went to when I died was Home. I wanted to stay Home. Coming back here is more—for lack of a better word—schooling. I came back to continue with the schooling I now have to finish." Sondra Boyd

> "Earth is the hard part. This is the University of Earth. I was shown that I applied and was accepted to this school. God doesn't cause bad things to happen. Before we come here we pick our lessons and plan how we will live our lives—just like we do before we go to college. He is always with us. When we learn our lessons and finish the job we came here to do, we get to graduate and go back home. Whether we die quickly or slowly, we all have to review our lives before we get to graduate." Mary Beth Willi

What if we saw our time on earth as a school where the course of our life (path we take) is actually the course of our life (lessons we are to experience) so we can learn how to love ourselves, our friends, our family, and our planet better? What if we knew that no matter how easy or hard Earth School/Camp is for us, we always get to go back home to Heaven?

Earthly hardships, challenges, and crises set us up for soul growth: Life's hardships help us develop and grow our souls. The things we hate the most as humans, problematic and painful things like debt, divorce, death, and natural disasters, are often the same experiences that stretch our souls the most.

> "We come here to experience all of the difficulties ON PURPOSE . . . We wanted to know what it was like to age, become sick, experience harsh emotions etc., that is why we come to this grand learning place as souls. That is the entire point. This answers the question of suffering on this planet such as why some children have cancer etc. It would be entirely pointless to come to Earth and incarnate into an enlightened body. You may as well stay on the Other Side. We come here to suffer. I don't know why souls want to learn about this but they are incredibly interested to learn about it." Leni D.

> "Our souls are here to learn lessons and we learn them through the difficulties in this life. By embracing those difficulties and seeing them as learning opportunities, realizing that by manifesting that love and compassion in this imperfect realm, that that is how we progress in that higher spiritual realm." Dr. Eben Alexander

Similarly, the people who make our life the most difficult are often our greatest teachers. While we struggle mightily to deal with them during our time here on earth and wonder why in God's name hardships happen to us compared to the bliss and beauty of Heaven, they force us to dig deeper, discover who we really are, and find out what really matters—and who really matters.

> "I realized that I had been angry with God for a long time. And I told him, 'You say you're this loving God and you want the best for your children and I call bull crap. I've seen what you've allowed my own children to go through. Here their dad abandoned them when they were just babies.' And him leaving me was hard enough and not deserved. You know I can take whatever he did to me but watching those kids talk to him on the telephone and then go to the mailbox every day to check for a gift that he said he was going to send that's never coming, and watch them walk back heartbroken every day, what kind of God allows that? I said, 'It would have been easier on all of us (and this is terrible to say) but it would have been easier if he died because I could have told the kids this story about what a wonderful man he was and how much he loved them, and they would have had at least that. But now they've got this man that's alive that is failing them in every way. And of course, children take that on and attribute it to something being wrong with them. And I really had held that against God and I was bitter and I wanted to be mad at Him. And He said, 'Oh,

you've completely misunderstood me. Let me show you something.' And we flash forward, and we're sitting in the bleachers and David, my oldest son, is sitting to my right, and Cole [her grandson] is older, he's like 5 or 6, and we're watching him play soccer and he's running up and down this field . . . And David looks at me and he says, 'Mom, I'm going to be the dad to him that I deserved.' And I was like, 'Wow! If it took his dad leaving for him to make that commitment, I get it. It's been worth it.'" Penny Wittbrodt

"I realized that even those who had seemingly hurt me had somehow moved me to the next level of my life in a positive way, even if I didn't feel like that at the time . . . Get in the habit of looking at your challenges as blessings. Instead of getting angry and frustrated when something isn't going the way you would like, ask yourself, 'If this were actually a gift from the universe, what would it be here to teach me?' You'll be amazed at how that shift in perspective can open you up to wisdom from within." Anita Moorjani

"We didn't come here just to experience all the happy things. We also came here to experience the difficult emotions because we learn from those and they enrich us in ways that we really can't get when we are out of body." Natalie Sudman

---

"If you are irritated by every rub, how will you be polished?"

Rumi, Sufi Poet

What if we viewed life's human hardships and the people we dislike or even detest as valuable teachers and spiritual development opportunities that polish us and have the potential to set us up for tremendous soul growth?

Our earthly life is recorded and leaves an imprint on the Universe: Our Life Review is proof that our entire life is somehow captured and played back to us at the end of our life to help us see the impact we had—and could have had. Christian religions often refer to the record of our life as the "Book of Life" while other religions call it the "Akashic Records." Whatever the case, the recording and replaying of our numerous life choices and situations reinforces the idea that earth is indeed a kind of spiritual school where we come to learn about love. We review our life and the many learnings we gained, both what to do and what not to do, through our Life Review.

> "I realized that everything that happened to me and every single thought I had, created an imprint. Every single event or thought influenced my life and the lives of those around me. Every feeling, every intention, every time I was aware of the light and gap between the pictures, everything counted." Romy

> "It began from the moment I was born in the hospital until the time I died and I watched everything. Moments that you forget about. Every moment of my life had been recorded, like a matrix. It was like everything was showing simultaneously of every conversation, of every person, every situation, every encounter. Every moment that we thought no one's watching. Everything is recorded . . . I didn't murder anyone, I didn't rob a store, I wasn't violent to people, but what I did see were these moments where I could have shined, where I could have helped someone that needed help." Peter Anthony

> "We carry our life's experience home from this world in the form of life data or memories, similar to that of a jet airliner which carries a flight data recorder, or a little black box as it is commonly known. As absurd as all of this may sound, each and every one of us has on board our very own little black box. Even though we may be unaware of it, from the very moment that we are born into this world we begin forming, recording, and storing memories or life data, right down to the smallest most intricate detail." Steve B.

How would we live if we knew that everything we did was captured and recorded and we would someday feel exactly how we made other people feel? (This critical question is one of the key ones of the entire book.)

THE LIFE REVIEW ENLIGHTENS US ABOUT OTHERS

The Life Review teaches us tons about other people and their role in our life. Be they dear friends and family members or detestable foes, each person plays a pivotal role in our life. Through the magic and miracle of our Life Review, we get to see how our interactions impact both them and us.

Relationships are critical: We learn the importance of our relationships with others in our Life Review. The movie of our life captures and allows us to see and analyze all of our interactions to learn which thoughts, words, and actions brought about love, joy, and peace, and which ones didn't.

"Too often we underestimate the power of a touch, a smile, a kind word, a listening ear, an honest compliment, or the smallest act of caring, all of which have the potential to turn a life around."

LEO BUSCAGLIA

"From what I saw and heard there, it is all about relationships and taking care of each other. Perfection is not expected of people, but learning is expected and considered good progress." Jean R.

"The thing that matters most to them is our relationships with each other. How we treat one another. Nothing else on earth really matters to them, there. Not politics, not making money, other than it's a helpful tool. Not the stock market. Just how we live with, and interact with, each other. That we do it well." Kim A.

"I understood instantly life was about people not pursuits . . . I realized how important people were in life, how important it was to accept them and love them." Laurelynn Martin

What if we lived with the understanding that our relationships are truly precious and infinitely more important than what much of popular culture currently defines as successful?

The little things are the BIG THINGS: Life Reviews teach us that the little things in life are truly the BIG THINGS. Our earthly accomplishments like job promotions, educational degrees, professional awards, and financial successes aren't the things featured or celebrated in our Life Reviews; it's all the little selfless acts of kindness that mean the most. Simple kindnesses mean so much to others.

"I was shown it is not the big things we do in life that make the difference. All the little things we do each day make the difference. Little acts of kindness mean so much to God." Mary Beth Willi

"I recall simple gestures having the most impact, like a spontaneous and genuine smile. For example, I smiled at a woman I passed on the street and it turned her day around. She had been feeling disheartened about life, and my smile changed her interactions later that day with her children and others." Debra Kaiser

"It all counts. During my NDE I learned that whatever the act may be, large or small, if it is done out of love, it is huge to God. Something as simple as just listening to another without saying anything, giving a hug for no reason, without thinking about it you empty your wallet into the hand of a homeless man, without thinking about it you offer a drink to someone who is hot and thirsty. A smile, giving a compliment just because. Reading a story to an Alzheimer's patient. None of these things are big acts of kindness. They are small but show great compassion. It was small things done without thought but things that changed the day of another." Sharon Milliman

"I saw every word, thought, and action deemed unimportant, insignificant to man. Yet, I now understand the things in life that mattered most to

God . . . I saw myself helping an elderly person with their groceries, comforting a friend in need, saying something kind when others were mean, standing up for the unwanted, advocating for those who couldn't find their voice, and being a patient listener to those who desperately needed to be heard. I was giving the homeless money when I didn't have money to give and putting others, often complete strangers, first over my own needs because my heart told me it was the right thing to do. It was having a huge heart for all animals, giving love to them, rescuing and caring for them in times of need . . . A great majority of these things I did not remember I had done because they were mostly things I did when no one was looking. But God was looking . . . God placed in my heart the value of the little things, the loving things we did for each other." Erica McKenzie, RN

What if we focused more on doing the little things in life than worrying about the big things? What if we looked to do simple little kindnesses for friends, family, and complete strangers whenever possible?

We are all one big interconnected body of humanity: Life Reviews demonstrate we are one big interconnected body of humanity and need to value and treat each other accordingly. Just as our fingers don't attack our toes because they look different and have different shapes, functions, and abilities, so too should we not attack or condemn others because they might look different than us or have an uncommon way of contributing to the world. A Life Review humanizes everyone—making it hard to demonize people of different races, nationalities, religions, sexual orientations, and politics. We see ourselves as one greater body of humanity through the Life Review. It helps us realize we are all interconnected and on the same team.

"Interconnectedness exists between all living beings and the Divine Consciousness at all times. We are always connected to everyone else . . . Once you feel this interconnection you cannot help but know compassion for everyone. Compassion leads us to truly care for the wellbeing of any person, regardless of race or background. As compassion grows within so do patience, understanding, and tolerance in every situation we experience . . . I recall my Life Review and seeing those ribbons and slivers of light that connect us to one another, how my actions and life experiences affected others." David Bennett

"Everything that you do to others you will experience yourself from their point of view, there is no you and I, just all is one, but in this lifetime our perception limits it to our experience of this body. We are all 'God' experiencing itself from different points of view." Justin U.

"Ever since I had my NDE, I feel human above all, and I see others the exact same way. I no longer primarily see people as male or female, gay or straight, rich or poor, tall or short, blonde or brown, in work or unemployed, omnivorous or vegetarian, and so on. I am now sharply aware of their human side." Marion Rome

What if we lived our life in a way that didn't rank, judge, or demonize others but honored them as fellow souls and respected them for the path they're on and the unique role and contribution they make to the world? What if we treated everyone as a valuable teammate rather than a stranger, opponent, or enemy?

"We are caught in an inescapable network of mutuality."

Martin Luther King, Jr.

What we do to others, we do to ourselves: We indelibly learn that what we do to others, we actually do to ourselves. We see and feel the full effect of the Golden Rule in our own Life Review. We also feel whatever karma we put out into the world, boomerangs back directly to us. There is no more perfect form of empathy and justice than experiencing ourselves exactly what we did and said to others.

"Every act, every thought, every feeling, every emotion—directed toward another—whether you know the person or not—will later be experienced by you. What you send out, returns . . . What could be a more perfect form of justice than this; everything you do becomes yours. It is not that we are rewarded for our good deeds or punished for our cruel ones; it is simply that we receive back what we have given out, and exactly as we have done it." Dr. Ken Ring

"It is patently obvious to me that when you hurt or deceive someone else or selfishly benefit at the expense of another, you are in reality only damaging yourself. Unfortunately, a great many people only realize this after their death, much to their regret." Malcolm Miller

What if we lived with and acted upon the knowledge that however we treated others we actually treated ourselves?

Fear, pain, and ego cause most hurtful behaviors: By being able to see exactly why people do things and what motivated them, we often see people hurt us because they hurt themselves. Unfortunately as humans, it is often easier to force our pain on others rather than constructively and maturely deal it with ourselves.

"Recognize that when someone has done something hurtful to you, it's usually a sign that they're suffering themselves. If you stay invested in other people's pain, you'll carry it around with you as if it were really yours—when, of course, it isn't. Take the opportunity to transcend the petty, destructive, and unconscious things that we humans can sometimes do, usually in an effort to enhance or 'protect' ourselves, and instead try to see them as opportunities to deal with someone's pain (maybe your own?) with generosity and compassion." Robert Kopecky

"I understood that when I had hurt others, those acts came from my own pain, my own fears, my own ignorance, and my own lack of awareness . . . My NDE enabled me to understand that people hurt others either out of ignorance or because they are in pain." Anita Moorjani

What if we understood that people who hurt us and others act from their own pain, ignorance, frustration, anger, and fears?

We can better empathize with hurt people and forgive them: When we realize people are hurting, we don't need to react to situations and fight fire with fire but can instead respond to situations with calmness, understanding, empathy, and love. We don't have to get caught up in and escalate someone else's drama. If we can empathize with someone's plight and pain, even if they may have hurt us in the process, we find it easier to forgive them. We take things less personally and can rise above the hurtful situation.

"I asked God why there had been so much pain in my life, and where had He been while I was suffering and so afraid? He then told me to hold his hand while he showed me something. I don't know exactly how to describe what happened next. The only way I know how to describe it as follows: Have you ever seen a pond where, as matter decays on the bottom of the pond, and bubbles rise to the surface? Well, as God held my hand I could see great chunks of memories, many of which I had repressed, as they were so painful, come floating up in front of me. I saw myself as a boy, getting physically and emotionally abused by my father. I saw myself in grade school, being mocked and ridiculed by other boys and girls, for I had been a loner and an object of ridicule. I saw myself suffering at the hands of nuns and teachers who only knew how to humiliate and denigrate me. The memories were terrible, and watching them, I felt so much sorrow and compassion for me, as a child. He then told me to look closely, and it was then I could see a light around my body during every one of the events. I could feel God's love for me as a little boy. He told me that He had always been right next to me, and he had never left my side. I was overwhelmed by his love for me at this point, it was completely overwhelming. It was then that everyone who had ever hurt me, (from my

> childhood all the way to some of the personalities in the monastery I was having trouble dealing with), I saw they too had a light around their bodies. I could see that we were all wounded children and the reason we were here was to love and forgive one another and to help one another through this spiritual journey. I could feel the love and compassion that God felt for not only me, but for everyone I had ever encountered. I was filled with compassion and forgiveness for everyone. God then held me tightly to Him, and told me that He would be with me always, and to not lose faith in Him. He told me there was nothing I could do for Him to leave me, and to know that: all was well." John K.

What if we were able to empathize with and forgive the people who hurt us rather than hold grudges and/or seek revenge against them?

THE LIFE REVIEW ENLIGHTENS US ABOUT OURSELVES

Finally, our Life Review provides us with tremendous insights into our own personalities, problems, motivations, fears, life patterns, etc. We see deeply into our hearts, minds, and souls and understand ourselves at a whole new level.

We gain tremendous insights into ourselves: The Life Review provides us with remarkable insight into our own motivations, struggles, fears, yearnings, personalities, etc. We come to see how certain people and events impacted us. We also see patterns that reoccur throughout our life with a whole new understanding.

> "In every scene of my childhood, I could feel my intense desire for approval and love. It appeared from the scenes of my childhood that I was driven by a need to be loved while I explored and discovered the world around me. I would work hard in school to win approval from teachers. Teachers who made me feel loved got everything I had to give in return. Teachers who didn't love me only frustrated me in my need to be perfect for them." Howard Storm

We see we have choices in how to respond to people and situations: The Life Review shows us that we always have choices in how we want to respond to the thousands of people and situations we encounter throughout our lifetime. We can react quickly and callously out of fear, frustration, anger, and selfishness and see how it typically escalates and exacerbates the situation. Or we can consciously and compassionately respond out of love, kindness, and forgiveness and see how it often diffuses the situation and brings about a sense of peace.

"I saw the choices I'd made in my life. Those choices, like the ripples, made little waves in the world around me. They affected other people. They affected my future. And somehow affected my past, too. Good or bad, my choices had an impact. We have the power to change the world immediately around us through the effective use of our own thoughts, words, feelings, and actions. If we choose to use all of these carefully, with love in our hearts and positive intentions, we can have powerfully positive lives. But if we make choices with an uninformed, negative, or malicious state of mind, or negative intent and not aligned with Spirit, our choices can easily hurt or destroy ourselves or others." Nancy Rynes

There are no mistakes, only lessons: One of the biggest enlightenments NDErs gain is that there are no mistakes, only lessons. From Heaven's viewpoint, everything we do on earth is a valuable learning opportunity. By seeing the multitude of effects we create in our Life Review through our seemingly innocuous words and actions, we see, and more importantly, feel exactly how we impact the world. Through this first-hand experience of feeling our own words and actions courtesy of the Life Review, we learn precisely what brings more love and understanding into the world and what doesn't. It is all a valuable learning opportunity.

"I realized that no real mistakes had been made in my life. Each experience was a tool for me to grow by. Every unhappy experience had allowed me to obtain greater understanding about myself, until I learned to avoid those experiences. So the review quickly changed from a negative experience to a very positive one. My perspective of myself was changed, and I saw my sins and shortcomings in a multi-dimensional light. Yes, they were grievous to me and others, but they were tools for me to learn by, to correct my thinking and behavior." Betty Eadie

"There are no mistakes, only lessons. We come here to learn lessons, teach lessons, or both. I was shown that I chose the lessons I wanted to learn before I came here. We will keep repeating the same lesson until we learn it—and sometimes we need to back up, rethink our decisions and then make different choices and then move on. In the midst of my worst 'mistakes' were the best lessons." Mary Beth Willi

"I saw my life. I saw things that I thought were mistakes. But in those loving arms it was flowing: 'There are no mistakes. That's your judgment of it—not Mine. Everything's in perfect order . . .' All that was flowing to me was: 'Look how much we love you. Look how much we honor your choices. Look how much we honor your life.'" Jeff Olsen

Our life matters and makes a difference: The Life Review clearly shows us how much our life matters. It matters in so many ways to all the people we regularly interact with like family and friends. Our thoughts, feelings, and actions create a powerful Ripple Effect on them. Further, as we saw in the Life Review examples, our thoughts, words, and actions can even impact people across space, time, and generations as we either set up people for success or failure.

> "This scene pops up . . . I'm in this grocery store in this little town we used to live in and there's a woman in the checkout lane in front of me and she's 72 cents short. She's rifling through her purse and she's trying to figure out what she's going to put back. And I remember being so moved by that as a single mom—because I've done it. I've been at the grocery store and thought, 'Well, David really likes macaroni and cheese and maybe I'll put the mouthwash back.' You know, you're trying to sort out the things you absolutely have to have. And I'm like, 'Hold on, hold on, I've got it.' I'm fishing through my purse and I hand her the money and she was overwhelmed and embarrassed, she's like, 'Thank you, thank you so much!' And I'm like, 'It's okay, I've been there, it's okay.' And instead of just leaving it like that, God's like, 'Let me show you. I want you to see every Ripple Effect of your kindness.' And so He flashes to this scene and this woman is working in a food pantry. And this other woman comes in and she's this single mom with kids and she doesn't have enough food. And here's this woman that I helped working in this food pantry. And she's like, 'It's okay, it's okay. I'm going to help you. We've got it. We're going to help you. Don't be embarrassed. That's what we're here for.' And I saw this Ripple Effect of this 72 cents. I mean, how does it have that much meaning going forward? It was just incredible! And I had had no idea how much these small kindnesses rippled out. They changed the world in small but meaningful ways." Penny Wittbrodt

> "I learned that everything we do matters. Even the person you smile to on your way to the bakery or work. Even the creatures big and small that you bend over to pet. Nothing goes unnoticed. It all matters. My purpose is to stand up for the meek, to be compassionate, but most of all is to love." Melinda G.

> "The experience has profoundly affected me. I see my current life as something brand new . . . I feel a new and intense gratitude when I wake up each and every morning. Things that used to bother me don't matter. People matter. Life matters. Love matters. Knowing and standing for the truth matters." Yvonne N.

> "Seeing my life left me with the impression that my life mattered." Grace Bulbuka

Enlighten Yourself Summary

Just one of these enlightenments can significantly change our viewpoint on ourselves, life, death, the Afterlife, and God. Imagine what our life would be like if we adopted just a couple of them moving forward.

How much more confident and less scared would we be?

How much more comforted and less worried would we be?

How much more inclusive and less judgmental would we be?

How much more loving and less selfish would we be?

These significant enlightenments from the Life Review motivate and encourage us to change our thinking and behavior. When we see and understand the world, God, Heaven, and death differently, we do life differently.

Our next chapter shows us how NDErs and those who learn about the Life Review operate much differently because of this profound and priceless knowledge. We learn that no matter what the situation, problem, or question, love is always the best answer.

> "I was only 5 years old when I had my NDE but nevertheless had a Life Review. I remember that I was surprised that my short life still had impacted others as much as it had. The overall lesson is as clear to me as if it was yesterday, even if it happened almost 50 years ago. The lesson was to always choose the most loving option in any situation." Lisa Meyler

---

"Let love be the answer to all of life's questions (even the really, really hard ones)."

Cleo Wade, Author of *Heart Talk*

ENLIGHTEN YOURSELF
PRACTICAL REFLECTIONS AND EXERCISES

ENLIGHTEN YOURSELF EXERCISE #1
Exploring Your Views and Paradigms

Through what paradigms and lenses do you view the world?

How do those paradigms either help you or hurt you?

What are your views about life after death and how are they similar or different to what NDErs say?

What are your views about God and how are they similar or different to what NDErs say?

What are your views about our life on Earth and how are they similar or different to what NDErs say?

ENLIGHTEN YOURSELF EXERCISE #2
Transforming Mistakes into Lessons

What are some of the biggest mistakes you've felt you've made in your life?

How can you reframe and transform them from harmful mistakes into valuable life lessons?

ENLIGHTEN YOURSELF EXERCISE #3
Mourning or Celebrating Our Deceased Loved Ones

What have your beliefs and feelings been about the death of a loved one?

Have you worried about them and wondered if they are okay?

How does what NDErs tell us about death and the Afterlife influence your beliefs and feelings?

ENLIGHTEN YOURSELF EXERCISE #4
Embracing Your Enlightenments

Which of the enlightenments do you already believe and why?

Which of the enlightenments are you struggling to believe and why?

How would being open to some of the enlightenments impact your life?

ENLIGHTEN YOURSELF EXERCISE #5
Most Impactful NDEr Quote

Which of the NDEr quotes from this chapter most impacted you and why? When you reflect on the quote in relation to your own life, how does it lead you to think and feel?

Love

6.
EXEMPLIFY LOVE

"The Being of Light presents the dying with a panoramic review of everything they have ever done. That is, they relive every act they have ever done to other people and come away feeling that love is the most important thing in life."

Dr. Raymond Moody, Author of *Life After Life*

Reinee Pasarow's Life Review

"The greatest of all the actions which I reviewed was something that had taken place when I was a teenager. It was something I had forgotten all about; something that I had not given much importance to.

I used to work as a volunteer at a day camp for mentally challenged children. I spent all summer, going eight hours a day, every day to this day camp.

On one very hot day, I had taken a child aside. And this was not a charming or a particularly lovable child. In fact, he could at times be very difficult, obnoxious, and abrasive, and was often rejected by both the children and the counselors in the camp.

I took him aside because I wanted this child to know what it was like to feel loved. He was a child of God, and although my intent was not religiously motivated in any formal way, I just wanted this child to know what it was like to feel loved.

I sat him on a wall, and gave him some punch, sang to him, and rocked him back and forth. He had been very agitated and rather than being rejected again, I simply wanted him to feel loved.

This experience was the greatest of all actions. Re-experiencing this filled with me with unspeakable and incomprehensible joy. It was not an action that anyone had noticed, and it was not an action that I even recalled. It was not an action that I had done with any thought of reward. It was simply an action motivated by love—selfless love—and that was the most meaningful thing I could have ever done."

> *"Do the best you can until you know better. Then, when you know better, do better."*
>
> **Maya Angelou,** Poet

The Life Review Calls and Challenges Us All to Do Better

By making it this far in the book, we can't help but know better. We can't help but know that every one of our thoughts, words, and deeds has an undeniable and indelible impact on others and the world around us—not just in the moment but over time—many times across people, neighborhoods, cities, countries, continents, our planet, and even generations.

We can't help but realize that every second of the day we can choose to have a positive or negative impact on the people, pets, plants, and planet around us. We can't help but know that our life matters. We can't help but know that we are called to share and spread love rather than hate—and we will hold *ourselves* accountable for doing so in our Life Review. And finally, we can't help but know that what we do to others—we ultimately do to ourselves.

Now that we clearly know better after learning about our powerful impact in the Life Review—we are called, encouraged, and ultimately challenged to:

- DO BETTER
- TO LIVE BETTER
- TO LOVE BETTER

Not because we have to or we selfishly don't want to feel the discomfort and pain in our Life Review, but because now that we know better we:

- deeply and sincerely want to do better
- see our interconnections with each other
- want to create a positive Ripple Effect for good in the world
- don't want to be one of those hurt people who hurt people
- want to stop the cycle of violence, abuse, alcoholism, criticism, negativity, and/or judgment in our family

- want to emulate and emanate God's unconditional love for us in the world
- feel good about selflessly serving our fellow travelers on this earthly journey

"I awoke and then received or became conscious of my Life Review . . . The experience changed my entire life and freed me of all guilt and shame and made me DESIRE to do the right thing, not because I was told to but because I understood energetically why and how I participate in everything." Sara A.

"My encounter with the Light radically changed my values, habits, aims, and purposes. In one split second, I was no longer a woman whose life was dominated by a past of fear, guilt, and a belief that God did not love me. I KNEW GOD LOVED ME! Knowledge replaced belief. I was brand new; I felt energized and ready and willing to face a future secure in the knowledge that what I had just experienced was real and truthful . . . I became very loving toward God, self, and others, not in the old way that says if you are nice to me, I'll be nice to you. Instead my actions speak more of unconditional love, the love that says I love you, no strings attached." Nancy Clark

"The love I received from that Living Benevolence was of such a nature, so big, so unspeakable, that it's not even a choice that I make to share my love as much as I can with others in the earthly world." Marion Rome

Up until now, we've all been doing the best we can with the limited awareness and knowledge we had about our impact on others and the world. As amazing spiritual beings effectively disguised as fallible human beings with limited awareness of our powerful spiritual nature, many of us slept-walked and stumbled our way through life with a limiting veil over our eyes and heart not truly knowing or realizing the tremendous impact we have on each other and the world.

"You are not just a drop in the ocean,
you are the mighty ocean in the drop."

Rumi, Sufi Philosopher

Now, through the lessons learned from hundreds of Life Reviews, we know more—WAY MORE!!!

Now we fully understand that we will evaluate our own life and ultimately hold ourselves accountable based on how well we lived fully and fearlessly and loved everyone and ourselves unconditionally.

NDErs come back from Heaven deeply, profoundly, and permanently changed people. Hopefully we are too after learning from their powerful Life Reviews.

> "As you can imagine, an experience like that changes you. I'm not the same person I used to be. I experience much more grace toward others, even in minor situations. When I feel cheated or taken advantage of, when an erratic driver cuts me off in traffic, I am able to feel a gentleness toward the perpetrator that I didn't before. When someone treats me rudely or disrespectfully, I remind myself that the person is, at that moment, the sum total of all his or her burdens and joys, successes, and failures . . . My Life Review had come to a close, but its impact would ripple through my life in countless ways." Dr. Mary Neal

> "I knew I was getting an opportunity to change my life, change my children's lives, change my husband's life, and change the world because of what I had witnessed." Virginia Drake

> "Think of the aftereffects of an NDE like rebooting your computer. Except when you reboot from an NDE, your life is no longer version 2.0. Now it's version 20.0." Debra Diamond

---

"Your time as a caterpillar has expired.
Your wings are ready."

Anonymous

A Powerful Reboot or Reset Button

Experiencing a Life Review, as well as learning about them and applying their wisdom, often becomes a powerful reboot to our personal operating system or spiritual reset button in our life. It resets our heart, mind, soul, priorities, values, personality, relationships, and virtually everything about us. Enlightened by the paradigm-shifting lessons of the Life Review, we see the world, ourselves, others, God, life, and death differently, realize what we do really matters to someone and/or something, make choices with greater awareness, operate at a higher spiritual level, and live more lovingly—and honestly, we should! There should be no going back to the largely fearful, ego-driven, selfish person we may have been before learning about the Life Review and all the enlightenments it engenders.

This critical, substantial, and essential change in perspective can leave us somewhat shell-shocked and overwhelmed at first to realize there's so much more to life, death, and the Afterlife than we realized, had been taught, and/or had previously lived by.

> "I had traveled on the most incredible journey. I crossed over the threshold into the realm of the next life. And, in that time, I once again became reacquainted with profound knowledge gained through an occurrence known as a near-death experience, or an NDE. Once back in the physical world there was an abrupt, inexplicable, and almost frightening change inside of me. My experience seemed to have opened up a completely new dimension within my mind leaving an indelible imprint of a completely different view and interpretation of life. The physical world in which we live and nearly everything in it was oh so different from before the incident. It isn't every day that a person undergoes a single experience that abruptly changes a multitude of things in his or her life. And because of this abrupt change, everything that I had learned to believe in or thought about life in terms of both physical and spiritual dimension had instantly been thrown into disarray." Steve

Having a Life Review or learning about them often leaves us a bit bewildered about where we go from here equipped with this new-found knowledge. But this chapter provides a way forward and pathway with our enhanced perspective. We learn how to act on our new enlightenments, become more of the loving soul we want to be and less of the ego-based, selfish, and stressed out human that came to earth as part of our original factory-setting to see if we could evolve and grow to a higher level of love.

> "The review of my life was essentially an opportunity to learn more about myself. It provided me with a burst of clearer consciousness, leaving me with the definite impression of what I needed to do in the future to grow into a more complete human being. My loving side was there for me to examine, but so was my selfish side." Malcolm Miller

Experiencing or Learning About A Life Review Changes Us

Many NDErs and those who learn about Life Reviews often view and do life differently. Knowing we will feel the emotional, psychological, and in some cases, physical pain we cause others deeply impacts us. The potential for causing others pain powerfully motivates us to live more consciously and act more compassionately because we know the gravity of our words and actions. Conversely, the joy we can help others feel because of a simple kind thing we could do fuels a self-perpetuating cycle of kindness and love.

> "Since my NDE, my values have changed. My beliefs have changed. My personality has changed. What I will tolerate from others has changed. My attitude toward life is different. It took off in a completely different direction. I'm smarter, more adventurous, more open, more forgiving, more aware, more alive . . . I have no fear of death because I know we don't die. I had lived life unconsciously, waiting to be told what to do, what to think, who to be, where to go or not go, what is true and not. But in the light, I saw face to face and my spiritual nature was reawakened. I was no longer afraid, no longer alone, no longer incomplete or unsure of who I really am." Diane Goble

> "Having that experience has changed my life and changed the way that I view life or how I live my life . . . it's how it impacts you so that you live life differently. It changes the way you view life and the way you experience life. It changes the way you interact, or the way you handle your own self. So then your life changes trajectory." Anita Moorjani

> "My experience was the catalyst that transformed me into a completely different person than what I was at the time of my NDE. It was so real that it completely changed my life. I can't live a 'normal' life because I think differently and I am driven to find ways to help people have more peace and contentment in their lives—to have more love in the world." Teri R.

> "I still make mistakes with my words and actions, but when it happens now I give myself a moment to re-center, ask myself what the real issue is under that anger or reaction (always fear of something) and go back to the person to change the experience with honesty even when it is embarrassing to my ego to do so. If I must face those words coming from me impacting another the way they experienced them . . . then I must go back and have that discussion again this time with honesty and love, so that I can forgive myself when I have the review again." Jennifer Tielking

Further, we realize the multiplicative impact of our actions. Not only do we influence a single person, the cascading Ripple Effect of our actions eventually spreads out to dozens of others, all positively or negatively affected because of our single action.

> "I saw that the love we express ripples out, creating an everlasting beauty that is often unbeknownst to us at the time. I saw this happen when I spoke a heartfelt word, thought a truly kind thought or gave undivided attention to someone." David Oakford

The Me Before and the Me After the Life Review

After learning about NDEs, I noticed the knowledge of Life Reviews created a significant change in my thinking and behavior. In many ways, I felt like I had my own low-grade NDE and personal transformation.

> "I had a Life Review; it was the biggest effect of all things toward my personality and life. It just changed me so much . . . Now I have the me before my NDE and the me after." Rich Raymond

> "The Life Review portion of the near-death experience is, I believe, the greatest agent for change." Dannion Brinkley

With my family, I half-jokingly refer to the me before as "Old Jeff" and the me after as "New Jeff". Unfortunately, for the first 42 years of my life, my hard-wired, default-setting of Old Jeff too often drove my human mode of unconsciously reacting to people and situations. I was often impatient, stubborn, selfish, materialistic, elitist, and judgmental. However, New Jeff now tries to speak, think, and act from a Higher Perspective with the lessons from the Life Review on the forefront of his mind as much as possible. Of course, I'm not always successful responding as New Jeff rather than Old Jeff as my family and friends will certainly attest, but I'm doing my best to put myself in other people's shoes and compassionately respond to people and situations from my higher, more enlightened self rather than react solely from my human ego.

Honestly, I am hopeful you too, after reading, reflecting on, and taking this powerful and paradigm-shifting Life Review information into your heart, mind, and soul, will find a similar Old You before learning about *Your Life's Ripple Effect* and a New You after you learned about it. New You will find yourself becoming a much more conscious, considerate, charitable, and compassionate soul who exemplifies love and short-circuits your own ego-based, selfish, unkind, and mean behavior.

> "On the Other Side, you will have the opportunity to become every person you have ever loved or harmed. Knowing that, how will you change the way you treat the people and the animals or even the plants and possessions in your life? All of us need to give some serious consideration to this." Dannion Brinkley

> "After returning to my physical existence, the Life Review haunted me and I wanted to change my way of living to being more understanding, less competitive, and more charitable." David Bennett

The New You After the Life Review

Interestingly, NDEr Dannion Brinkley had multiple NDEs throughout his lifetime from a lightning strike, brain surgery, and heart surgery. Talk about a guy who's had some adversity in his life. The movie *Saved by the Light* chronicles Dannion's first NDE. In his first Life

"Use me, God. Show me how to take who I am, who I want to be, and what I can do, and use it for a purpose greater than myself."

DR. MARTIN LUTHER KING, JR.

Review, he saw how much of a violent jerk he had been to friends and family members. He experienced their physical and emotional pain and vowed to be a better human being. After his first NDE and Life Review, he started a hospice program for veterans called the Twilight Brigade where he and other volunteers comfort dying veterans at their bedside during their final hours. In his subsequent Life Reviews, Dannion experienced all of the peace and comfort he and the Twilight Brigade brought to thousands of struggling veterans during their time of need.

> "When I went through my first panoramic Life Review, I became the people I had hurt physically and emotionally, feeling every nuance of the damage I had caused. However, during my next two reviews, I was able to experience the peace and enormous gratitude of my hospice patients when they took their last breath in my arms . . . The Life Review that came with the second near-death experience was wonderful. Unlike my first, which was filled with mayhem, anger, and even death, this one was a pyrotechnic display of good deeds." Dannion Brinkley

Dannion's story reminds us that we too, no matter what harmful, hurtful, or horrendous words we have said or deeds we have done in the past day, week, month, year, or decade, can choose loving words and actions moving forward today, tomorrow, next week, and so on for the rest of life. Not only will we make the world a better place and evolve as a soul—but we will experience their positive Ripple Effects in our Life Review and counterbalance and possibly neutralize our previous unloving actions. There is no time like the present to be the person we want to be.

"The best time to plant a tree was 20 years ago.
The second-best time is now."

Chinese Proverb

---

10 WAYS THE LIFE REVIEW CHANGES US

Having a Life Review or learning about them changes who we are, how we think, and how we act going forward. Based on what we learn from NDErs, here are the 10 most common ways we can positively change following the knowledge of the Life Review:

1. makes us much more aware of our impact on others

2. short-circuits our unloving thoughts, words, and deeds
3. encourages us to share and spread love
4. compels us to make amends and right wrongs
5. inspires us to live purposely and share our gifts
6. rearranges our priorities and values
7. reveals our interconnection with everyone and everything
8. motivates us to treat everyone and everything with love and respect
9. moves us to be more giving and generous with others
10. encourages us to live a life that is true to ourselves

1. Makes Us Much More Aware of Our Impact on Others

The Life Review awakens, expands, and deepens our understanding of the impact we have on others. Once we realize all the things we do to others will not only be experienced by them but also ourselves, we are a million times more conscious of and careful about the words we use with others and how we treat them. We now more fully comprehend the impact of our thoughts, words, and actions and want to do nothing to upset, harm, or hurt the beautiful and fragile souls around us.

> "My NDE made me understand the true meaning of life and of human relations . . . I am much more aware of the effect of every single one of my words and actions will have on others on a deep soul level, and also because I now know with absolute certainty that ultimately it's me that I am hurting in an unimaginable way from a human perspective." Marion Rome

> "I am more aware of trying to do things that will not do harm. I attempt to have a better understanding of each individual's experience so that I can be more compassionate." Rebecca P.

> "I am currently sixty years of age and numerous times have I reflected on my NDE. This NDE has been the most personally meaningful and significant experience I've ever encountered in all my sixty years . . . I became more sensitive towards people, more loving and understanding. These are all positive changes when it comes to relating to any and all of the world's creatures." Albert S.

> "Be careful what you do in life, because you have to see yourself do it again when you die. The difference is that this time you are on the receiving end." Dannion Brinkley

2. Short-circuits and Reduces Our Unloving Thoughts, Words, and Deeds

After learning about the powerful impact of the Life Review, we too should proceed with much more caution, compassion, sensitivity, understanding, and empathy when we deal with our fellow human beings, animals, and environment. We can start by adopting the doctor's Hippocratic Oath of "first, do no harm."

Rather than reacting with frustration, irritation, resentment, or retribution, we can hopefully catch ourselves and consider the Golden Rule, "How would I want someone to treat me in this situation?" As we now know, we will actually feel ourselves exactly how we treated them. The Life Review teaches us to pause when we are frustrated, reflect on how we would want to feel, and lead with love rather than quickly and callously react with ego, anger, or fear.

> "I became more tolerant of others, less reactive, and had more compassion for my fellow human beings, even those that commit what we consider in our relative world to be unforgivable crimes." Helen S.

3. Encourages Us to Serve and Spread Love

After experiencing or learning about the Life Review, hopefully we all want to create and spread more love around our home, school, church, workplace, community, etc. Seeing the positive and virtually unending Ripple Effect a simple word of encouragement or random act of kindness creates should inspire and motivate us all to generate more of them. When we know how much a simple act of kindness means to people, it is easy to do more of them.

Our family will never forget the kindness and outpouring of support we received when our daughter broke her back from a climbing accident. So many people reached out to her and us during this traumatic time. People showed up at the hospital, brought huge teddy bears, made meals, sent texts and cards, and offered to help in any way they could. We felt their love and concern and it helped us all survive a really tough time. Because we felt how meaningful and helpful it was, we committed to do the same for others when they experienced tough times.

"Love becomes real in this world through our actions,
since God both expresses and experiences life through us."

Rob Gentile, Author of *Quarks of Light*

> "Remember that when you have your Life Review as I did, you will see the times in your life when you had opportunities to express your loving self to others but didn't. This is a very, very painful Life Review process so I urge you to use the opportunities that come your way to lessen this painful review. Remember, we are here to learn how to love unconditionally . . . Your purpose as a human being is to grow in love and to allow the Light of God within you to be expressed through you." Nancy Clark

> "For the first time in my earthly existence, making others feel loved and cared for mattered more to me than anything else. My NDE made me realize how important it is to give love, and to show it whenever possible . . . I now show my love at all times . . . I stopped waiting for special occasions or particular reasons to let those close to me know about my love for them." Marion Rome

Don't wait for special occasions to tell people you love them. Don't wait until the end of the project to thank people for their hard work. Don't wait until someone's funeral to realize how important they were to you. Say it now. Do it now. You'll all be glad you did.

4. Compels Us to Make Amends and Right Our Wrongs

NDEr Nancy Rynes, author of the fabulous book *Awakenings from the Light,* said one of the very first things she wanted to do when she came back to life after her NDE was to make amends with everyone she had hurt, especially her sister. Nancy re-experienced a situation in her Life Review when she was 17 years old where she said something mean and hurtful to her sister—and felt it fully in her Life Review.

> "I examined a point in my life where I said something intentional to spite my sister. It was just one of those spiteful sibling comments that was awful. And she was really hurt by that. In this review, not only could I see it like it was a video, but then I dove into it. I was back in it again. But I wasn't back in it only from my viewpoint, I could experience her viewpoint at the same time. So I was experiencing her hurt and her feelings of the betrayal at the same time that I was spewing this garbage out at her. I could feel like it was me, like I was hit with the stuff I was spewing out. I can feel how horrible she was feeling. She was just devastated by what I said. And to me, it wasn't that bad. But to her, it was. And I had done it intentionally." Nancy Rynes

While still lying in the hospital bed following her accident and before even telling her sister of her remarkable NDE, Nancy felt compelled to apologize to her sister for the incident. Ironically, her sister had forgotten about the incident and didn't remember it until Nancy had mentioned it.

Experiencing all of the hurtful feelings our words and actions have created in others humbles us. Not only that, but it motivates and compels us to apologize to those we hurt and right the wrongs whenever possible. We now realize that something we didn't think was a big deal may have been to someone else. After seeing and feeling the pain others experienced, we desperately want to apologize to them and let them know the actions came from our own fear, pain, ignorance, ego, or spite.

> "After my experience, one of the first actions I did was write down a list of all the people that I could remember having hurt in my life. My negative Life Review had impacted me so strongly that my remorse pushed me to ask forgiveness . . . As I looked up people such as old friends and ex-girlfriends one by one, I realized that it was an expression of love to acknowledge their pain and say I was sorry for causing it." Rene Jorgensen

NDEr Mary Beth Willi strongly encourages us to make amends with people while we are still here on earth whenever possible.

> "We can change our Life Review every single second of every day—it is never too late to make things right. Despite how hard it is here to take responsibility for our actions and make amends it is much harder on us if we wait to do it on the other side." Mary Beth Willi

> "The pain you cause to others comes back to you in proportions beyond description once you die and find yourself in that parallel world where feelings—positive and negative—are heightened. The bigger the pain you cause in the earthly life, the more enhanced it is when you feel in the other—albeit all-forgiving—dimension." Marion Rome

As we reflect on our own life and the people we hurt, who are some people we may want to make amends with? Of course not everyone is going to be ready for our apology or even accept it, but after learning about the Life Review we now feel a strong motivation to right the wrongs we created in the world. Even if the other person is not in a place to grant forgiveness, acknowledging our wrongdoings demonstrates our willingness to own our behavior.

Knowing we will hold ourselves accountable for our unloving behavior, I felt compelled to send a 40-year belated apology note to a grade school classmate I had once bullied and ridiculed. I wrote: "I am sure it is a little strange to get a note from me because we haven't connected since our school days. However, this note and apology is long overdue. Decades overdue unfortunately. So I am hoping the phrase 'better late than never' might apply here. I am deeply and sincerely sorry for the way I treated you back in our grade school days. It was not right and I want you to know I am sorry about it. It is one of the biggest regrets I have as I look back on my life. There was no excuse for it—and despite the decades long delay—I want you to know I am sorry for my hurtful actions and hope you can forgive me for them." I felt badly for how poorly I had treated him but I also felt good to finally take full responsibility for it, own up to it, and apologize to him for it.

> "I have spent the last twenty-two years seeking out those I had wronged or hurt and made every effort to make amends. I have learned to forgive and made great strides in controlling the negative aspects of my personality." Stephen K.

Similarly, we also have to be willing to forgive others when they hurt us, as challenging as this can be at times. Despite the physical, emotional, psychological, and financial ways people may have hurt us through the years, we should remember that "hurt people hurt people" and try to be the more spiritually-evolved person and forgive them. Failing to forgive only weighs us down through life and drains our energy.

> "If possible, I strongly petition you to make amends or settle your differences as best that you can. Whether they lie within you or with another, it would be to an unselfish advantage to do so . . . Forgiveness has such tremendous healing powers and capabilities and, when exercised properly, is in and of itself a truly wonderful experience . . . Forgiving someone else doesn't necessarily mean that they in turn will be willing to forgive you. Ultimately, that is a choice that they and they alone will have to make. You and only you have the power to choose to forgive—no one else can do it for you—and it only works when you choose to use it. And so, by affording yourself this unique—design of the Great Divine favor—it will help alleviate a lot of energy depleting emotional pain, and thus help make your life in the moment more fulfilling." Steve B.

"To forgive is to set a prisoner free only to discover that the prisoner is you."

Lewis Smedes, Christian Author

---

5. Inspires Us to Live Purposely and Share Our Gifts

The Life Review teaches us that our life has a valuable and necessary purpose for the world and for our spiritual growth. It is our sacred responsibility and duty to find and fulfill these purposes during our time on earth. Rather than "wasting" our day on trivial matters, we seek to live a life that matters in accordance with our purpose.

The Life Review shows us how our life impacts so many others in a multitude of ways. Some of the value of our life's purpose we may see in the moment but most of the significant and ongoing impact we aren't even aware of until we see and feel it in our Life Review. Few of us realize the sheer impact we have on so many others, much like we only see the tip of the iceberg but don't realize 90% of it is below the surface. Similarly, most of us don't realize how important we are to our family, friends, co-workers, church, school, community, and the world and substantially discount and deny our impact and life's purpose.

> "As you sow, you shall reap. I found out that there was too little for me to reap. I guess that was why I wanted to go down and finish my earthly life. There was so much that I had to do. I had to improve as a human being. I had to go down to sow in order to reap. I hadn't sowed much until then. I could see that. I was really ashamed of seeing myself. First and foremost, I had to sow love. Today it is the most important commandment to me." Anni S.

> "The angels told me that I still had a purpose to fulfill, many people to influence, that I had someone whom I was supposed to marry and have a meaningful life. They said it would be hard, that there were lots of trials, but that I would get through all of them with success. They said the world needed me right now." Karie N.

Now that we know our life has essential meaning and purpose, we hopefully will live more purposely and intentionally. We now realize there are many lives we still need to positively encourage and impact, be they our own family members, friends, strangers, etc. People are counting on us to play our role and do our part by sharing our gifts and talents with the world. The world needs us right now.

> "I was given the message that it wasn't my time to be there and that I had things I needed to do here on this plane. I was upset by this news because this was the most indescribable, loving, and all-encompassing feeling I'd ever had and didn't want to return. I even remember protesting but being gently told that I had to come back to complete the things I was sent here to do." Demi B.

> "We reviewed my life. Then together we began to look at the things left undone." Rhonda I.

> "One thing I remember is that when I drifted in the light with God there was a point in time that I was begging him to take me with Him; I told Him that I did not want to go back and it was safe with Him. He asked me, 'Are you finished?' I thought about it and realized that I was not finished and if I came home with the Lord I would have unfinished business and my tasks would be incomplete. I was given a choice to stay or go and I chose to come back and finish." Elisa R.

Are you finished? If you are still here on earth, there are still people you need to impact and still things left undone in your life. There are still things you need to finish. It's likely time to do them or at least get started on them. The Universe is calling you.

"When I stand before God at the end of my life, I would hope that I would not have a single bit of talent left, and could say, 'I used everything you gave me.'"

Erma Bombeck, American Humorist

---

6. Rearranges Our Priorities and Values

After having or learning about a Life Review, many people's priorities change. The things they once valued, focused on, and fretted about transform from the superficial things of life to the simple, significant, and sacred things of life.

> "My values and belief system had changed. What used to be important was no longer important. Materialism, success, social status, competitiveness, and achievement didn't matter anymore. The most important focus was to follow through with my three main messages from my experience: 1. To love self and others unconditionally and nonjudgmentally with the love I received on the Other Side, 2. To always seek knowledge, and 3. To live my life's purpose." Laurelynn Martin

Most people become much less materialistic after learning about the Life Review. Rather than trying to keep up with the Joneses and thinking they need the latest and greatest of everything, they take stock of their life and re-evaluate what it really means to be successful. Instead of focusing on getting the material things in life like the big, beautiful house, fancy car, trophy spouse, corner office, etc., they realize true success means living out their life's purpose and giving their gifts to the world.

"I put a lot of emphasis on material things. I was quite wealthy at the time when this happened. I drove a fancy car and lived in a big house. In this Life Review, I realized how irrelevant all these things were. How little value they had. But moments like laughing and playing hide and seek with the children were very important all of a sudden." Anke Everitz

"Within the first week after my NDE, I was cleaning out my house, wanting to get rid of many things, a lot of decor, music CDs that I didn't find in harmony with the vibration I desired, etc . . . I lost my desire to want to shop as much as I had previously." Amy Call

"A purely loving act was the most wonderful thing I could have ever achieved in my life. This was much more meaningful than if I had won the Nobel Prize, or had been the wealthiest person on the planet, or had become the President of the United States." Reinee Pasarow

"Before I had my encounter with the Light, and like most people in Western societies, I always wanted more money, more and more clothes, IT gadgets, dinners in nice restaurants, holidays in faraway places and so on. I was the epitome of materialism . . . Don't get me wrong. I still enjoy owning nice things, but this idea is not central to my existence anymore. Instead, love, kindness, and compassion have become my top priority. As a direct result of my NDE, I am convinced that the more love you give in this life, the more wonderful the Afterlife." Marion Rome

As we examine our own priorities, values, finances, and shopping habits, are there things we really don't need that we buy primarily for appearances or out of habit? What material things can we become addicted to that we really don't need? How might we use these items to try to project an image of success to others or attempt to fill the emptiness in our soul when instead we could fill it by finding and fulfilling our purpose?

"Your religion is where your love is."

Henry David Thoreau, Philosopher

---

7. Reveals Our Interconnection with Everyone and Everything

The Life Review shows how interconnected we all are with everyone and everything. What happens to a fellow soul whether they be in New Orleans, New York, New Delhi, or Neuvo Leon is of our concern. The injustices our black and brown brothers and sisters face are injustices we all must work to solve. The endangered animal species on the verge of extinction should concern us all. The precious rain forests being annihilated around the world impact us all, especially as climate change escalates. We come to see that we are all intricately linked in some way to each other and our planet. It may not be immediately apparent, but what we do and say impacts a wide swath of people and our environment.

> "I've never lost that feeling that we are totally connected like a web or something, as if we're all the same person and what happens to one person in another part of the world affects me." Judith White

> "I came out of it thinking we are all connected on this planet, it doesn't matter our species, color, race or how much money we have . . . I have been a vegetarian for 27 years, I just can't be cruel to something we are so connected to that have the same feelings and emotions we do . . . It definitely changed my whole perspective on life." Karen

> "We are all connected as one spirit. We think that we do not have any responsibility to a stranger because we do not recognize them, but we do. In essence, we are the same as they, intertwined together like a complex wiring system." Casper

---

"First they came for the socialists, and I did not speak out—
because I was not a socialist.
Then they came for the trade unionists, and I did not speak out—
because I was not a trade unionist.
Then they came for the Jews, and I did not speak out—
because I was not a Jew.
Then they came for me—and there was no one left to speak for me."

Martin Niemoller, German Theologian

---

8. Motivates Us to Treat Everyone and Everything Lovingly and Respectfully

Because we know our words and actions matter, hopefully we treat everyone and everything with much more love and respect. We are much more polite, patient, and courteous to friends, family, and even strangers. We respect everyone no matter what their status, spiritual path, politics, or position might be in life.

> "I realized how important people were in life, how important it was to accept them and love them. And I finally understood the old Mohegan Indian

saying I had heard when I was in Girl Scouts, 'Never judge another squaw until you have walked a mile in her moccasins.'" Laurelynn Martin

"One of the benefits and burdens of remembering your death is a feeling of tremendous responsibility to always strive to do the right thing. To treat people with anything less than kindness, fairness, and respect carries a heavy price tag when you are able to remember who you really are. The intensity of emotion while witnessing my life story is one that I will never be able to translate appropriately." Dr. Mary Helen Hensley

We also are much more kind to all living beings including animals, insects, and plants. As an example, before learning about NDEs and the Life Review, Old Jeff killed lots of bugs by stepping on them, swatting them, and mercilessly spraying them with insecticides. Now, even with bees and wasps, which I previously hated, New Jeff respectfully ushers them back outside by trapping them in a clear plastic cup and releasing them back into the wild. I now find it hard to kill most any living being, even the creepy crawly ones. However, mosquitos are still a challenge for me.

"I value all life, even that of insects (I no longer kill flies and spiders, I catch them and release them outside). Because I know that I came to earth for a purpose, I believe that others have too. I have developed more respect and love for people." Chantal L.

"I stopped hunting although I don't condemn it, it's just not for me anymore—I don't even kill bugs. I fish but only catch and release. But I am not a vegetarian." Lee

"I became aware that all life forms are sacred and part of the Divine. From the smallest ant to the tallest tree, I feel so connected to the life-force that flows through everything. Every single life form that inhabits our world is part of the Divine . . . The bond I feel with animals is very, very strong." Nancy Clark

9. Moves Us to be More Giving and Generous with Others

Understanding our interconnection with everyone, the Life Review encourages us to be more giving and generous with our fellow humans, especially those experiencing challenges like poverty and homelessness. We are now much more conscious of people's struggles and willing to help with our time, treasure, and/or talents.

My approach to homeless people has changed completely since learning about Life Reviews. When I travel to a city with a lot of homeless people, I purposely make sure I have several \$5 and \$10 bills in my wallet or will offer to buy them a meal. I willingly give them not only money but my time and full attention. I will ask them their name, where they're from, and how they are doing. In addition to some money, I've also given several hugs. Instead of seeing them as the dregs of society, I look them in the eyes and see the Divine within them and encourage you to do the same. I think, "How would I feel if I were homeless and needed to beg for money to survive?"

> "I do tend to give a little more to charity now. Before, if somebody would pass me on the street and say, 'Hey, do you have a dollar?' I'd say, 'No! Get away from me, man. Go get a job!' I'm not that kind of person anymore. Now I might say, 'Here's $5. Go get yourself something to eat.' I'll do whatever I can do to help. I never used to be a generous person, I never looked to help anybody before. Now if someone needs my help, I'm more than happy to help." Paul Johnson

---

"Every charitable act is a stepping stone toward Heaven."

Henry Ward Beecher, Preacher

---

10. Encourages Us to Live a Life that is True to Ourselves

Finally, the Life Review shows us how important it is to live a life that is true to ourselves. So many of us live our lives worrying about what other people think of us. We think we need to act or live in a certain way for other people to like or accept us. We conform to conventional societal norms and standards of success even though they may not fit with our values or who we really are. We unconsciously follow the herd no matter where it goes. We fear being shunned or ostracized so we go along to get along.

NDErs realize that life is short and nothing to be wasted. They confidently stay true to themselves and follow the calling of their heart. They respect others but don't lose themselves in the process.

> "I suddenly realized that, without my NDE, I would probably have followed social rules to a tee. I would have kept doing a job I didn't like for the sake of money. I would have more than likely married my boyfriend so that I would not be a deviant in my circle of friends . . . I realized that I would have kept defining life success based on anything but the universal and unconditional love that I felt during my NDE and that is now central to my existence." Marion Rome

Exemplify Love Summary

Having or learning about a Life Review can't help but make us more conscious, compassionate, and caring people. We realize the tremendous impact we have on the world and deeply desire for it to be a beneficial one that creates a positive Ripple Effect for as many people as possible. Further, we learn that even our simple and seemingly smallest acts of kindness often make a significant difference to someone or something—and create a long-lasting Ripple Effect. Just as the Life Review changes the life of NDErs for the better, it can also positively change our life too when we act upon the lessons and exemplify love in our thoughts, words, and actions.

"Judge nothing, you will be happy.
Forgive everything, you will be happier.
Love everything, you will be happiest."

Sri Chinmoy, Indian Spiritual Teacher

EXEMPLIFY LOVE
PRACTICAL REFLECTIONS AND EXERCISES

EXEMPLIFY LOVE EXERCISE #1
Curb Your Critic and Bite Your Tongue

The Life Review encourages us to short-circuit and reduce our unloving reactions. Rather than criticizing people this week, commit to curb your inner critic, bite your tongue, and let it go. As radio show host Bernard Melzer once said, "Before you speak, ask yourself if what you are going to say is true, is kind, is necessary, is helpful. If the answer is no, maybe what you are about to say should be left unsaid."

Before speaking with anyone this week, ask yourself:

Is it true?

Is it kind?

Is it necessary?

Is it helpful?

If the answer is no to any one of these questions, it is much likely better left unsaid.

EXEMPLIFY LOVE EXERCISE #2
Share and Spread Love

The Life Review teaches us the simple things in life are often the most valuable and meaningful. What simple kindnesses can you do for a family member, friend, co-worker, neighbor, or complete stranger this week?

EXEMPLIFY LOVE EXERCISE #3
Making Amends and Extending Forgiveness

We all have people we'd like to make amends with, take full responsibility for our harmful words or actions, and ask for their forgiveness. This may be the perfect week to do so.

Who are the people in your life you would like to make amends with and ask for their forgiveness? When and how can you best do this in the next week? You may choose to write a letter, schedule a face to face meeting, make a phone call, or offer a silent prayer of forgiveness; whichever seems the most appropriate for the situation.

Further, who are the people that you may need to forgive in your life? How can you offer your forgiveness?

EXEMPLIFY LOVE EXERCISE #4
Find and Fulfill Your Purpose

The Life Review reminds us that our life has meaning and purpose for ourselves and others. As we examine our life, our purpose is often found at the intersection of our interests, talents, passions, and gifts as well as the needs of our neighborhoods, schools, churches, community, etc. We all are here to help each other and make the world better in some way.

How can you best use your gifts, talents, interests, and passions to positively contribute in some small yet significant way this week?

EXEMPLIFY LOVE EXERCISE #5
Reexamine Your Priorities

Invest the time this week to examine your priorities. Our priorities are often revealed and measured by the amount of time and money we spend/invest in them.

Who are the people you spend the most time with and why?

What are the things you spend the most time doing and why?

What are the things you spend the most time thinking about and why?

What are the things you spend the most money on and why?

How do your answers to these questions compare to the things you believe and say are the most important to you?

As you Evaluate Your Life, what would you like your priorities to be?

How can you better reallocate your time and money to your desired priorities?

EXEMPLIFY LOVE EXERCISE #6
Realize Your Interconnections

The Life Review shows us how our life is intimately interconnected and intertwined with everyone and everything else. We see that we are one big interconnected body of humanity.

How can you be more conscious and considerate of the impact your actions have on the people in your neighborhood?

How can you be more conscious and considerate of the impact your actions have on the people in your community?

How can you be more conscious and considerate of the impact your actions have on the world?

How can you be more conscious and considerate of the impact your actions have on the environment?

What needs, challenges, or crises have you overlooked or ignored because you thought it doesn't affect me or is not my problem? How can you support the people who suffer from these issues?

EXEMPLIFY LOVE EXERCISE #7
Treat Everyone Lovingly and Respectfully

The Life Review teaches us to treat everyone lovingly and respectfully rather than judge, demean, or demonize them. Their skin color, weight, age, sex, might be different than our own but they are so much more than their outer appearance. No matter what their race, culture, nationality, sexual orientation, religion, socio-economic class, politics, education level, etc., everyone is a worthwhile human being and sacred spiritual being and we need to treat them as such.

How can you treat people of a different race more lovingly and respectfully?

How can you treat people of a different religion more lovingly and respectfully?

How can you treat people of a different political party more lovingly and respectfully?

How can you treat people of a different sexual orientation more lovingly and respectfully?

How can you treat people of a different socio-economic class more lovingly and respectfully?

EXEMPLIFY LOVE EXERCISE #8
Most Impactful NDEr Quote

Which of the NDEr quotes from this chapter most impacted you and why? When you reflect on the quote in relation to your own life, how does it lead you to think and feel?

7.

HOW TO DO YOUR OWN LIFE REVIEW

"The two most important days in your life are the day you are born and the day you find out why."

Mark Twain

Nancy Clark's Life Review

"Please be aware that our Life Reviews at the end of our physical deaths reveal every thought, word, and deed that we have experienced during our entire lives. It's a feeling as if we are actually reliving those moments.

We get to feel what it was like for someone we manipulated, bullied, argued with, and so on. Actually feeling what the other person felt like when we were unloving towards them is not pleasant, believe me. On the other hand, it is a wonderful feeling to experience what someone felt like when we offered that person our love, support, and forgiveness!

If I have one message to shout from the rooftops to all who can hear me, I would say, 'Don't wait until you die to have your Life Review. Live your Life Review NOW!'

My Life Review was an outstanding lesson that catapulted my spiritual growth to new heights of consciousness, because I began to understand myself better, and understand my fellow human beings as well. With this understanding comes love, and responsibility, a responsibility to God, self, and others.

Your lifetime mission on earth is to know yourself as thoroughly as you can, and to love yourself and others without qualification. Treasure the knowledge of your Divine Self above all other knowledge. It is your personal truth . . .

Our lives right now are the lessons we are learning. We should make use of every opportunity to advance our soul's journey to the Light, NOW while there is still time . . .

So live your Life Review NOW! Then when you come to the end of your earthly life and return to the Light, your Life Review will be a virtuous one and you will have few regrets."

One of the primary purposes of this book is to encourage us all to do a Life Review now to benefit from it instead of waiting until the end of our human life. By consciously, comprehensively, and compassionately reviewing our life now, we can gain virtually all of the same benefits NDErs received when they did theirs in Heaven—and still have the chance to make the improvements, learn the lessons, do better, have more harmonious relationships, be more of the person we want to be, and live more lovingly during our remaining time on earth. By intentionally reviewing our life now and learning and applying these powerful and profound insights, we can more regularly exemplify love throughout the rest of our life for whatever time we might have left.

> "I wish everyone could have one—it would change the world! Everyone would understand each other, there wouldn't be conflict, and there wouldn't be chaos, and there wouldn't be greed and war . . . The Life Review is the ultimate teaching tool." Neev

In actuality, you've probably already done several partial Life Reviews of certain moments of your life as you contemplated many of the soul-stirring accounts and lessons from NDErs in this book and reflected on what your personal Life Review might be like. These short reflections and mini Life Reviews yield eye-opening and helpful insights and often positively and powerfully alter your attitude and actions going forward.

With these life-changing benefits in mind, you may wish to do a more in-depth and thorough Life Review. Of course it is up to you how intensive and comprehensive you would like be with your review. This final chapter provides you with a practical and proven framework to conduct, experience, and benefit from your own personal Life Review.

Determine If You are Mentally and Emotionally Ready

Ultimately, like it is in Heaven, a Life Review should be a positive and productive learning experience. An effective and balanced Life Review helps us see how we can bring more love into the world and what we can improve to help us minimize our unloving choices.

First, be sure to be proud of your loving choices, words, thoughts, and actions. Too often in reviewing our life we have a tendency to focus on our unloving behavior. However, focus on and give yourself credit for all the loving things you have done throughout your lifetime.

Dredging Up and Defeating Your Inner Demons

Conversely, as imperfect humans who are essentially wired to regularly act from their egos and make many mistakes, an in-depth Life Review will also focus on some unloving actions and dredge up emotional and complicated situations, people, issues, and even some "demons" you may have been avoiding or battling for months, years, or even decades. So many of us carry around excessive guilt over things we have and haven't done during our life. So many of us hold grudges and harbor resentments towards others that we vow we'll take to the grave. So many of us suffer from debilitating shame for things we've said and done. These things weigh on us mentally, physically, and emotionally and often cause depression and disease. Examining them and dealing with them through a Life Review can often help us resolve and release these negative attachments rather than allowing them to continue to haunt and harm us the rest of our life.

No doubt, engaging in a comprehensive and intensive Life Review is grueling and highly personal inner work. Make sure you are in a good spot mentally and emotionally before conducting a Life Review; and have the necessary personal and professional support readily available (your own angelic support team of friends/family/counselors) should you have a hard time processing some of your life's situations, choices, challenges, and relationships.

If you currently feel overwhelmed and stressed out, are in the throes of grief, and/or experiencing major life changes, it is best to wait to do your Life Review until you are in a better spot mentally and emotionally. If you are questioning whether the timing might be right, consult with a therapist or counselor to determine if this is the right time to do a Life Review.

It won't be easy taking a deep dive into who you have been, truthfully and transparently excavating and examining your past behavior, determining and coming to terms with your underlying motives, and revealing the core of who you have been as a human being to this point.

Like in Heaven, the goal is to unconditionally love yourself as you compassionately dredge up, carefully dissect, systematically dismantle, and ultimately defeat your inner demons using the 6 Lessons of the Life Review we detailed in the book.

Conducting your own Life Review while still in the flesh is extremely helpful and valuable soul development work if you want to fully understand how you've been wired as human being, how that wiring drove so much of your egoic and unloving behavior, and how you can effectively re-wire yourself so you can recognize and maximize your spiritual strengths and short-circuit and minimize your human shortcomings. Doing this deep inner work on your shadow side is both challenging and rewarding. The numerous benefits of a Life Review help you exponentially evolve as a soul and become a much more loving person who more regularly responds from a Higher Perspective of consciousness and compassion rather than a Human Perspective.

"If you have to fight a dragon, you should go to its lair before it comes to your village."

Jordan B. Peterson, Author of *12 Rules for Life*

Doing a Life Review Now Neutralizes Your Unloving Acts

Further, shamans believe doing this important spiritual work of an intensive Life Review now while human actually impacts our heavenly Life Review in a positive way by proactively processing and learning from our unloving behaviors. NDErs confirm this as well saying that we can essentially neutralize and make up for our unloving acts by taking full responsibility for them now and learning from them.

> "I understood every reason for everything I did in my life. And I also understood the impact I had on others. A part of me began to anticipate certain events, things in my life I would dread seeing again. But most of them didn't show up, and I understand that I had taken responsibility for these actions and had repented of them. I saw myself repenting of them, sincerely wanting God to remove the weight and guilt of those terrible actions. And He had. I marveled at His sublime love and that my misdeeds could be forgiven and removed so easily." RaNelle Wallace

> "It is important that we take responsibility for our actions and make amends as we go along. As hard as it is to make amends here on Earth, it is much harder to view and feel the hurt we caused others in God's loving

presence when you can no longer do anything about it. What goes around really does come around and we will have to take responsibility for our actions at the end of our lives if we do not take the responsibility and make amends as we go along." Mary Beth Willi

"I was surprised when I realized that wrong deeds for which I felt remorse and repented of were not in my Life Review. Those things were gone! Vividly, however, I realize I could have repented for the wrong deeds I was still seeing, such as seeking revenge, being easily provoked, or doing things that worked against my own life's progression." Dr. Joyce Brown

Conducting a Life Review now rather than waiting until we physically die allows us to experience and take total responsibility for our unloving actions. We see the situations, feel how they impacted others, understand the underlying motives, learn the valuable lessons, and live more lovingly the rest of our days because of them. In essence, by processing our life now, extracting the wisdom, and acting on the lessons, we can defuse and often even erase the necessity of re-experiencing the unpleasantness of it in our Life Review because we accept full responsibility for it, learn from it, forgive ourselves for it, and act on it.

"To know thyself is the beginning of wisdom."

Socrates

---

10 Commitments to Ensure Your Life Review is Positive and Productive

Before you begin your Life Review, promise yourself to abide by these essential guidelines by putting your initials in each of the boxes to signify your full commitment to them. Be sure to refer back to them often, especially when your Life Review gets especially difficult, raw, revealing, and gut-wrenching. If you can't make and keep these promises to yourself, don't do the Life Review!

I promise to:

- ☐ use this Life Review as a positive and productive learning experience for my soul's growth
- ☐ remember God loves me fully and unconditionally—there is absolutely nothing, zip, zilch, nada that could ever change this no matter what choices I've made in my life

- ☐ trust that God and those in Heaven do not judge me in any way—I am the only one who evaluates myself and my life
- ☐ equally examine the loving ("good") things I've said and done as well as the unloving ("bad") things I've said and done
- ☐ balance out remembering and listing the loving and unloving words and actions (don't list more than three unloving things until I balance it with at least one loving thing)
- ☐ be gentle with myself and realize I did the best I could with what I knew, was taught, or believed at the time
- ☐ understand at my core I am a marvelous spiritual being who is having a temporary human experience with built-in challenges and adversities to learn and grow
- ☐ understand as a human being I have been pre-wired with a certain personality that interprets and reacts to the world in an often unconsciously pre-set way—but a Life Review can help me realize and rewire how I consciously choose to interpret and respond to people and challenges in a more loving way (move from Human Perspective to Higher Perspective)
- ☐ focus much more on the positive changes and love I can exemplify going forward from this Life Review than criticize myself and get depressed over the unloving words and actions I many times unwittingly did in the past
- ☐ have a trusted friend and/or professional counselor on standby and speed-dial when I have challenging or traumatic situations/relationships to review and process

Again, be sure to agree to these 10 Commitments before starting your review.

Recommended Time Frame: One to Two Weeks

Give yourself at least a week or two to complete the Life Review process, investing an hour or two each day, as it will take a good amount of time to remember, list, analyze, and grow from your life's multitude of experiences. This is not a process to rush so take your time with it. Unfortunately, the lightning-fast, super-efficient Life Review version we'll experience in Heaven is just not available here on earth so go at your own pace.

6 LESSONS OF THE LIFE REVIEW

You'll find a practical, six-step process mirroring the 6 Lessons of the Life Review we discussed in this book to guide your personal Life Review. Like the review you'll have in Heaven, be unconditionally loving with yourself rather than harsh, critical, and judgmental.

STEP 1: EXAMINE YOUR LIFE

Once you have committed to the essential guidelines and made a solemn and sacred pact with yourself to ensure your Life Review is a positive and productive experience that will be extremely valuable for you throughout the rest of your life, you can begin by examining your life.

Contemplating and Cataloging Your Life

You will likely find it helpful to group your many life experiences by decades to organize your life's events. Use the grid provided to help you catalog your life with the loving and unloving situations you can remember from each decade of your life.

Examine the situations that come to mind for each of the decades of your life.

What situations come to mind when you made loving choices and helped someone or something?

What situations come to mind when you made unloving choices and hurt someone or something?

Depending on the strength of your memory, look to list roughly 6-10 loving choices and 6-10 unloving choices for each of the decades if possible. You will likely start with an initial list of events to examine and more will likely bubble up over time so you can always add them to the list. Don't forget about or discount the little kindnesses you've done. (Remember, God and the angels rejoiced when the young boy simply poured his bucket of water on the parched ground around the tree.)

You may not be able to remember quite as many events, situations, and relationships when you were younger as compared to more recent ones, but do the best you can with what comes to mind.

DECADE	LOVING SITUATIONS
0-10 YEARS	
11-20 YEARS	
21-30 YEARS	
31-40 YEARS	
41-50 YEARS	
51-60 YEARS	
61-70 YEARS	
71-80 YEARS	
81-90 YEARS	
91-100 YEARS	

DECADE	UNLOVING SITUATIONS
0-10 YEARS	
11-20 YEARS	
21-30 YEARS	
31-40 YEARS	
41-50 YEARS	
51-60 YEARS	
61-70 YEARS	
71-80 YEARS	
81-90 YEARS	
91-100 YEARS	

Triggering Memories

While many of your life's most emotional and significant moments will readily come to mind, there will be many events and people you may not remember. You can use the following ideas to help you trigger both loving and unloving memories to reflect on for your Life Review.

Ways to help trigger memories:

- Look at pictures or video of different stages of your life
- If practical, physically visit the areas or your life. Visit your hometown, walk by the schools you attended, drive by the places you lived, park outside of where you once worked. Physically going to the places often triggers memories you may have forgotten. See what memories bubble up and list them
- Listen to music from various eras of your life
- The goal of these various methods is to spark memories of things, events, and people you may have forgotten

STEP 2. EXPERIENCE YOUR LIFE

Once you've created your initial list of loving and unloving events and situations for the various decades of your life, take them one by one and try to re-envision them. Again, if some of these situations are especially difficult or traumatic for you to even think about let alone relive, be sure to consult with a trained professional before reviewing them.

Ideally, you can try to re-experience your situations from four perspectives, as the shamans suggest:

- Perspective #1: see the situation from your own viewpoint
- Perspective #2: try to see the situation from the viewpoint of the others involved
- Perspective #3: observe the situation from an objective observer viewpoint as if you were an invisible drone hovering over the situation
- Perspective #4: finally, view the situation as if God viewed it with unconditional love, infinite wisdom, and full forgiveness

You can use the questions below to consider the various viewpoints.

- What do you think it was like for the other(s) to experience that situation from their point of view?

- How and why did they see things differently than you did?
- How might their perspective be understandable from their point of view?
- How would someone who saw the situation from an outside, third-person perspective view the situation?
- How would the Divine see the situation?

Once you experienced the situation from multiple perspectives, also try to determine the Ripple Effect the situation might have had on yourself and others both near and far over the short and long term.

- What kind of immediate and extended Ripple Effect might the situation have had on others?
- How did this event positively or negatively impact or influence others?

STEP 3. EMPATHIZE WITH OTHERS

As you put yourself in other people's shoes and see situations from their unique perspective, try to feel the emotions they likely felt in the situation. Empathize with them to feel their joy, elation, relief, confidence, pride, and other positive emotions when you made loving choices. Alternately, try to feel their pain, embarrassment, fear, rage, resentment, frustration, and other negative emotions when you made unloving choices. Experience and sit with these emotions in an effort to feel how your words, choices, and actions led others to feel.

If you have a hard time feeling what they likely felt, imagine if someone said or did to you what you said or did to them. How would you feel or react in a similar situation if it happened to you? Considering how you would feel if the situation were reversed can often help you see and feel what they likely felt in the same situation.

- What emotions did they likely feel in that situation and why?
- How did those emotions impact them, you, and the situation?

What is it like to be your own spouse, child, friend?

I found the most powerful and penetrating Life Review questions were contemplating what it was like to be my own spouse, child, parent, sibling, friend, neighbor, and co-worker. These questions, when explored humbly and answered honestly, revealed the most difficult yet valuable information on how I made others feel during my lifetime to this point.

- How would I feel if I was married to me?
- How would I feel if I was parented by me?
- How would I feel if I was my own mom/dad?
- How would I feel if I was my own sister/brother?
- How would I feel if I was my own friend?
- How would I feel if I was my own neighbor?
- How would I feel if I was supervised by or worked with me?

Empathize with these people in regard to how you have related to them to this point.

Do they feel like you unconditionally love them and bring out the best in them—or something else?

Depending on your relationship with them, their willingness to be honest with you, and your own courage and comfort level to potentially hear some challenging but helpful feedback, you may want to at some point ask them point blank: "How do you feel when you're with me?"

If this question scares or disheartens you, you probably already know the answer about how you make them feel. Explore your fear or sadness to ask this question and what you can learn from it—and how it might inform and motivate you to be more loving, accepting, and positive towards them.

Don't ask them the question (How do you feel when you're with me?) if you aren't willing to openly listen to and fully accept their answer without judgment or argument. Even more importantly, don't try to discount, downplay, or deny their real feelings. Hear them out, paraphrase their answer to ensure you understand it, let it marinate in your heart, mind, and soul, and ultimately let it motivate you to be more unconditionally loving moving forward.

STEP 4. EVALUATE YOUR LIFE

After feeling how others felt, objectively evaluate how well you responded to the various people and situations of your precious life to this point. Remember, hindsight is always 20/20. Determine if you reacted to the situations you listed from your Human Perspective (ego) or responded to the situation from your Higher Perspective (Essence). Did you callously react out of fear or compassionately respond out of love?

- How would you evaluate your choices and behavior in each situation?
- What different choice could you have made and what impact might it have had?
- What recurring themes and patterns do you see in your choices, relationships, and situations that seem to happen over and over again until you learn the lesson?

3 Primary Ways to Evaluate Your Life Thus Far

1. How well have I loved others and myself unconditionally?
2. How well have I lived my life fully and fearlessly?
3. How well have I fulfilled my life's purpose(s)?

How well did I love others and myself unconditionally?
Be sure to consider how well you loved others and yourself unconditionally. Many people struggle to share unconditional love with people they dislike or see as different than themselves. A significant number of people find loving themselves as their biggest challenge. They are super hard on themselves and don't allow for the natural and normal mistakes, problems, and imperfections we have as humans. They constantly compare themselves to other people who they feel are better than them, smarter than them, prettier than them, in better shape than them, richer than them, have more friends than them, are a better parent than them, etc. They critically evaluate everything they do and say with perfection as the standard.

- What would the most loving choice have been in the situation?
- How would you have responded if you came from unconditional love?

As I reflected on my Life Review, I definitely saw how I could have done much better in numerous situations with multiple people. I learned how my pre-set personality motivated many of my actions. While these actions felt comfortable for me based on my personality, I realized they weren't for others. There were also times when I withheld love because I thought it might not be appropriate for a male to be unconditionally loving and express it openly.

I learned that most of my unloving moments resulted from my own fears, frustrations, and pains. It wasn't the situations, people, or relationships themselves which caused my reactions to them, but how I viewed and interpreted them. I realized I often fearfully reacted from my Human Perspective rather than lovingly responded from my Higher Perspective. At the core of my unloving behavior I discovered I was often hurt, scared, and/or uncomfortable and took those negative feelings out on others instead of patiently and productively processing them myself.

My unloving thoughts, words, and actions came from:

- my fears
- my insecurities
- my pain
- my embarrassment
- my doubts
- my selfishness
- my ignorance
- my frustration
- my discomfort and awkwardness
- my impatience
- my need to look competent or perfect
- my need to bolster myself and feel superior to others
- my fear of looking stupid or inadequate
- my desire to have things a certain way

As you do your own Life Review, my guess is you too will discover that many of your unloving actions also originated from your fears, insecurities, frustrations, etc. Our forceful yet fragile ego is a normal and natural part of being human but most often is the root cause of our unloving behavior. Doing this hard personal and spiritual work reveals how often we act from our Human Perspective, both consciously and unconsciously. However, spiritual growth and development also shows we can strive to override and overcome our human ego with the enlightening knowledge and consistent application of the wisdom of the Life Review, as we are doing with this intensive exercise.

How well did I live my life fully and fearlessly?

Invest the time to evaluate how well you lived your life fully and fearlessly.

- Did you live a life being true to yourself or did you let your fears hold you back?
- Did you worry too much about what others thought of you or were you comfortable being yourself even though it may have gone against the grain and subjected you to the negative judgments of others?

I realized many times I worried about and feared what others would think of me and this concern limited my behavior. I also discovered that I was afraid to share my purpose with the world and my fears held me hostage for a few years before I finally broke through them.

How well did I fulfill my life's purposes?

Finally, consider how well you found and fulfilled your life's purposes. Each of us typically has a few significant purposes during different phases of our life. Part of our purpose may be linked to our career, another part to our hobbies, and often our purpose is found in our relationships with family members and friends. For many, a big part of our purpose is to parent our kids and/or help a friend through some adversity like a difficult divorce, the loss of a child, or cancer diagnosis. These purposes tap into our gifts, talents, and interests and serve others and the world in a valuable and necessary way.

As I reviewed my life, professionally I felt like I served a valuable purpose for the first 30 years of my career. However, it took me a while to understand and accept my evolving calling and purpose in sharing this book and the *10 Life-Changing Lessons from Heaven* with the world. My fears kept me from embracing the change. For many years I felt like I was trying to drive with the emergency brake on.

Personally, I have the sacred privilege of being a husband and dad to a beautiful family. Overall, I feel like I have done a decent job with this purpose but there were numerous times when I could have been better and done better. Moving forward, I am making an effort to be better in these essential areas.

Move Forward Instead of Trying to Change the Past

As you Evaluate Your Life, no matter what hurtful words you said and/or harmful actions you demonstrated in the past, don't look back and beat yourself up for what you have or haven't done. Realize and accept the fact that you did the best you could with what you knew at the time. We all have thousands of words we wish we could take back and hundreds of actions we deeply regret. It's a natural and normal part of being "perfectly imperfect" as humans and happens to everyone. God intentionally built our mistakes into the process for us to learn and grow.

Realize the bell has been rung—don't waste precious time trying to unwring it. The toothpaste has been squeezed out of the tube—don't expend valuable energy trying to put it back in. Those words and actions are in the past. Learn from them—exactly as the Life Review encourages us to do. Make amends. Ask for forgiveness. Forgive yourself and others and move on. Let it go.

Put your full focus and valuable energy on the positive Ripple Effect you can create right this moment, the rest of today, tomorrow, next week, next month, next year, and for the rest of your life. You have so much good you can do right in front of you; in your own home, at your workplace, in your school, in your community, etc., as we will focus on with the Exemplify Love step. Focus your mind on those things and commit to creating a positive Ripple Effect moving forward with your life. That's specifically what God and Heaven want you to do: move forward with love in your heart. They aren't holding your "mistakes" against you and neither should you.

> "You're going to be asked when the time comes, 'How much did you love?' What matters is how much did you love when you were here. You get opportunities every day. If you screw up one day, that's okay because tomorrow is going to be another day, and you're going to have opportunities again." Sharon Milliman

> "In our essence, we are powerful and loving beings, and we are given countless opportunities to act from that love, endless chances to learn and grow by offering and receiving love. It felt as if we are living inside a grand game, which is perfectly designed to always give us another opportunity to get it right this time." Debra Kaiser

STEP 5: ENLIGHTEN YOURSELF

An effective Life Review enlightens you about what works and what could work better. By seeing situations and relationships from multiple perspectives and deeply feeling the emotions involved, you learn so much more about yourself, others, and the value of love.

As you look at your life, what are the major lessons you have learned:

- What did you learn about yourself in that situation?
- What did you learn about others in that situation?
- What did you learn about the importance of love in that situation?

These valuable lessons form the foundation of the more spiritually evolved person you want to be moving forward. They will also provide you with the motivation to act and speak differently.

Familiarize Yourself with the Enneagram

As you review and evaluate your life, you will likely find similar patterns of thoughts and behavior underlying your decisions and responses. I found the Enneagram, a well-established and researched personality profile which reveals powerful and accurate psychological and spiritual insights, extremely helpful as a framework to help me recognize and explain the typical thoughts that drove my choices, words, and actions. If you are not already familiar with the Enneagram, which details nine personality types, I encourage you to learn more about it online and through various books like *The Road Back to You* as a primer or *The Complete Enneagram* and *The Spiritual Dimension of the Enneagram* if you are already familiar with it. I found the Enneagram tremendously enlightening and amazingly on point in helping me recognize the common motivations behind my behavior. I think you will find it super helpful and enlightening in processing your Life Review and evaluating your life in regard to your particular personality.

Seeing Your Parents as People with Unique Personalities

The Life Review enlightened me about the pivotal role my parents played in my life as they shaped my motivations, fears, values, etc. I saw how much I wanted to please them and thought I had to be successful to earn their love. The review helped me see them as human beings with their own unique personalities, challenges, strengths, and weaknesses and the effect those things had on me. It helped me appreciate everything they brought to my life as well as understand and forgive them for the ways they may have made my life more challenging, likely without even realizing it until having their own Life Reviews.

- What influence and impact did your parents or primary care givers have on your life?
- How did they shape your motivations, fears, and values?
- What strengths and challenges did they have as human beings and how did they impact you?
- How can you appreciate them for what they brought to your life?
- How can you forgive them for the challenges they may have brought to your life?

Patterns with Challenging People

Further, a thorough Life Review virtually brings you face to face with the people you've found challenging in life be they a former roommate, ex-lover, nosy neighbor, difficult co-worker, or archrival. Whether they realize it or not, they played the starring role of villain, nemesis, or antagonist in the movie of your life, and provided you with a significant amount of drama and turmoil to learn from and overcome.

As I looked at the challenging people I experienced conflict with or struggled to be around during my lifetime, I found many of them had similar styles and personalities. These insights combined with enlightenments about my own personality helped me see why we disagreed on issues and how we may have been better able to resolve them without the tense moments, heated arguments, and/or ongoing resentment.

- Who are the most challenging people you have dealt with in your life and why?
- Are there any consistent patterns to the people and personalities that have been hard for you to deal with?
- What can you learn from them and about yourself?
- How can you better deal with these kinds of people moving forward?

STEP 6: EXEMPLIFY LOVE

The ultimate step in the Life Review process is to live more lovingly based on the insights and enlightenments we gain from our review. We leave the bliss and beauty of Heaven and put ourselves through the emotional wringer and gauntlet of life and the Life Review so we can grow as a soul and become more loving people. Witnessing and processing our Life Review consciously compels us to love more, live more, give more, and forgive more. We aspire and commit to live much more from a Higher Perspective than from a Human Perspective.

- How will what you learned from each life situation positively impact your thoughts, words, and actions moving forward?
- Who would you like to thank for the positive impact they made on your life and how will you best express your gratitude?
- Who would you like to make amends with for how you may have harmed them and how and when will you best express your remorse?
- Who are you consciously going to be nicer to (or at least tolerant of) that you may not have been in the past and why?
- Who are you going to share your forgiveness with who may have hurt you?
- How are you going to consciously share and spread more love with yourself and others?
- How are you going to find and fulfill your purpose?

As you complete your intensive and comprehensive Life Review, summarize the main loving actions you commit to doing moving forward. It can be as simple as:

My loving strategies moving forward:

- ♥ Focus more on collaborating with people and not making everything into a competition
- ♥ Value relationships with people more than results
- ♥ Be more authentic, real, honest, and vulnerable with people
- ♥ Share my fears, frustrations, failures, and fallibilities

"I shall tell you a great secret, my friend.
Do not wait for the last judgment,
it takes place every day."

ALBERT CAMUS

- See everyone as equal, worthwhile, and valuable—as amazing spiritual beings disguised as imperfect human beings
- Actively support and advocate for the marginalized and downtrodden of the world
- Be more patient with others—efficiency may be my preference but it isn't for others
- Ask for forgiveness from the people I have hurt in some way
- Even though I love my way, others don't, remember there is not only one right way

Invest the time to summarize your main takeaways and action items from your Life Review. This summary provides you with a succinct way to capture the attitudes and actions you want to Exemplify Love with moving forward. Post them somewhere you will see them often to keep them on the top of your mind and grade yourself regularly to monitor your progress.

Incorporate A Daily or Weekly Life Review

Once you have listed, posted, and committed to your loving strategies, you can continually evaluate and enlighten yourself on a weekly and even daily basis. NDEr Dannion Brinkley recommends doing a Daily Life Review.

> "On an almost daily basis I consciously have a Life Review. This doesn't mean that the Life Review I have is the intense variety I had during my near-death experiences. What I do to have a Life Review is reflect on my daily actions. By having this sort of pre-death Life Review, I am able to strip away the ego, through which so many of us filter our actions, and look honestly at who I am. I often joke that we are having a near-death experience right now because we are living our Life Review right now. That makes the Life Review the most obvious aspect of the near-death experience to use in building your empathy, sensitivity, and direction on a daily basis. It also means that we don't have to wait until we die to receive the benefits of a Life Review." Dannion Brinkley

At the end of each day as you prepare for bed, you can do a mini-Life Review of your day. Examine your words and actions throughout the day to see where you may have acted with love and where you didn't. Put yourself in the other people's shoes and attempt to feel their emotions as they interacted with you. Evaluate how well you lived with unconditional love. Learn lessons from your interactions and vow to apply them the next day when you awake.

If a Daily Life Review is too much for you, you can do a Weekly Life Review. At the end of each week, perhaps sometime on a Sunday, you can reflect on your previous week and do a Weekly Life Review using the same six lessons.

1. Examine your thoughts, words, and actions over the past week.
2. Experience your week from other peoples' perspectives.
3. Empathize with those you interacted with during the week to experience their feelings.
4. Evaluate how well you loved others and yourself, lived fearlessly, and served your purpose.
5. Enlighten yourself about what you learned about love and living life fully and fearlessly.
6. Exemplify love in your thoughts, words, and actions this week based on what you learned.

How to Do Your Own Life Review Summary

Our final chapter provided you with a practical and proven framework to conduct your own comprehensive, intensive, and instructive Life Review. While likely mentally grueling and emotionally gut-wrenching, hopefully the experience was also tremendously spiritually enlightening and practically helpful. Hopefully the lessons you learned on how you lived your life thus far both informed and motivated you to live more lovingly and fearlessly for whatever time you have left on this earth. Apply the lessons to your life and not only will you become more of the person you aspire to be, you will also create a positive Ripple Effect that you will be proud of when you have your Life Review in Heaven with God and your guides by your side.

REALIZE YOUR RIPPLE EFFECT AND EXEMPLIFY LOVE

As we come to the end of this book, we all now fully realize our life does way more than just "flash" before our eyes when we physically die and transition to Heaven. Our comprehensive Life Review provides us with the marvelous and miraculous opportunity to examine all of our life's choices, see how they impacted others, feel the emotions they felt, evaluate how much love our actions brought to the situation, learn what a loving choice would be, and live life with much more love, compassion, kindness, and forgiveness.

Knowing that we'll ultimately hold ourselves accountable for our Life Review motivates us to make our life matter—for ourselves, our family, our friends, our community, and the world.

Thank you for going on this sacred journey. I hope it was beneficial for you and all you will impact with your precious life.

If you would like to share any feedback or suggestions on how to improve this book or how it has impacted you, please email me at jeff@LifeLessonsFromHeaven.com to share your experience and stories.

Realize Your Ripple Effect and Exemplify Love!

With unconditional love and immense gratitude,

Jeff Janssen

"Enough words have been exchanged;
Now at last let me see some deeds!
Something useful should transpire . . .
So get on with it!"

Johann Wolfgang von Goethe

ABOUT THE AUTHOR

After almost suffering a widowmaker heart attack at the relatively young age of 42, author Jeff Janssen sought answers to Life's Biggest Questions like: who am I, why are we here, and what happens to us when we die? His way too close brush with death put him on a serious quest to discover solid and soul-satisfying answers. Jeff's research led him to the stories of Near-Death Experiences (NDEs). After studying over 3,500 NDE accounts, Jeff synthesized their findings into the *10 Life-Changing Lessons from Heaven* so that he and others could benefit from their profound wisdom. Because learning about the Life Review had such a profound impact on his life, he then wrote *Your Life's Ripple Effect*. Jeff also has written a book for kids who have lost a loved one called *What You'll Learn in Heaven*.

Jeff has shared these life-changing lessons with numerous groups including parents who have had children pass away as part of Helping Parents Heal, formerly incarcerated women as part of A New Way of Life, members of the International Association of Near-Death Studies (IANDS), and people from all religious backgrounds and faiths through his Soul Peeps Discussion Groups.

Jeff worked over 30 years in the sports world as a highly respected leadership and championship culture coach helping professional, college, and high school teams from all sports. He has consulted with Olympic gold medal winning athletes and helped over 30 teams win NCAA National Championships at colleges such as Arizona, Arkansas, Colorado, Illinois, Michigan, North Carolina, Notre Dame, South Carolina, and Stanford. A popular speaker and prolific writer, Jeff has spoken to and inspired tens of thousands of people across the world and written 20 books including *The Team Captain's Leadership Manual*, *How to Build and Sustain a Championship Culture*, and *What It Takes to Win Championships*.

Jeff lives in the Raleigh/Durham NC area with his lovely wife Kristi and their children Ryan and Jillian and dog Trey. They enjoy reading, traveling, nature walks, eating at great restaurants, and watching sports.

For additional info on Jeff and his programs and resources, visit LifeLessonsFromHeaven.com.

APPRECIATIONS

This book is the result of the Ripple Effect of many. I am honored and humbled to thank the many people who contributed.

Thank you to all the NDErs who share their sacred Life Reviews. Each of your life-changing experiences is an essential piece of the puzzle for understanding what comes next in Heaven and how best to live and love on earth now. Thanks especially to Nancy Rynes and Jeff Olsen for your guidance and your valued friendship.

Thank you to Dr. Ken Ring for adding his wealth of wisdom to make this book better. Ken's book *Lessons from the Light* was the first to delve deeply into the Life Review and is the gold standard of NDE books. I appreciate his help and friendship and am honored to stand on his shoulders.

Thank you to Jeff and Jody Long from the Near-Death Experience Research Foundation for compiling and sharing all the NDEs on NDERF.com. Thanks to Kevin Williams, David Sunfellow, and IANDS for your committed study of NDEs.

Thank you to Tammy Shain and Cathy Shaw who supported this purpose from the beginning. Thank you to all of the Soul Peeps who provided their valuable insights: Melissa Herrin, Emily Graham, Roseanne Chee, Brenda Horn, Carrie Brody, Catherine Hubbard, Marie Garcia, Bobbie Christiansen, Barb and Wayne Morrison, Cindy Dalgleish, Kim Mancuso, Amy Popp, Jenny Dalton-Hill, Beth Matkom, Steph Conard, and Julie Domina. Thank you to Sherry Roberts and Melody Christian for your graphic design talents to make this book come alive.

Thank you to my wonderful family for your love and support. I wish I knew much earlier what I know now from the Life Review as a husband and father but I am doing my best to apply it. Ryan and Jill, I love you both unconditionally and am privileged and proud to be your dad. Kristi, thanks for your unconditional love, friendship, and support through the decades. I am a very fortunate soul.

Finally, thank you dear reader for investing your precious time to read this book. I hope it encourages you to act upon your powerful Ripple Effect. If you are so moved, I encourage you to write a review of it so others can learn about their Ripple Effect too. THANK YOU!

NOTES

For a list of Recommended Readings on NDEs visit lifelessonsfromheaven.com/recommended-readings-on-near-death-experiences/

Introduction

Deroan. *Deroan fde*. NDERF.org. http://www.nderf.org/Experiences/1deroan_fde.html

Fenimore, A. (1995). *Beyond the darkness*. New York, NY: Bantam.

RaNelle Wallace quoted in Williams, K. (2016). *RaNelle Wallace's near-death experience*. http://www.near-death.com/experiences/notable/ranelle-wallace.html

Miguel A. *Miguel A. nde*. NDERF.org https://www.nderf.org/Experiences/1_miguel_a_nde.html

Gallup, G., & Proctor, W. (1982) *Adventures in immortality: a look beyond the threshold of death*. New York, NY: McGraw Hill.

Brinkley, D., & Brinkley, K. (2008). *Secrets of the light: lessons from heaven*. San Francisco: HarperOne. p. 118-119 and x.

Dr. Diane Morrissey quoted in Williams, K. (2016). *Dr. Diane Morrissey's near-death experience*. https://www.near-death.com/experiences/notable/dianne-morrissey.html

Rome, Marion (2014). *Beyond sight: the true story of a near-death experience*. Scotts Valley, CA: CreateSpace.

Ring, K. (2006). *Lessons from the light: what we can learn from the near-death experience*. Needham, MA: Moment Point Press.

Neal, M. (2012). *To heaven and back: a doctor's extraordinary account of her death, heaven, angels, and life again: a true story*. NewYork, NY: WaterBrook. p. 57.

Ring, K. (2006). *Lessons from the light: what we can learn from the near-death experience*. Needham, MA: Moment Point Press. p. 147.

Casper. *Casper nde*. NDERF.org https://www.nderf.org/Experiences/1casper_nde.html

Call, A. Amy Call nde. NDERF.org http://www.nderf.org/Experiences/1amy_c_nde_4720.html

What is Heaven Like?

Steve B. Steve B nde. NDERF.org https://www.nderf.org/Experiences/1steve_b_nde.html

Julio M. Julio M nde. NDERF.org https://www.nderf.org/Experiences/1julio_m_nde.html

Lupo, L. (2018). *Remember, every breath is precious: how dying taught me how to live*. Surrey, U.K. White Crow Books. p. 5-6.

Jorgenson, R. (2007). *Awakening after life: a first hand guide through death into the purpose of life*. Charleston, SC: Booksurge Publishing. p. 25.

Clark, N. (2012). *Hear his voice*. Fairfield, IA: 1st World Publishing. p. 163-164.

Juana DB. Juana DB nde. NDERF.org https://www.nderf.org/Experiences/1juana_db_nde.html

Moorjani, A. (2016). What if heaven is here and now? https://www.healyourlife.com/what-if-heaven-is-here-and-now

Panagore, P. (2015). *Heaven is beautiful: how dying taught me that death is just the beginning*. Newburyport, MA: Hampton Roads Publishing. p. 86.

Pasarow, R. (2018). *Answers from heaven: the near-death experience of Reinee Pasarow*. CreateSpace Independent Publishing. p. 17.

Craig, H. Grief 2 growth [Audio podcast episode 32]. https://www.grief2growth.com/grief-2-growth-podcast-episode-31-heidi-craig-her-nde-and-3-life-lessons-from-it/

Rose, D. IANDS NDE Radio with Lee Witting. https://www.youtube.com/watch?v=vHklG2DgREs

Loran, G. Loran G nde. NDERF.org https://www.nderf.org/Experiences/1loran_g_nde.html

Nichole BD. Nichole BD nde. NDERF.org https://www.nderf.org/Experiences/1nichole_bd_nde.html

Barbara S. Barbara S. nde. NDERF.org. https://www.nderf.org/Experiences/1barbara_s_nde.html

Katherine I. Katherine I. nde. NDERF.org. https://www.nderf.org/Experiences/1katherine_l_nde.html

Mary Lu R. Mary Lu R. nde. NDERF.org. https://www.nderf.org/Experiences/1mary_lu_r_nde.html

Yazmine S. Yazmine S. nde. NDERF.org. https://www.nderf.org/Experiences/1yazmine_s_nde.html

Alexander, E. (2014). *Map of heaven: how science, religion, and ordinary people are proving the afterlife.* New York, NY: Simon & Schuster.

Clark, N. (2012). *Divine moments: ordinary people having spiritually transformative experiences.* Fairfield, IA: 1st World Publishing. p. 102.

Giroux, D. (2021). *Why heaven was so shocking.* [Video] YouTube. www.youtube.com/watch?v=NBS55IZcrxo

Carl D. Carl D. nde. NDERF.org. https://www.nderf.org/Experiences/1carl_d_nde.html

John S. John S. nde. NDERF.org https://www.nderf.org/Experiences/1john_s_nde_3876.html

Hausheer, J. (2021) *Three physicians' near-death experiences.* IANDS Conference.

Katherine I. Katherine I. nde. NDERF.org. https://www.nderf.org/Experiences/1katherine_l_nde.html

Diane C. Diane C. nde. NDERF.org https://www.nderf.org/Experiences/1diane_c_nde.html

Gentile, R. (2021). *Quarks of light: a near-death experience.* Fresno, CA: Ignite Press. p. 106.

Heather V. Heather V nde. NDERF.org http://www.nderf.org/Experiences/1heather_v_nde.html

Miller, M. (2021). The impossible dream. https://iands.org/research/nde-research/nde-archives31/newest-accounts/1579-australian-man-is-taken-on-guided-journey-of-the-universe.html

Rodonaia, G. NDERF.org https://www.nderf.org/Experiences/1george_rodonaia_nde.html

Daniel A. Daniel A nde. NDERF.org https://www.nderf.org/Experiences/1daniel_a_nde.html

Brandy M. Brandy M. nde. NDERF.org https://www.nderf.org/Experiences/1brandy_m_probable_fde.html

Mohammed Z. Mohammed Z. nde. NDERF.org https://www.nderf.org/Experiences/1mohammad_z_nde.html

Moorjani, A. https://www.afterlifetv.com/2015/05/26/anita-moorjanis-extraordinary-near-death-experience-2/

Mohammed Z. Mohammed Z. nde. NDERF.org https://www.nderf.org/Experiences/1mohammad_z_nde.html

Kason, Y. (2021) Let's talk near death—pt 1: the near death experiences & spiritual experiences of Dr. Yvonne Kason. [Video]. Youtube. www.youtube.com/watch?v=KcUP41XeUoI

Olsen, J. (2012). *I knew their hearts: the amazing true story of a journey beyond the veil to learn the silent language of the heart.* Plain Sight Publications. p. 35-37.

Moorjani, A. https://www.afterlifetv.com/2015/05/26/anita-moorjanis-extraordinary-near-death-experience-2/

Gentile, R. (2021). *Quarks of light: a near-death experience.* Fresno, CA: Ignite Press. p. 108.

John S. John S. nde. NDERF.org. https://www.nderf.org/Experiences/1john_s_nde_3876.html

Leonard. Leonard nde. NDERF.org. https://www.nderf.org/Experiences/1leonard_nde.html

Nightingale, J. Juliet N. nde. NDERF.org. https://www.nderf.org/Experiences/1juliet_n_nde.html

Tom Sawyer quoted in Ring, K. (1985). *Heading toward omega: in search of the meaning of the near-death experience.* New York, NY: Harper Perennial. p. 58-59.

Wallace, R. (1994). *The burning within.* Warren, MI: Gold Leaf Press. p. 105-106.

Mehne, S. (2021). *I was welcomed by the light | Sabine Mehne's near death experience.*
[Video]. Youtube. www.youtube.com/watch?v=E-IBPltVcL0

Gentile, R. (2021). *Quarks of light: a near-death experience.* Fresno, CA: Ignite Press. p. 106.

Bethards, B. quoted in Williams, K. (2016). Homecoming and the near-death experience. https://near-death.com/homecoming/

Thomas, K. (2017, September 9). We don't die radio show [Audio podcast episode 32]. https://www.youtube.com/watch?v=QWgw1xAEolY

Milliman, S. Sharon M. nde. NDERF.org. https://www.nderf.org/Experiences/1sharon_m_nde_7925.html

Alma. (August 2020). The Bark.com. Near-death experiences: will our dogs be waiting for us? by Scott Janssen https://thebark.com/content/near-death-experiences-will-our-dogs-be-waiting-us

Examine Your Life—Chapter 1

Bennett, D. (2020) David Bennett NDE. https://ndestories.org/david-bennett/

Bennett, D. (2011). *Voyage of purpose: spiritual wisdom from near death back to life*. Rochester, VT: Findhorn Press.

Grace Bulbulka quoted in Williams, K. (2016). *Grace Bulbulka's near death experience*. http://www.near-death.com/experiences/notable/grace-bubulka.html

Larry. Larry's NDE. NDERF.org. https://www.nderf.org/Experiences/1larry_nde.html

John F. John F. nde. NDERF.org https://www.nderf.org/Experiences/1john_f_nde.html

Brian T. *Brian T. nde*. NDERF.org Retrived from https://www.nderf.org/Experiences/1brian_t_probable_nde.html

Miller, M. (2021). The impossible dream. https://iands.org/research/nde-research/nde-archives31/newest-accounts/1579-australian-man-is-taken-on-guided-journey-of-the-universe.html

Andy Petro quoted in Sunfellow, D. (2016.) *Love the person you're with: life-changing insights from the most compelling near-death experiences ever recorded.* Scotts Valley, CA: CreateSpace. *http://lovethepersonyouarewith.com/videos/AndyPetro/*

Traci P. Traci P. nde. NDERF.org. https://www.nderf.org/Experiences/1traci_p_fde.html

Bryan C. Bryan C. nde. NDERF.org. https://www.nderf.org/Experiences/1bryan_c_nde.html

Dougherty, N. (2002). *Fast lane to heaven: a life-after-death journey*. Newburyport, MA: Hampton Roads Publishing. p. 34.

Nightingale, J. Juliet N. nde. NDERF.org. https://www.nderf.org/Experiences/1juliet_n_nde.html

Mary. Mary's nde. NDERF.org. https://www.nderf.org/Experiences/1mary_nde.html

Mike. (2020, November). Life review shows his encouragement of others. https://www.iands.org/research/nde-research/nde-archives31/newest-accounts/1493-life-review-shows-his-encouragement-of-others-2.html

Neal, M. (2012). *To heaven and back: a doctor's extraordinary account of her death, heaven, angels, and life again: a true story*. NewYork, NY: WaterBrook. p. 57.

Larry. Larry's NDE. NDERF.org. https://www.nderf.org/Experiences/1larry_nde.html

David D. David D. nde. NDERF.org. https://www.nderf.org/Experiences/1david_n_possible_nde.html

Eadie, B (1992). *Embraced by the light*. Warren, MI: Gold Leaf Press p. 112.

Thomas, K. Karen's nde. NDERF.org. https://www.nderf.org/Experiences/1karen_t_nde.html

Lynnclaire Dennis quoted in Williams, K. (2016). Lynnclaire Dennis' near-death experience. http://www.near-death.com/experiences/notable/lynnclaire-dennis.html

Anonymous NDEr. https://iands.org/research/nde-research/nde-archives31/newest-accounts/1339-life-review-exchanging-loving-kindness-with-all.html

Rachel F. Rachel F. nde. NDERF.org. https://www.nderf.org/Experiences/1rachel_f_nde.html

Daniel A. Daniel A nde. NDERF.org https://www.nderf.org/Experiences/1daniel_a_nde.html

Nel quoted in Ring, K. (2006). *Lessons from the light: what we can learn from the near-death experience.* Needham, MA: Moment Point Press. p. 150.

Rodonaia, G. NDERF.org https://www.nderf.org/Experiences/1george_rodonaia_nde.html

Samantha H. Samantha H. nde. NDERF.org. https://www.nderf.org/Experiences/1samantha_h_nde.html

Glauco S. Glauco S. nde. NDERF.org. https://www.nderf.org/Experiences/1glauco_s_nde.html

Birgit S. Birgit S. nde. NDERF.org. https://www.nderf.org/Experiences/1birgit_s_fde.html

Nilda P. Nilda P. nde. NDERF.org. https://www.nderf.org/Experiences/1nilda_p_nde.html

Fazzi, M. (2021). *Am I dead now?—no one seemed to be able to answer my question | Manuela Fazzi's nde.* [Video] YouTube. www.youtube.com/watch?v=yl3OS7aA1gg

Greg L. Greg L. nde. NDERF.org. https://www.nderf.org/Experiences/1greg_l_nde.html

Mary. Mary's nde. NDERF.org. https://www.nderf.org/Experiences/1mary_nde.html

Sandy D. Sandy D. nde. NDERF.org. https://www.nderf.org/Experiences/1sandy_d_nde.html

Vernon C. Vernon C. nde. NDERF.org. https://www.nderf.org/Experiences/1vernon_c_nde.html

Grady R. Grady R. nde. NDERF.org. https://www.nderf.org/Experiences/1grady_r_nde.html

Koppi H. Koppi H possible nde. NDERF.org. https://www.nderf.org/Experiences/1koppi_h_possible_nde.html

Barker, T. Tricia B. nde. NDERF.org. https://www.nderf.org/Experiences/1tricia_b_nde.html

Hensley, M.H. (2015). *Promised by heaven: a doctor's return from the afterlife to a destiny of love and healing*. New York: NY. Atria. p. 8-10.

Willy, C. (2019). *Chapter 87—Cecil Willy—it's going to be ok.* [Video] YouTube. www.youtube.com/watch?v=vcPE6pmNMNw&t=69s

Bennett, D. (2011). *Voyage of purpose: spiritual wisdom from near death back to life*. Rochester, VT: Findhorn Press.

Dr. Diane Morrissey quoted in Williams, K. (2016). Dr. Diane Morrissey's near-death experience. https://www.near-death.com/experiences/notable/dianne-morrissey.html

Cree Dean quoted in Williams, K. (2016). Cree Dean's suicide near-death experience. https://near-death.com/cree-deans-nde-suicide/

Betty Eadie quoted in Bailey, L. & Yates, J. (1996). *The near death experience: a reader*. Florence, KY: Routledge. p. 56.

Virginia Drake quoted in Dominguez, H. (2016). *Consciousness continues: near-death experiences and the aftereffects.* Independently published. p. 40.

Call, A. Amy Call nde. NDERF.org http://www.nderf.org/Experiences/1amy_c_nde_4720.html

Katherine I. Katherine I. nde. NDERF.org. https://www.nderf.org/Experiences/1katherine_l_nde.html

Brown, J. (2014). *Heavenly answers for earthly challenges*. Mesquite, NV: Davidson Press.

Niels W. Niels W. nde. NDERF.org. https://www.nderf.org/Experiences/1niels_w_nde.html

Storm, H. (2005). *My descent into death: a second chance at life.* New York, NY: Harmony.

Odell H. Odell H. nde. NDERF.org. https://www.nderf.org/Experiences/1odell_h_nde.html

Barker, T. Tricia B. nde. NDERF.org. https://www.nderf.org/Experiences/1tricia_b_nde.html

Brinkley, D., & Brinkley, K. (2008). *Secrets of the light: lessons from heaven*. San Francisco: HarperOne. p. 10-11.

Juliet Nightingale quoted in Williams, K. (2016). Juliet Nightingale's near-death experience. https://www.near-death.com/experiences/notable/Juliet-nightingale.html

Koppi H. Koppi H possible nde. NDERF.org. https://www.nderf.org/Experiences/1koppi_h_possible_nde.html

Farr, S., & Sawyer, T. (1993). *What Tom Sawyer learned from dying*. Newburyport, MA: Hampton Roads Publishing. p. 30.

Martin, M. (2022). Near-death experiences facebook group. www.facebook.com/groups/417838578320702

Brinkley, D. (2021). Life and Near Death Experiences with Dannion Brinkley [Video] YouTube. www.youtube.com/watch?v=rDrDYPzbvlc&t=908s

Experience Your Life—Chapter 2

Farr, S., & Sawyer, T. (1993). *What Tom Sawyer learned from dying*. Newburyport, MA: Hampton Roads Publishing.

Neev quoted in Ring, K. (2006). *Lessons from the light: what we can learn from the near-death experience.* Needham, MA: Moment Point Press. p. 148.

Ring, K. (2006). *Lessons from the light: what we can learn from the near-death experience*. Needham, MA: Moment Point Press. p. 154.

Andy Petro quoted in Sunfellow, D. (2016.) *Love the person you're with: life-changing insights from the most compelling near-death experiences ever recorded.* Scotts Valley, CA: CreateSpace. *http://lovethepersonyouarewith.com/videos/AndyPetro/*

Dannion Brinkley quoted in Bailey, L. & Yates, J. (1996). *The near death experience: a reader*. Florence, KY: Routledge. p. 69.

Oakford, D. (2007). *Journey through the world of spirit.* Reality Press.

Robert, C. (2020). Near-death experiences facebook group. www.facebook.com/groups/417838578320702

Whitfield, B. (2010). *The natural soul.* Muse House Press. p. xi-xii, 5.

Neev quoted in Ring, K. (2006). *Lessons from the light: what we can learn from the near-death experience.* Needham, MA: Moment Point Press. p. 22.

Oakford, D. (2007). *Journey through the world of spirit.* Reality Press.

Beckman, D. (2012). Dr. Jeffrey Long—near death experiences. https://www.youtube.com/watch?v=LwyVFW9kT8k

Carol I. Carol I. nde. NDERF.org. https://www.nderf.org/Experiences/1carol_i_nde.html

Neev quoted in Ring, K. (2006). *Lessons from the light: what we can learn from the near-death experience.* Needham, MA: Moment Point Press. p. 155.

Rachel F. Rachel F. nde. NDERF.org. https://www.nderf.org/Experiences/1rachel_f_nde.html

Justin U. *Justin U. nde.* NDERF.org. Retried from https://www.nderf.org/Experiences/1justin_u_nde.html

Josiane Antonette quoted in Williams, K. (2016). Josiane Antonette's near death experience. http://www.near-death.com/experiences/notable/josiane-antonette.html

Mohammed Z. Mohammed Z. nde. NDERF.org https://www.nderf.org/Experiences/1mohammad_z_nde.html

Mohammed Z. Mohammed Z. nde. NDERF.org https://www.nderf.org/Experiences/1mohammad_z_nde.html

Anonymous NDEr via IANDS. https://iands.org/ndes/nde-stories/iands-nde-accounts/1167-liver-failure-shows-me-all-animals-and-plants-have-souls.html

Anthony, P. (2017) Peter Anthony—near death experience: back in a moment. https://www.youtube.com/watch?v=LamlFhFnlLE

Brown, J. (2014). *Heavenly answers for earthly challenges.* Mesquite, NV: Davidson Press. p. 90.

Neal, M. (2014) *Mary Neal—the gift of life.* IANDS presentation. Newport, CA.

Lee C. Lee C. nde. NDERF.org. https://www.nderf.org/Experiences/1lee_c_ndes.html

Oakford, D. (2007). *Journey through the world of spirit.* Reality Press.

Pasarow, R. (2018). *Answers from heaven: the near-death experience of Reinee Pasarow.* CreateSpace Independent Publishing. p. 30.

Brown, J. (2014). *Heavenly answers for earthly challenges.* Mesquite, NV: Davidson Press. p. 116.

Rynes, N. (2015). *Awakenings from the light: 12 life lessons from a near death experience.* Scotts Valley, CA: CreateSpace.

Brinkley, D., & Brinkley, K. (2008). *Secrets of the light: lessons from heaven.* San Francisco: HarperOne. p. 114.

Farr, S., & Sawyer, T. (1993). *What Tom Sawyer learned from dying.* Newburyport, MA: Hampton Roads Publishing.

Craig, H. Grief 2 growth [Audio podcast episode 32]. https://www.grief2growth.com/grief-2-growth-podcast-episode-31-heidi-craig-her-nde-and-3-life-lessons-from-it/

Eadie, B (1992). *Embraced by the light.* Warren, MI: Gold Leaf Press p. 113.

Katie W. Katie W. nde. NDERF.org. https://www.nderf.org/Experiences/1katie_w_nde.html

Anonymous NDEr. https://iands.org/ndes/nde-stories/iands-nde-accounts/1165-sixty-years-in-heaven-thirty-minutes-earth-time.html

Jorgensen, R. (2017). Chapter 7—near-death-like experiencer Rene Jorgensen—the full consequences of my actions. http://lovethepersonyouarewith.com/videos/renejorgensen/

Parti, R. (2016). *Dying to wake up: a doctor's voyage into the afterlife and the wisdom he brought back.* New York, NY: Atria Books. p. 41-42.

Parti, R. (2016). *Dying to wake up: a doctor's voyage into the afterlife and the wisdom he brought back.* New York, NY: Atria Books. p. 155-157.

Wittbrodt, P. Grief 2 growth [Audio podcast episode 29]. https://www.grief2growth.com/grief-2-growth-episode-29-penny-wittbrodt-near-death-experience-wife-mother-grandmother/

Anni S. Anni S. nde. NDERF.org. https://www.nderf.org/Experiences/1anni_s_nde.html

Annie. Annie nde. NDERF.org. https://www.nderf.org/Experiences/1annie_nde.html

Craig, H. Grief 2 growth [Audio podcast episode 32]. https://www.grief2growth.com/grief-2-growth-podcast-episode-31-heidi-craig-her-nde-and-3-life-lessons-from-it/

Empathize with Others—Chapter 3

Webb, R. (2013). Consciousness continues. https://www.amazon.com/gp/video/detail/B01N59JX39?ie=UTF8&language=tr_TR

Brinkley, D., & Brinkley, K. (2008). *Secrets of the light: lessons from heaven.* San Francisco: HarperOne. p. 190.

David Beckman quoted in Dominguez, H. (2016). *Consciousness continues: near-death experiences and the aftereffects.* p. 42.

Carol I. Carol I. nde. NDERF.org. https://www.nderf.org/Experiences/1carol_i_nde.html

Martin, L. (1996). *Searching for home: a personal journey of transformation and healing after a near-death experience.* St Joseph, MI: Cosmic Concepts.

Tielking, J. Near-death experiences facebook group. www.facebook.com/groups/417838578320702

Sandra Rogers quoted in Williams, K. (2016). Sandra Rogers' suicide near death experience. https://near-death.com/sandra-rogers-suicide-nde/

Miller, M. (2021). The impossible dream. https://iands.org/research/nde-research/nde-archives31/newest-accounts/1579-australian-man-is-taken-on-guided-journey-of-the-universe.html

Renfrow, C. (2015). *Cami Renfrow nde.* Quoted in https://ndestories.org/cami-renfrow/

Jorgenson, R. (2007). *Awakening after life: a first hand guide through death into the purpose of life.* Charleston, SC: Booksurge Publishing. p. 96.

Farr, S., & Sawyer, T. (1993). *What Tom Sawyer learned from dying.* Newburyport, MA: Hampton Roads Publishing.

Farr, S., & Sawyer, T. (1993). *What Tom Sawyer learned from dying.* Newburyport, MA: Hampton Roads Publishing.

Rome, Marion (2014). *Beyond sight: the true story of a near-death experience.* Scotts Valley, CA: CreateSpace.

Rome, Marion (2014). *Beyond sight: the true story of a near-death experience.* Scotts Valley, CA: CreateSpace.

Sassano, C. (2013). Life after four deaths. http://www.naturaltransitions.org/wp-content/uploads/2011/10/NTM-Vol24-Life_after_four_deaths.pdf

Goran Grip quoted in Ring, K. (2006). *Lessons from the light: what we can learn from the near-death experience.* Needham, MA: Moment Point Press. p. 157.

Fazzi, M. (2021). *Am I dead now?—no one seemed to be able to answer my question | Manuela Fazzi's nde.* [Video] YouTube. www.youtube.com/watch?v=yl3OS7aA1gg

Panagore, P. (2015). *Heaven is beautiful: how dying taught me that death is just the beginning.* Newburyport, MA: Hampton Roads Publishing. p. 86-87.

Anonymous NDEr quoted in Ring, K. (2006). *Lessons from the light: what we can learn from the near-death experience.* Needham, MA: Moment Point Press. p. 159.

Scott Drummond quoted in Cheney, A. (2021). *The near-death experience of Scott Drummond.* [Video] YouTube. https://www.youtube.com/watch?v=B7vEdwuJBEg

Jean R. Jean R nde. NDERF.org http://www.nderf.org/Experiences/1jean_r_nde_6166.html

Wallace, R. (1994). *The burning within.* Warren, MI: Gold Leaf Press.

Brinkley, D. & Perry, P. (1995). *At peace in the light: the further adventures of a reluctant psychic who reveals the secret of your spiritual powers.* New York, NY: HarperCollins. p. 7.

Mohammed Z. Mohammed Z. nde. NDERF.org https://www.nderf.org/Experiences/1mohammad_z_nde.html

Helen S. Helen S nde. NDERF.org https://www.nderf.org/Experiences/1helen_s_ste.html

Cami Renfrow. Cami R nde. NDERF.org https://www.nderf.org/Experiences/1cami_r_nde.html

Philip S. Philip S. nde. NDERF.org. https://www.nderf.org/Experiences/1philip_s_nde.html

Smith, D. Duane S. nde. NDERF.org. https://www.nderf.org/Experiences/1duane_s_nde.html

Ruth. Ruth nde. NDERF.org. https://www.nderf.org/Experiences/1ruth_nde.html

Roger C. Roger C. nde. NDERF.org. https://www.nderf.org/Experiences/1roger_c_nde.html

Milliman, S. Sharon M. nde. NDERF.org. https://www.nderf.org/Experiences/1sharon_m_nde_7925.html

Brown, J. (2014). *Heavenly answers for earthly challenges*. Mesquite, NV: Davidson Press. p. 74.

Everitz, A. (2020). *Nine days of eternity | Anke Evertz: a profound near-death-experience during a coma.* [Video] YouTube. www.youtube.com/watch?v=O2whJPweTkQ&t=1633s

Amphianda Baskett quoted in Sunfellow, D. (2016). Love the person you're with: life-changing insights from the most compelling near-death experiences ever recorded. Scotts Valley, CA: CreateSpace. p. 144.

Call, A. Amy Call nde. NDERF.org http://www.nderf.org/Experiences/1amy_c_nde_4720.html

Oakford, D. (2018). *Soul bared: a metaphysical journey*. Maryland: Publish America. p. 51.

Farr, S., & Sawyer, T. (1993). *What Tom Sawyer learned from dying*. Newburyport, MA: Hampton Roads Publishing.

Farr, S., & Sawyer, T. (1993). *What Tom Sawyer learned from dying*. Newburyport, MA: Hampton Roads Publishing. p. 35-36.

Rome, Marion (2014). *Beyond sight: the true story of a near-death experience.* Scotts Valley, CA: CreateSpace.

Brinkley, D. & Perry, P. (1995). *At peace in the light: the further adventures of a reluctant psychic who reveals the secret of your spiritual powers.* New York, NY: HarperCollins. p. 9-10.

Kopecky, R. (2014). *How to survive life (and death): a guide for happiness in this world and beyond.* Newburyport, MA: Conari Press. p. 46.

Casper. Casper nde. NDERF.org https://www.nderf.org/Experiences/1casper_nde.html

Miller, M. (2021). The impossible dream. https://iands.org/research/nde-research/nde-archives31/newest-accounts/1579-australian-man-is-taken-on-guided-journey-of-the-universe.html

Whitfield, B. (2010). *The natural soul.* Muse House Press.

Evaluate Your Life—Chapter 4

Olsen, J. (2018). Personal communication.

Brinkley, D. & Perry, P. (1995). *At peace in the light: the further adventures of a reluctant psychic who reveals the secret of your spiritual powers.* New York, NY: HarperCollins. p. 137.

Rosenblit, D. quoted in Williams, K. (2016). David Rosenblit's near-death experience. https://www.near-death.com/experiences/notable/daniel-rosenblit.html

Oakford, D. (2018). *Soul bared: a metaphysical journey*. Maryland: Publish America.

Panagore, P. (2015). *Heaven is beautiful: how dying taught me that death is just the beginning.* Newburyport, MA: Hampton Roads Publishing. p. 81.

Ian McCormack quoted in Sharkey, J. (2014). *A glimpse of eternity*. CreateSpace Independent Publishing.

Leonard. Leonard nde. NDERF.org. https://www.nderf.org/Experiences/1leonard_nde.html

Brown, J. (2014). *Heavenly answers for earthly challenges*. Mesquite, NV: Davidson Press. p. 88.

Storm, H. (2005). *My descent into death: a second chance at life.* New York, NY: Harmony. p. 86.

William R. William R. nde. NDERF.org. https://www.nderf.org/Experiences/1william_r_nde_8726.html

Call, A. Amy Call nde. NDERF.org http://www.nderf.org/Experiences/1amy_c_nde_4720.html

Katherine I. Katherine I. nde. NDERF.org. https://www.nderf.org/Experiences/1katherine_l_nde.html

Whitfield, B. (2010). *The natural soul.* Muse House Press. p. 5.

Thomas, K. (2018). Near death experiencces facebook group. https://www.facebook.com/groups/returnfromdeath/

Miller, M. (2021). The impossible dream. https://iands.org/research/nde-research/nde-archives31/newest-accounts/1579-australian-man-is-taken-on-guided-journey-of-the-universe.html

Storm, H. (2005). *My descent into death: a second chance at life.* New York, NY: Harmony. p. 86.

Panagore, P. (2015). *Heaven is beautiful: how dying taught me that death is just the beginning.* Newburyport, MA: Hampton Roads Publishing. p. 86.

Storm, H. (2005). *My descent into death: a second chance at life.* New York, NY: Harmony.

Kemkaram, K. Near-death experiences facebook group. www.facebook.com/groups/417838578320702

Clark, N. (2017). *Reflections from the light; what I learned about life's purposes.* First World Publishing. p 109.

Eadie, B (1992). *Embraced by the light.* Warren, MI: Gold Leaf Press p. 115.

Valvita Jones quoted in Williams, K. (2016). Linda Stewart's near-death experience. https://www.near-death.com/religion/christianity/valvita-jones.html

Goran Grip quoted in Ring, K. (2006). *Lessons from the light: what we can learn from the near-death experience.* Needham, MA: Moment Point Press. p. 157.

Susan Finlay quoted in Rudolph, I. (2019). Your life in review is coming—no hidden secrets!! https://ivanrudolph46.medium.com/your-life-in-review-is-coming-no-hidden-secrets-9af49af2e647

Mary Beth Willi. Mary W nde. NDERF.org http://www.nderf.org/Experiences/1mary_w_nde.html

Rome, Marion (2014). *Beyond sight: the true story of a near-death experience.* Scotts Valley, CA: CreateSpace.

Bybee, J. (2021). God asked him 3 questions during his near death xxperience. *www.youtube.com/watch?app=desktop&v=e0jCYOxPD3U&feature=youtu.be*

Linda Stewart quoted in Williams, K. (2016). Linda Stewart's near-death experience. http://www.near-death.com/experiences/notable/linda-stewart.html

McKenzie, E. (2015). *Dying to fit in.* Erica McKenzie. p. 89.

Lisa M. Lisa M nde. NDERF.org http://www.nderf.org/Experiences/1lisa_m_nde.html

Leonard. Leonard nde. NDERF.org. https://www.nderf.org/Experiences/1leonard_nde.html

Mary Beth Willi. Mary W nde. NDERF.org http://www.nderf.org/Experiences/1mary_w_nde.html

Giroux, D. (2021). *Why heaven was so shocking.* [Video] YouTube. www.youtube.com/watch?v=NBS55IZcrxo

Rome, Marion (2014). *Beyond sight: the true story of a near-death experience.* Scotts Valley, CA: CreateSpace.

PMH Atwater quoted in Ring, K. (2006). *Lessons from the light: what we can learn from the near-death experience.* Needham, MA: Moment Point Press.

Riki E. Riki E. possible nde. NDERF.org. https://www.nderf.org/Experiences/1riki_e_possible_nde.html

Ritchie, G. & Sherrill, E. (2006). *Return from tomorrow.* Ada. MI: Revell. p. 58-65.

Bybee, J. (2021). *God asked him 3 questions during his near death experience.* [Video] YouTube. www.youtube.com/watch?app=desktop&v=e0jCYOxPD3U&feature=youtu.be

Linda G. Linda G. nde. NDERF.org. https://www.nderf.org/Experiences/1linda_g_nde.html

Hensley, M.H. (2015). *Promised by heaven: a doctor's return from the afterlife to a destiny of love and healing.* New York: NY. Atria. p. 8.

Glenda H. *Glenda H. nde.* NDERF.org. Retrived from https://www.nderf.org/Experiences/1glenda_h_nde_3045.html

Aubier, Julie quoted in Sunfellow, D. (2018). NDEs & the purpose of life. http://the-formula.org/ndes-the-purpose-of-life/

Craig, H. (2018). The near-death experience of Heidi Craig. https://www.youtube.com/watch?v=YSa3El8VFOo

Miller, M. (2021). The impossible dream. https://iands.org/research/nde-research/nde-archives31/newest-accounts/1579-australian-man-is-taken-on-guided-journey-of-the-universe.html

Brinkley, D. & Perry, P. (1995). *At peace in the light: the further adventures of a reluctant psychic who reveals the secret of your spiritual powers.* New York, NY: HarperCollins. p. 66.

Peck, L. quoted in Sunfellow, D. (2021) Nde stories—Louisa Peck *https://ndestories.org/louisa-peck/*

Reinee Pasarow quoted in Williams, K. (2016). Reinee Pasarow's near-death experience. https://www.near-death.com/experiences/notable/reinee-pasarow.html

Brinkley, D., & Brinkley, K. (2008). *Secrets of the light: lessons from heaven.* San Francisco: HarperOne. p. 114.

Mergner, Y. (2020). Near-death experiences facebook group. www.facebook.com/groups/417838578320702

Clark, Nancy (2012). *Divine moments: ordinary people having spiritually transformative experiences.* Fairfield, IA: 1st World Publishing. p. 38.

Clark, Nancy (2012). *Hear his voice.* Fairfield, IA: 1st World Publishing. p. 80.

Barbara S. Barbara S. nde. NDERF.org. https://www.nderf.org/Experiences/1barbara_s_nde.html

Lynnclaire Dennis quoted in Williams, K. (2016). Lynnclaire Dennis' near-death experience. http://www.near-death.com/experiences/notable/lynnclaire-dennis.html

Meyler, L. (2019). Near Death Experiences Facebook Group. https://www.facebook.com/groups/returnfromdeath/

Pasarow, R. (2018). *Answers from heaven: the near-death experience of Reinee Pasarow.* CreateSpace Independent Publishing. p. 29.

Darryl quoted in Ring, K. (1985). *Heading toward omega: in search of the meaning of the near-death experience.* New York, NY: Harper Perennial. p. 71.

Peter Anthony quoted in Cheney, A. (2018). *The near-death experience of Peter Anthony.* [Video] YouTube. www.youtube.com/watch?v=5XrA79_T_R0&list=PLgAXPFXpvUXi1bZYoi9b2uVTllsr2oy5c&index=3&t=587s

Katherine I. Katherine I. nde. NDERF.org. https://www.nderf.org/Experiences/1katherine_l_nde.html

Barry. Barry nde. NDERF.org. https://www.nderf.org/Experiences/1barry_fde.html

Johnson, I. Grief 2 growth [Audio podcast episode 59]. https://www.grief2growth.com/grief-2-growth-podcast-isabella-johnson-do-we-soul-plan-tragedy-ep-58/

Mary Jo Rapini. Mary Jo R NDERF.org http://www.nderf.org/Experiences/1mary_jo_r_nde.html

Storm, H. (2005). *My descent into death: a second chance at life.* New York, NY: Harmony. p. 34-35.

Everitz, A. (2020). *Nine days of eternity | Anke Evertz: a profound near-death-experience during a coma.* [Video] YouTube. www.youtube.com/watch?v=O2whJPweTkQ&t=1633s

Moorjani, A. (2012). *Dying to be me: my journey from cancer, to near death, to true healing.* Carlsbad, CA: Hay House. p. 66.

Brinkley, D. & Perry, P. (1995). *At peace in the light: the further adventures of a reluctant psychic who reveals the secret of your spiritual powers.* New York, NY: HarperCollins. p. 38.

Kim A. Kim A. nde. NDERF.org. https://www.nderf.org/Experiences/1kim_a_nde.html

Rynes, N. (2015). *Awakenings from the light: 12 life lessons from a near death experience.* Scotts Valley, CA: CreateSpace. p. 166.

Mary Beth Willi. Mary W nde. NDERF.org http://www.nderf.org/Experiences/1mary_w_nde.html

Calvert, O. *Experiencer Oliver John Calvert.* Retrieved by http://lovethepersonyouarewith.com/references/experiencer-oliver-john-calvert/

Clark, Nancy (2012). *Hear his voice.* Fairfield, IA: 1st World Publishing. p. 81.

Dougherty, N. (2002). *Fast lane to heaven: a life-after-death journey.* Newburyport, MA: Hampton Roads Publishing. p. 34.

Lisa M. Lisa M nde. NDERF.org http://www.nderf.org/Experiences/1lisa_m_nde.html

Darlene Holman quoted in Williams, K. (2019). Darlene Holman's dream near-death experience. https://near-death.com/darlene-holman/

Schaeffer, K. Near-death experiences facebook group. www.facebook.com/groups/417838578320702

Brinkley, D., & Brinkley, K. (2008). *Secrets of the light: lessons from heaven.* San Francisco: HarperOne. p. 193.

Thomas, K. (2018). Near Death Experiences Facebook Group. https://www.facebook.com/groups/returnfromdeath/

Edwards, N. My near-death experience. https://reprogramyourlife.org/articles

William. William's story. Shared Crossing Project. https://www.sharedcrossing.com/williams-story.html

Bo Katzman, B. (2020). *Two minutes of eternity—an extraordinary near death experience | Bo Katzman's nde.* [Video] YouTube. https://www.youtube.com/watch?v=8iNucPVPGw4

Singer, M. (2007). *The untethered soul: the journey beyond yourself.* Oakland, CA: New Harbinger. p. 159.

Chantal L. Chantal L. nde. NDERF.org. https://www.nderf.org/Experiences/1chantal_l_nde.html

Casper. Casper nde. NDERF.org https://www.nderf.org/Experiences/1casper_nde.html

Vido. Vido nde. NDERF.org. https://www.nderf.org/Experiences/1vido_nde.html

Brinkley, D. & Perry, P. (1995). *At peace in the light: the further adventures of a reluctant psychic who reveals the secret of your spiritual powers.* New York, NY: HarperCollins. p. 137.

Rosenblit, D. quoted in Williams, K. (2016). David Rosenblit's near-death experience. https://www.near-death.com/experiences/notable/daniel-rosenblit.html

Storm, H. (2005). *My descent into death: a second chance at life.* New York, NY: Harmony.

Vander Yacht, J. Near-death experiences facebook group. www.facebook.com/groups/417838578320702

Brown, J. (2014). *Heavenly answers for earthly challenges.* Mesquite, NV: Davidson Press. p. 100.

Colin F. Colin F. nde. NDERF.org. https://www.nderf.org/Experiences/1colin_f_nde.html

Archie M. Archie M. nde. NDERF.org. https://www.nderf.org/Experiences/1archie_m_nde.html

James G. James G. nde. NDERF.org. https://www.nderf.org/Experiences/1james_g_probable_nde.html

William R. William R. nde. NDERF.org. https://www.nderf.org/Experiences/1william_r_nde_8726.html

Karen B. Karen B. nde. NDERF.org. https://www.nderf.org/Experiences/1karen_b_nde.html

McKenzie, E. (2015). *Dying to fit in.* Erica McKenzie. p. 72.

Oakford, D. (2018). *Soul bared: a metaphysical journey.* Maryland: Publish America.

Moorjani, A. (2021). Anita Moorjani—2nd Buddha at the gas pump interview. [Video] YouTube. www.youtube.com/watch?v=f_XkHCFuWhg

Wallace, R. (1994). *The burning within.* Warren, MI: Gold Leaf Press. p. 107.

Casper. Casper nde. NDERF.org https://www.nderf.org/Experiences/1casper_nde.html

Frances W. Frances W. nde. NDERF.org. https://www.nderf.org/Experiences/1frances_w_nde.html

Brinkley, D., & Brinkley, K. (2008). *Secrets of the light: lessons from heaven.* San Francisco: HarperOne. p. 172.

Enlighten Yourself—Chapter 5

Romy. Romy nde. NDERF.org. http://www.nderf.org/Experiences/1romy_nde.html

Moorjani, A. (2012). *Dying to be me: my journey from cancer, to near death, to true healing.* Carlsbad, CA: Hay House.

Jean R. Jean R nde. NDERF.org http://www.nderf.org/Experiences/1jean_r_nde_6166.html

Brown, J. (2014). *Heavenly answers for earthly challenges.* Mesquite, NV: Davidson Press. p. 87-88.

Glenda H. *Glenda H. nde.* NDERF.org. Retrived from https://www.nderf.org/Experiences/1glenda_h_nde_3045.html

Neal, M. (2018). Death brings context to life | Dr. Mary Neal | TedxJacksonHole. [Video] YouTube. www.youtube.com/watch?v=C-M9zR17egA

V. V. nde. NDERF.org. https://www.nderf.org/Experiences/1v_nde.html

Karen Brannon quoted in Williams, K. (2016). Karen Brannon's near-death experience. https://near-death.com/reincarnation-and-the-nde/

Mary H. *Mary H. nde.* NDERF.org. Retrived from https://www.nderf.org/Experiences/1mary_h_nde.html

Brinkley, D., & Brinkley, K. (2008). *Secrets of the light: lessons from heaven.* San Francisco: HarperOne. p. 16.

Leni D. Leni D. nde. NDERF.org https://www.nderf.org/Experiences/1leni_d_ndelike.html

Parti, R. (2016). *Dying to wake up: a doctor's voyage into the afterlife and the wisdom he brought back.* New York, NY: Atria Books. p. 59.

Wittbrodt, P. (2021). *Life to afterlifte death and back 2.* [Video] YouTube. https://www.youtube.com/watch?v=65eyvshsx5U

Judy G. Judy G. nde. NDERF.org. https://www.nderf.org/Experiences/1judy_g_nde_8329.html

PMH Atwater quoted in Hugenot, A. (2012) *The death experience: what it is like when you die.* Dog Ear Publishing. p. 136.

Nightingale, J. Juliet N. nde. NDERF.org. https://www.nderf.org/Experiences/1juliet_n_nde.html

Brenda I. Brenda I. nde. NDERF.org. https://www.nderf.org/Experiences/1brenda_i_ndes.html

Craig quoted in Ring, K. (2006). *Lessons from the light: what we can learn from the near-death experience.* Needham, MA: Moment Point Press.

Romy. Romy nde. NDERF.org. http://www.nderf.org/Experiences/1romy_nde.html

Rose, D. IANDS NDE Radio with Lee Witting. https://www.youtube.com/watch?v=vHklG2DgREs

Rodonaia, G. (2013) *Dr. George Rodonaia—NDE.* [Video] https://ndestories.org/dr-george-rodonaia/

McVea, C. (2013). *Waking up in heaven: a true story of brokenness, heaven, and life again.* Brentwood, TN: Howard Books.

John K. John K. ste. NDERF.org. https://www.nderf.org/Experiences/1john_k_ste.html

Kason, Y. (2021) *Let's talk near death—pt 1: the near death experiences & spiritual experiences of Dr. Yvonne Kason.* [Video]. Youtube. www.youtube.com/watch?v=KcUP41XeUoI

Goble, D. Diane G. nde. NDERF.org. https://www.nderf.org/Experiences/1diane_g_nde.html

Eadie, B (1992). *Embraced by the light.* Warren, MI: Gold Leaf Press p. 121.

Neal, M. (2012). *To heaven and back: a doctor's extraordinary account of her death, heaven, angels, and life again: a true story.* NewYork, NY: WaterBrook. P. 134.

Carry G. Carry G. nde like. NDERF.org. https://www.nderf.org/Experiences/1carry_g_ndelike.html

Petro, A. (2014). *Alive in the light: remembering eternity.* Outskirts Press.

Brett D. Brett D. nde like. OBERF.org. https://www.oberf.org/brett_d_ndelike.htm

Moorjani, A. (2016). *What if this is heaven?: how our cultural myths prevent us from experiencing heaven on earth.* Carlsbad, CA: Hay House. p. 113.

Milliman, S. (2017). Let's talk near death: Sharon Milliman. https://www.youtube.com/watch?v=Q5RlgozR0Hs

Panagore, P. (2015). *Heaven is beautiful: how dying taught me that death is just the beginning.* Newburyport, MA: Hampton Roads Publishing. p. 86.

Rynes, N. (2015). *Awakenings from the light: 12 life lessons from a near death experience.* Scotts Valley, CA: CreateSpace. p. 89.

Whitfield, B. (2010). *The natural soul.* Muse House Press. p. 8.

Judy G. Judy G. nde. NDERF.org. https://www.nderf.org/Experiences/1judy_g_nde_8329.html

Ryan Rampton quoted in Sunfellow, D. (2016.) *Love the person you're with: life-changing insights from the most compelling near-death experiences ever recorded.* Scotts Valley, CA: CreateSpace. p. 70.

Weber, S. (2020). *The place between here and there: a true and beautiful near-death experience.* Independently published.

Steve B. Steve B nde. NDERF.org. https://www.nderf.org/Experiences/1steve_b_nde.html

Sondra Boyd quoted in Dominguez, H. (2016). *Consciousness continues: near-death experiences and the aftereffects.* p. 143.

Mary Beth Willi. Mary W nde. NDERF.org http://www.nderf.org/Experiences/1mary_w_nde.html

Leni D. Leni D. nde. NDERF.org https://www.nderf.org/Experiences/1leni_d_ndelike.html

Alexander, E. (2015, June 4). Neurosurgeon's near death experience: doctor says heaven is real. After Life TV with Bob Olson. https://www.afterlifetv.com/tag/dr-eben-alexander/

Wittbrodt, P. Grief 2 growth [Audio podcast episode 29]. https://www.grief2growth.com/grief-2-growth-episode-29-penny-wittbrodt-near-death-experience-wife-mother-grandmother/

Moorjani, A. (2016). *What if this is heaven?: how our cultural myths prevent us from experiencing heaven on earth.* Carlsbad, CA: Hay House. p. 111 and 60.

Sudman, N. (2012). *Application of impossible things: a near-death experience in Iraq*. Ozark Mountain Publishing.

Romy. Romy nde. NDERF.org. http://www.nderf.org/Experiences/1romy_nde.html

Anthony, P. (2017) Peter Anthony—near death experience: back in a moment. https://www.youtube.com/watch?v=LamlFhFnlLE

Steve B. Steve B nde. NDERF.org. https://www.nderf.org/Experiences/1steve_b_nde.html

Jean R. Jean R nde. NDERF.org. http://www.nderf.org/Experiences/1jean_r_nde_6166.html

Kim A. Kim A. nde. NDERF.org. https://www.nderf.org/Experiences/1kim_a_nde.html

Martin, L. (1996). *Searching for home: a personal journey of transformation and healing after a near-death experience*. St Joseph, MI: Cosmic Concepts. p. 18-19.

Mary Beth Willi. Mary W nde. NDERF.org http://www.nderf.org/Experiences/1mary_w_nde.html

Debra Kaiser (2020) quoted in David Sunfellow's The Formula.org. https://the-formula.org/a-childs-near-death-experience-that-covers-all-the-bases/

Milliman, S. (2019). Near Death Experiences Facebook Group. https://www.facebook.com/groups/returnfromdeath/

McKenzie, E. (2015). *Dying to fit in*. Erica McKenzie. p. 73.

Bennett, D. (2011). *Voyage of purpose: spiritual wisdom from near death back to life*. Rochester, VT: Findhorn Press. p. 56, 84.

Justin U. *Justin U. nde*. NDERF.org. Retried from https://www.nderf.org/Experiences/1justin_u_nde.html

Rome, M. (2015). *Through the light: after-effects of a near-death experience*. Scotts Valley, CA: CreateSpace.

Ring, K. (1985). *Heading toward omega: in search of the meaning of the near-death experience*. New York, NY: Harper Perennial. p. 70.

Miller, M. (2021). The impossible dream. https://iands.org/research/nde-research/nde-archives31/newest-accounts/1579-australian-man-is-taken-on-guided-journey-of-the-universe.html

Kopecky, R. (2014). *How to survive life (and death): a guide for happiness in this world and beyond*. Newburyport, MA: Conari Press. p. 7.

Moorjani, A. (2016). *What if this is heaven?: how our cultural myths prevent us from experiencing heaven on earth*. Carlsbad, CA: Hay House. p. 88.

John K. John K. ste. NDERF.org. https://www.nderf.org/Experiences/1john_k_ste.html

Storm, H. (2005). *My descent into death: a second chance at life*. New York, NY: Harmony. p. 32.

Rynes, N. (2015). *Awakenings from the light: 12 life lessons from a near death experience*. Scotts Valley, CA: CreateSpace.

Betty Eadie quoted in Bailey, L. & Yates, J. (1996). *The near death experience: a reader*. Florence, KY: Routledge. p. 56.

Mary Beth Willi. Mary W nde. NDERF.org http://www.nderf.org/Experiences/1mary_w_nde.html

Olsen, J. (2012). *I knew their hearts: the amazing true story of a journey beyond the veil to learn the silent language of the heart*. Plain Sight Publications. p. 102.

Wittbrodt, P. Grief 2 growth [Audio podcast episode 29]. https://www.grief2growth.com/grief-2-growth-episode-29-penny-wittbrodt-near-death-experience-wife-mother-grandmother/

Melinda G. Melinda G. nde. NDERF.org. https://www.nderf.org/Experiences/1melinda_g_nde.html

Yvonne N. *Yvonne N. probable nde*. NDERF.org. https://www.nderf.org/Experiences/1yvonne_n_probable_nde.html

Grace Bulbulka quoted in Williams, K. (2016). *Grace Bulbulka's near death experience*. http://www.near-death.com/experiences/notable/grace-bubulka.html

Meyler, L. (2019). Near Death Experiences Facebook Group. https://www.facebook.com/groups/returnfromdeath/

Exemplify Love—Chapter 6

Moody, R. (1975) *Life after life*: Harlan, IA: Guideposts.

Pasarow, R. (2018). *Answers from heaven: the near-death experience of Reinee Pasarow*. CreateSpace Independent Publishing.

Sara A. Sara A. probable nde. NDERF.org. https://www.nderf.org/Experiences/1sara_a_probable_nde.html

Clark, Nancy (2012). *Hear his voice.* Fairfield, IA: 1st World Publishing. p. 96.

Rome, M. (2015). *Through the light: after-effects of a near-death experience.* Scotts Valley, CA: CreateSpace.

Neal, M. (2012). *To heaven and back: a doctor's extraordinary account of her death, heaven, angels, and life again: a true story*. NewYork, NY: WaterBrook.

Virginia Drake quoted in Dominguez, H. (2016). *Consciousness continues: near-death experiences and the aftereffects.* Independently published. p. 79.

Diamond, D. (2016). *Life after near death: miraculous stories of healing and transformation in the extraordinary lives of people with newfound powers*. Newburyport, MA: New Page Books. p. 74.

Steve. Steve nde suicide. NDERF.org. https://near-death.com/steves-nde-suicide/

Miller, M. (2021). The impossible dream. https://iands.org/research/nde-research/nde-archives31/newest-accounts/1579-australian-man-is-taken-on-guided-journey-of-the-universe.html

Diane Goble quoted in Sartori, P. & Walsh, K. (2017). *The transformative power of near-death experiences: how the messages of ndes can positively impact the world.* London, UK: Watkins Publishing. p. 125.

Moorjani, A. (2021). Anita Moorjani—2nd Buddha at the gas pump interview. [Video] YouTube. www.youtube.com/watch?v=f_XkHCFuWhg

Teri R. Teri R. nde. NDERF.org. https://www.nderf.org/Experiences/1teri_r_nde.html

Tielking, J. (2020). Near-death experiences facebook group. www.facebook.com/groups/417838578320702

Oakford, D. (2018). *Soul bared: a metaphysical journey*. Maryland: Publish America.

Raymond, R. Near-death experiences facebook group. www.facebook.com/groups/417838578320702

Brinkley, D. & Perry, P. (1995). *At peace in the light: the further adventures of a reluctant psychic who reveals the secret of your spiritual powers.* New York, NY: HarperCollins. p. 7.

Brinkley, D., & Brinkley, K. (2008). *Secrets of the light: lessons from heaven*. San Francisco: HarperOne. p. 193.

Bennett, D. (2020) David Bennett NDE. https://ndestories.org/david-bennett/

Brinkley, D., & Brinkley, K. (2008). *Secrets of the light: lessons from heaven*. San Francisco: HarperOne. p. 190.

Rome, M. (2015). *Through the light: after-effects of a near-death experience.* Scotts Valley, CA: CreateSpace.

Rebecca P. Rebecca P. nde. NDERF.org. https://www.nderf.org/Experiences/1rebecca_p_nde.html

Albert S. Albert S. probable nde. NDERF.org. https://www.nderf.org/Experiences/1albert_s_probable_nde.html

Brinkley, D., & Perry, P. (1994). *Saved by the light: the true story of a man who died twice and the profound revelations he received.* New York: Villard. p. 165.

Helen S. Helen S nde. NDERF.org https://www.nderf.org/Experiences/1helen_s_ste.html

Gentile, R. (2021). *Quarks of light: a near-death experience*. Fresno, CA: Ignite Press. p. 169.

Clark, Nancy (2012). *Hear his voice.* Fairfield, IA: 1st World Publishing. p. 174.

Rome, M. (2015). *Through the light: after-effects of a near-death experience.* Scotts Valley, CA: CreateSpace.

Wade, C. (2018). Heart talk: poetic wisdom for a better life. New York: NY. Atria.

Rynes, N. (2021). Nancy Rynes—Buddha at the gas pump interview. [Video] YouTube. www.youtube.com/watch?v=isOYm03muBU&t=3s

Jorgenson, R. (2007). *Awakening after life: a first hand guide through death into the purpose of life*. Charleston, SC: Booksurge Publishing. p. 127-128.

Mary Beth Willi. Mary W nde. NDERF.org http://www.nderf.org/Experiences/1mary_w_nde.html

Rome, M. (2014). *Beyond sight: the true story of a near-death experience.* Scotts Valley, CA: CreateSpace.

Stephen K. Stephen K. nde. NDERF.org. https://www.nderf.org/Experiences/1stephen_k_nde.html

Steve B. Steve B nde. NDERF.org https://www.nderf.org/Experiences/1steve_b_nde.html

Anni S. Anni S. nde. NDERF.org. https://www.nderf.org/Experiences/1anni_s_nde.html

Karie N. Karie N. nde. NDERF.org. https://www.nderf.org/Experiences/1karie_n_nde.html

Demi B. Demi B. nde. NDERF.org. https://www.nderf.org/Experiences/1demi_b_nde.html

Rhonda I. Rhonda I. nde. NDERF.org. https://www.nderf.org/Experiences/1rhonda_j_nde.html

Elisa R. Elisa R. nde. NDERF.org. https://www.nderf.org/Experiences/1elisa_r_nde.html

Martin, L. (1996). *Searching for home: a personal journey of transformation and healing after a near-death experience.* St Joseph, MI: Cosmic Concepts. p. 28.

Everitz, A. (2020). *Nine days of eternity | Anke Evertz: a profound near-death-experience during a coma.* [Video] YouTube. www.youtube.com/watch?v=O2whJPweTkQ&t=1633s

Call, A. (2017). Amy Call | NDE. [Video] *https://ndestories.org/amy-call/*

Pasarow, R. (2018). *Answers from heaven: the near-death experience of Reinee Pasarow.* CreateSpace Independent Publishing. p. 30.

Rome, M. (2015). *Through the light: after-effects of a near-death experience.* Scotts Valley, CA: CreateSpace.

Judith White quoted in Dominguez, H. (2016). *Consciousness continues: near-death experiences and the aftereffects.* p. 42.

Karen. Karen fde. NDERF.org. https://www.nderf.org/Experiences/1karen_fde.html

Casper. Casper nde. NDERF.org https://www.nderf.org/Experiences/1casper_nde.html

Martin, L. (1996). *Searching for home: a personal journey of transformation and healing after a near-death experience.* St Joseph, MI: Cosmic Concepts. p. 19.

Hensley, M.H. (2015). *Promised by heaven: a doctor's return from the afterlife to a destiny of love and healing.* New York: NY. Atria. p. 11.

Chantal L. Chantal L. nde. NDERF.org. https://www.nderf.org/Experiences/1chantal_l_nde.html

Lee. Lee probable nde. NDERF.org. https://www.nderf.org/Experiences/1lee_probable_nde.html

Clark, Nancy (2012). *Hear his voice.* Fairfield, IA: 1st World Publishing.

Paul Johnson quoted in Dominguez, H. (2016). *Consciousness continues: near-death experiences and the aftereffects.* p. 128.

Rome, M. (2014). *Beyond sight: the true story of a near-death experience.* Scotts Valley, CA: CreateSpace.

How to Do Your Own Life Review—Chapter 7

Clark, N. (2017). *Reflections from the light; what I learned about life's purposes.* First World Publishing. p 110-112.

Neev quoted in Ring, K. (2006). *Lessons from the light: what we can learn from the near-death experience.* Needham, MA: Moment Point Press. p. 24.

Peterson, J. B., Doidge, N., & Van, S. E. (2018). *12 rules for life: An antidote to chaos.*

Wallace, R. (1994). *The burning within.* Warren, MI: Gold Leaf Press. p. 92.

Mary Beth Willi. Mary W nde. NDERF.org http://www.nderf.org/Experiences/1mary_w_nde.html

Brown, J. (2014). *Heavenly answers for earthly challenges.* Mesquite, NV: Davidson Press. p. 86.

Sharon Milliman quoted in Dominguez, H. (2016). *Consciousness continues: near-death experiences and the aftereffects.* p. 114.

Debra Kaiser (2020) quoted in David Sunfellow's The Formula.org. https://the-formula.org/a-childs-near-death-experience-that-covers-all-the-bases/

Brinkley, D. & Perry, P. (1995). *At peace in the light: the further adventures of a reluctant psychic who reveals the secret of your spiritual powers.* New York, NY: HarperCollins. p. 145.

PHOTO CREDITS

Cover—image by Arek Socha of pixabay.com
Introduction—image by Arek Socha of pixabay.com
What Is Heaven Like?—image by Kareni of pixabay.com
Examine Your Life—image by Gerd Altmann of pixabay.com
Experience Your Life—image by Alexas Fotos of pixabay.com
Empathize with Others—image by Terri Sharp of pixabay.com
Evaluate Your Life—image by Succo of pixabay.com
Enlighten Yourself—image by Anja of pixabay.com
Exemplify Love—image by Pexels of pixabay.com
How to Do Your Own Life Review—image by Wolfgang Eckert of pixabay.com